The Better Parts of a Life

The Better Parts of a Life

An Autobiography

Robert S. Lancaster

Proctor's Hall Press
Sewanee, Tennessee

ISBN: 0-9627687-1-5

Published by Proctor's Hall Press
Proctor's Hall Road
P.O. Box 856
Sewanee, Tennessee 37375-0856

Cover Design by Dick Posan, Two P's Design

Printed and bound in the United States of America

To the memory of my teacher Elizabeth Gwinn
and to Sewanee men and women
whose lives reflect the Sewanee vision.

Contents

Introduction

The title of Dr. Robert S. Lancaster's rich and evocative memoir is *The Better Parts of a Life*, but readers of these sprightly pages need not be committed fans of "the Red Dean" (as I am) for an emendation of this thoroughly apt title to occur to them. "The Better Parts of a *Good* Life," or, to echo a distinctly Wordsworthian tone in the writing, "The Better Parts of a *Good Man's* Life," are titles that would fit even more snugly and truthfully.

Of course, just as the memoir itself is disarmingly modest about his own personal and professional achievements, Dr. Lancaster's title risks only as much as he would permit by way of self-regard or positive claim. But whatever the elements that go to make up "the good life," Dean Red's has been enviably rich in them, and this account of his experiences, these impressions and recollections from his long and notable career, give many of these elements full and vivid play.

Literally as well as metaphorically, the very heart of Dean Red's character is manifest in the book's first line: "I have always been thankful to have been born." Taking the mysterious fact of life itself as a wonderful if unmerited gift, he shows in these pages how steadily and responsively he is able to *affirm* the essential goodness of life— not only to find life-quickening good in seemingly ordinary or every-day experience, but to ratify with deep emotional power a whole range of intense and life-affirming responses.

It is entirely characteristic of him to evoke, for example, a vivid youthful impression from haymaking, the "aromatic" newly-cured timothy hay having "in its odor the sweetness of spring rain, the promise of a June day, the melancholy tinge of dying grass. No wonder that throughout history it is associated with wanton errancy, with erotic delights." Likewise, that he can describe so poignantly what it is like at nine or ten years old, or twenty-one, or much later in life, to fall in love—and summarize his feelings, in all seriousness, by asserting that "If heaven is what they say it is, it must be something like being in love."

More surprising, no doubt, at least to anyone not close friend or family, would be his response to events not at all personally immediate. Hearing the news of Hiroshima and Nagasaki, he immediately weeps: "Not many of my companions felt as I did. For me the world would never the be the same. . . . It was not a question of pity. I did not blame the president who had made the decision. My feelings and sadness had to do with the passing of an era. . . . I sensed the coming of fear and unease. I belonged to the earth and the sea and the sky, and somehow these were in danger."

Red Lancaster's "thankfulness" for the gift of life, and for having been fortunate enough to live it so abundantly, underscores and penetrates everything about him, and hence everything about this book. In it, his unselfconsciously reiterated words of praise and value form a revealing cluster: "sprightly," "vibrant," "energetic," "outgoing," "spirited," "high-spirited." He is first attracted to Ernestine Desporte ("Tine," his wife for nearly fifty years) because she is "impudent, strong-willed, filled with laughter," and "danced as lightly as a maple leaf in a south breeze."

"By nature," he announces, "I am a romantic"—an identification repeatedly confirmed both in the selection and telling of his experiences: "While visiting [my cousin Dr. Phlegar in Washburn, Tennessee] one spring, I had a wonderful and strange experience. The day was clear and cool, with little wind. I decided to climb Clinch Mountain, which rose above Dr. Phlegar's house. After a leisurely but demanding climb to the top, I lay down on one of the rocks that dotted the summit. Suddenly all was so peaceful, so quiet that I was carried away. Time flowed by me easily and silently. I became a part of all creation, of all being. My mind soared away into the clouds. How long I lay in this state I do not know. I came to and began to feel the breeze, to see the two vultures sailing the air streams above. The experience sobered me, remained with me a long time. For once, though, I experienced peace; perhaps I had a glimpse of heaven."

Dean Red writes here, then, very much as he has lived: with an avid and constantly refreshed delight in the natural world and in his fellow creatures, whether animal or human; with a sense even in adversity of his good fortune; with strongly-held convictions but also with an abiding good humor; and with a scrupulous care for the just articulation of his ardent mind and spirit that connects his own temper with, say, the ideal of a classical orator—not merely a man who speaks unusually well, but an unusually good man, speaking.

I don't invoke the word *orator* casually. During my undergraduate days at Sewanee, several figures who at one time or another took the podium in All Saints' Chapel (most commonly at Tuesday noon, when attendance was required) have proved memorable: David Collins, Chaplain, genially earnest, slyly didactic, as ready with a slang phrase out of pop culture or sports as a cadence from the Psalms; John Webb, Dean of Men, low-key and deadpan, whose barbs of dry wit were so acerbically deft that it could be hours later before the sting fully registered; Gaston Bruton, Provost, laconic and direct, choosing his diction for its denotative accuracy as carefully as a surgeon his instruments; Edward McCrady, Vice-Chancellor, whose classical training and musical ear meant that his periods were as resonant as they were ordinate, at once pointed and allusive.

But of them all, only Dean Lancaster's rhetoric and tone either rose to, or risked failing at, eloquence. Partly posture, partly vocal pitch and timbre, partly echo of political stump-speaking before the day of microphones and amplification, partly an upswung half-syllable "uh" sound on the final word of a phrase (a vocal tic distinctive to his way of speaking not easy to describe but instantly recognizable), partly a readiness to invoke the ringing phrase, the rhetorically heightened cadence: whatever the mix of elements, Dean Red's eloquence always italicized the given moment as a significant *occasion*. For him, the risk of sounding florid and orotund had to be taken in order to aim for what would be stirring, fervent, and memorable, and, often enough, in touch with the sublime.

Fortunately, Red has deigned to include in his memoir, not his Founders' Day speeches or one of hundreds of others he might have chosen, but a Sewanee Academy graduation talk rich in his characteristic *eloquentia,* as in this summary passage (a personal and pedagogical credo of sorts) near its close:

> These memories I recall that we may weave together the strands in the rope of our inheritance. It is a thick rope and heavy with meaning. Of the many, I have recalled only a few, and I have said nothing of those millions who in their humble but sturdy lives have borne the burdens and kept faith in our inheritance: faith in Reason, the principle of quick intelligence; the dignity and worth of man as a free-willing child of God; the ultimate responsibility of men for their choices; the brotherhood of all men; the eternal worth of every individual for whom organizations and governments exist; power held in trust under law; progress over linear time; the principle of human equality—all men equal in the sense all coins are equal because they have upon them the insignia of authority; the redemption of the world by our Lord Jesus Christ.

And Red is certainly one of those who has "kept faith" with these principles and values, most conspicuously in the lifetime of achievements made in and for Sewanee. Some of these are material and palpable: Rebel's Rest, the 1866 log home of Major Fairbanks now renovated and refurbished as the University's guest house, and the Bishop's Common, the student center endowed and dedicated to the memory of Bishop Juhan, are two structures for which Dean Red is directly responsible. Other efforts also issued in tangible benefits, such as his decisive role, alongside Bishop Juhan, in meeting the Ford Foundation challenge in the 1960s, which added $10 million to Sewanee's resources.

Perhaps inevitably in such a long and unstinting life in one institution, however, so many of Red's other efforts and achievements fall into the category of "those little, nameless, unremembered acts/ Of kindness and of love" that make up, in Wordsworth's phrase, "the best part of a good man's life"—acts literally "unremembered" here in Dean Red's memoir, because they were done immediately, without calculation or self-regard, and then forgotten just as quickly in moving at once to the next challenge.

But if the particular deeds themselves have by now become "nameless," the general impact of their beneficence and virtue have not. Dean Red began by helping to keep the Sewanee Military

xii

Academy open and solvent during the Great Depression, taking on whatever tasks the institution required. As dean of the college, his administrative partnership with Dr. McCrady and Dr. Bruton spanned in the years from 1957 through 1969 a remarkable period. The college increased the number, diversity, and quality of its students. Growing resources and expanding programs led to Sewanee's most ambitious building program ever, from the completion of the Chapel and renovation of Walsh Hall to the construction of Guerry Hall, duPont Library, Woods Laboratories, Juhan Gymnasium, Snowden Forestry Building, and several dormitories. A distinguished teaching faculty already in place (including Dean Red himself as a professor of politics) was improved steadily by the addition of new scholars, and the college's academic stature, both in fact and by reputation, was continually enhanced through the period of his tenure.

Readers of this memoir familiar with Sewanee, in one or another of its phases since Dean Red's first year in 1931, will not only find evocation and reinforcement of their own rich memories of the place but will especially appreciate Dean Red's easy-going, back-and-forth, allusive way of treating his experiences of it. Readers who happen not to know Sewanee, though their responses will necessarily be different, will nonetheless discover readily enough the peculiar charm and character of the place, in the main because Dean Red's love and care and knowledge of it are so indelibly inscribed throughout.

Early in the memoir, Dr. Lancaster remembers what it was like coming to terms with his conspicuously red hair. "Put him on a stump," one of his father's contemporaries had joked, "and the woodpeckers would feed him!" Gradually he comes to feel that red hair is a distinct virtue, and that it is "a gross calumny to attribute a bad disposition and a fierce temper to redheads":

> To me it is a sure sign of energy and sensitivity and usually goes with an outgoing, good disposition. . . . Give me a red-haired boy with a freckled face, a sure smile, britches too big for him, and bare feet, and I will trade you any old black-headed or brown-haired for him, sight unseen, as the knife swappers used to say.

Whether that's exactly what we feel about redheads in general doesn't matter: for certain that's what we feel about Red Lancaster. We wouldn't swap him, or the good luck to have known him, for anyone else. The better parts of his life have permanently enabled and enriched the better parts of hundreds of Sewanee lives. And how good it is to have this lively record of who he has been among us! *Ecce quam bonum vita virorum!*

Douglas Paschall
Morgan's Steep
Sewanee, Tennessee
August 1990

Chapter One

From the Blue Ridge

I have always been thankful to have been born. There will be a time when no babies are born on this planet. The sun will have cooled; the earth will no longer labor with life. Only the scars will be left to testify to the insatiable activity of men. But I was born into a green world of grass and trees and flowing streams and floating clouds, into the comfort of my mother's breast.

I have few early memories so my first years must have been secure. I am told that I was a very active baby, very strong and restless, once even pushing my way out of the cradle, that old cradle that contained and pacified the energy of ten babies. I was the fifth. When I was little more than a year old I became very sick with pneumonia. Life had its claims, and I recovered, learned once again to take halting steps, began to take again the strong but plain food that mothers in the Blue Ridge Mountains fed their babies. For it was in these mountains I was born one night in July in 1909. As men count, I was born in the twentieth century, but we lived in the eighteenth century or partly astraddle of the eighteenth and nineteenth—by inclination, attitude, and lifestyle.

Of my forebears I know something but not enough. They fade out in the shadowy beginnings of life on the frontier. I am Robert Lancaster. My father was Robert Lancaster. His father was Robert Lancaster, whose father was Thomas, whose father was John. When and how my remote ancestors made their way from England to America I do not know. I have never seriously inquired. I have always cherished my family name, though. I have liked the sound of it. Sometimes in my dreams I have associated myself with John of Gaunt and that splendid Plantagenet tribe that set afire all England and half of Europe. By nature, you see, I am a romantic.

My grandfather married Octavia Underwood, who was born of the marriage of Joshua Underwood and Delilah West. It is from the West side of my father's family that we have inherited the remnant of land that we still own in Floyd County, Virginia, and the old log houses built in 1796. It is from the Underwoods that the men in the family have inherited the hunting streak. My father told me that old Joshua was a real stem-winder, taking off to the woods for a week at a time with only a bag of salt and a little corn, returning with haunches of fat deer. That he could not write his name I know, for I have a deed signed with his mark. He made his mark, too, on many a fat buck and many a gasping trout, and many a chunk of hard, sweaty work. To raise a family and prosper after a fashion was no easy job in the mountains of Virginia. He is buried in the Pine Creek cemetery in Floyd County and I hope my grandchildren visit his grave as I have done to keep alive memories. Men without memories are lost. Pity the poor man who knows not whence he came. He is apt to be a barbarian though he may not know it. Memories sweeten life, bring security, and though they be bittersweet, memories fix values and make character.

Of my grandfathers I know all too little. My paternal grandfather, Robert Lancaster, died before I was born. He must have been a godly man whose sins, like him, were Calvinistic and rather stern. He served as a private in the War between the States in Pelham's Horse Artillery attached to Jeb Stuart's cavalry. He carried cannon balls and tended the mobile guns. In Richmond after the Peninsula Campaign he contracted dysentery and almost died. I think that his sickness and recovery affected him powerfully and led him to religion. I have a much-used Bible that he read during his sufferings. He was furloughed home and never returned to the fighting. My father told me that my grandfather carried the old Kentucky rifle as a boy of ten following the wagon that carried the household goods on the journey from Bedford County. I can scarcely believe it because the rifle is very heavy. If this story is true, he was a stout boy. That he was a patient, hard-working, just man I cannot doubt, for I have heard this from old men who knew him.

They spoke of him with a kind of respect that is usually reserved for men of character and substance.

My maternal grandfather was John Connor Barnard. I remember him but faintly. My memory is of a short, very portly man with great bushy eyebrows and a long flowing mustache. He was a spirited, enterprising, sprightly man, filled with sharp wit, shrewd and at the same time adventuresome. He bought land adjoining my father's people and made a living principally by making and selling whiskey and brandy. He had the first bonded brandy warehouse in the state. The government kept a gauger in attendance upon his operations, who lived in the house and must have gained more knowledge of the business of selling whiskey and brandy than the government ever knew of. I have heard of barrels tapped from below the floor and filled several times under the same seal. At first the business was profitable, but my grandpa Connor had a taste for politics. He ran for the office of county treasurer in Floyd County and was the first Democrat to be elected to that office—and the only one since. He was not a good overseer of those who worked for him, was often away, busy with his own rather than the County's business. He was defeated for a second term principally as a result of a rally at which too much whiskey was consumed. Soon thereafter he moved to Roanoke, Virginia, having lost his farm and brandy business in a successful attempt to repay funds to an estate which he was administering for the family of a friend, the investments for which turned out poorly. That he was honest no one doubted. That he had a flair for attracting men to his side is evident. He sired a family of three sons and six daughters. All of them were spirited; all of them had a quick tongue; one of them, my mother, was the kindest, the happiest, the most selfless woman I have ever known.

On my mother's side I am kin to the Turners and the Woods as well as the Barnards. My maternal grandmother was Mary Elizabeth Turner, the daughter of Samuel Turner and Rachel Wood. Of the Turners I know little. They were typical frontier people, big-boned, tough-minded Scotch-Irish people with a capacity for sadness and burden-bearing and a taste for corn liquor and a love of land. Rachel Wood, my great-grandmother, I remember well. She lived nearly a hundred and two years, broke her hip in her nineties and lived to walk again. It was she who could say: "Arise, my daughter, and go to thy daughter, for thy daughter's daughter has a daughter." Once when already old by year count alone she was attacked in the barnyard by a buck sheep.

She simply sat on his back and rode him around the barnyard for a turn or two. He never charged her again. When I was in college I returned home for a visit and went to see Grandma Turner. She was in bed and by her account doing poorly. She had by her bedside a glass with some whiskey and rock candy, her usual medicine. When she was a hundred years old, her family gave her a birthday party attended by a host of descendants and friends and well-wishers. A photographer from the newspaper came to take her picture. She was much against having her picture made. Said she: "When I was young and pretty nobody wanted to take my picture. Now that I am old and ugly everybody wants it. I reckon you can take it, but it won't be worth looking at." I am glad that I have a vivid memory of Grandma Turner. It is a comfort to know that I have some of her genes. Her stories of life in the Blue Ridge so many years ago bind me to the region, give me a sense of my own worth and will to live.

The grandfather of Grandma Turner was Richard Wood, the only one of my ancestors about whom I know much. In the 1700s he lived near Wood's Gap in Patrick County, Virginia. He is buried at County Line with his four wives about him. He was a pioneer in the area who farmed, kept a tavern, and acquired a frontier competence. He must have been uxorious; surely he was manly and a vibrant soul even in his extreme age. Upon the death of his third wife his children provided him with a housekeeper to whom he took a fancy. He married her in his late seventies much to their disgust. In answer to the question "Why, Papa, why?" he answered, "I found a cabbage among the collards." It is from this cabbage, Rachel Cockerhan or lately Cochran, that I am descended. From her name came my mother's; from her my own Rachel, who is the fifth with her name.

Some years ago the Wood clan used to gather at the tomb of Father Dickie for yearly family reunions. I have seen more than a thousand descendants come from all over the country to celebrate in the shade of the memory of Father Dickie. Stories would be told, speeches made, babies kissed, liquor drunk, and food by the basketful consumed. Some came in what my mother used to call "flivvers," some in Cadillacs. Some walked. But whatever their place and lot in life, they remembered that they were a clan, one people. There was no crisis of self-identity among these people. Few of them knew what a psychiatrist was. They had ills of body and mind—some of them. This they knew. They knew also how to endure and how to die.

I have said that I grew up astraddle the eighteenth and nineteenth centuries. It is a fact. When I was a little boy we did the everyday things the way they had been done since time out of mind. Let me first look at the relationship between man and animal. To start with take the cows. They were milked by hand—all too often by my hand; they were driven to pasture in the summer, brought home to the milking lot in evening; penned up at night in the winter in stables wet and aromatic from their own droppings; fed hay and fodder, occasionally chop and nubbins; they had names like members of the family—Daisy, Polly; they shared in the corporate life. When the harvest was good they had more, just like the family. Further, they had to be milked or their bags would spoil. Men felt responsible for their animals. How different this form of ownership is from the form that has come to characterize the twentieth century. Now a man feels no responsibility for the share of stock in a corporation or the bond of an insurance company. Ownership has become impersonal, devoid of responsibility, cool, deadly.

Ah, yes, cows were a very necessary part of my family. In my earliest memory we milked, strained the milk through a wire mesh to remove anything undesirable, and then placed it in the cool running water of the spring house to await the rising of the cream. This we skimmed off, placed in another jar to sour for churning. What we did not eat we sold to Mr. Ingram, the huckster. The skimmed milk we fed to the pigs, mixed with chop ground from our own wheat, oats, and buckwheat. How they loved it! I would take a goblet and a piece of corn bread to the spring and steal the sweet creamy milk before it soured. I can still taste that wonderful creamy mixture of cornbread and milk. Later we bought a second-hand cream separator from Abe Proffit, the blacksmith, and separated the cream from the milk while it was still fresh and foaming.

Of cows I have the fondest memories. My brother Albert, five years my senior, used to go with me to drive the cows from one field to another. I suppose I should say that I tagged along with him. At any rate we were driving the cows peacefully up the dirt road one day when a puffing, coughing red monster burst over the hill raising a cloud of dust. I leaped over the rail fence. The cows put their tails over their backs and bawled fearfully. Albert sought sanctuary in the woods. "What is it, what is it?" I yelled.

With much authority, as though such monsters were everyday

apparitions to him, he replied, "That's an automobile. I think it belongs to Paige Lawrence in Floyd."

That was my first introduction to automotive vehicles. I think it was the first the cows ever saw, too. They gave milk that night, but I tasted some, and it had the taste of lingering fear. Even as a child I knew the taste of lingering fear.

Of the horses I can say they were beasts of burden, and they were looked after because they were necessary and because they were horses. My father had a respect and a fondness for horses that I never developed. He fed them, at times shod them, worked them, cursed them and praised them. The bond between man and horse was different from the bond between man and cow. The horse was a kind of servant. The cow simply a beast, a producer of milk and calves. We kept only a necessary pair of horses. Occasionally a colt came along. This was always a great event, almost like the coming of a new baby to the family. The horses ploughed the land, pulling an old Syracuse or Oliver Chill. With the horses the land was harrowed, laid-off, drilled. The corn was cultivated with a double-shovel or a five-footed cultivator that ran between the rows. The wagon, a clumsy four-wheeled affair, was drawn by horses. The wagon served many purposes, and of all the vehicles until the automobile came along it was the most useful and even gay.

I cannot remember learning to ride. Babies from the time they could walk could also ride after a fashion. I rode when I could, walked when I had to. Many a turn of corn I shelled in the granary and carried barebacked to Charlie Glaspy's mill to be ground into meal, from which was made the staple, ever-eaten strengthener-of-life, brown-crusted cornbread. A horse understands man as no cow ever could. I do believe that cows have a peculiar fondness for children, though, that no horse has. A horse tolerates children. A horse respects and fears and in some cases loves man. Our horses had such names as Selim, Dan, Daisy. My uncle had a horse named Kemper, poor four-footed beast that had his hooves ruined from foundering on rye. His owner, my Uncle Jud, never gave him the attention he needed. As a boy I thought that my Uncle Jud ought to have foundered on the rye instead of the horse. Though I never developed the love for horses that my father had, I did like and enjoy and use them. Sixty years past my childhood I can still get on a horse without fear and ride him hell-for-leather, as I have done on hunting trips. The point is that horses were a man's life when I was young. The automobile came along and spoiled the relationship for me.

Thanks be to God that I grew up in a hunting and dog-loving family. It might have happened that I was born into a penurious, dime-pinching, religious-on-Sunday family that fattened on Calvinism and gave no dog food. There were a few people like that in my community, but very few. My father was a hunter, my Uncle Albert was a hunter, my early companions were hunters. What more natural than that I should be a hunter, a lover of dogs. The earliest family dog that I remember well was a black and tan hound named Tray, and, dimly, another before him called Rock. After Tray we had a succession of dogs—hounds, bird dogs, the shepherd Kazan whom I loved most. Once we had an Airedale. By the time I was twelve I could handle a bird dog and kill a quail on the wing.

I believe I was nine years old, on my first hunting venture alone, when I killed my first squirrel with a single-shot .44 caliber shotgun. Before that I had shot ground squirrels and even a cock quail with a .22 rifle. I remember the occasion well. I had gone into the woods above John Nichols's place about seven in the morning of a September day. Coming near a large hickory tree, I heard the patter of cuttings falling on green leaves. My heart leaped, and I shivered with anticipation. Far up in the tree I caught a glimpse of old bushy-tail. I sighted and shot, and down fell the gray body. I ran most of the way home to show my trophy. Only a few years after that my father permitted me to take the double-barreled Ithaca into the woods. Before breakfast and after the cows were milked one morning, I went into the woods on the hill above the house and shot a squirrel from a tree only to have two fall. Another I had not seen was in my line of fire. My father had heard me shoot once. Imagine my satisfaction in pretending that I had planned it that way. So delighted was I that I asked if I might take one of the squirrels to school to give it to my teacher, Miss Annie Bell Kyle. I was allowed to take it wrapped in one of my mother's Sunday napkins to my teacher. She almost fainted when I gave it to her but she was lady enough to thank me for it. Oh, I was young. To be young, impulsive, happy; feel the spring of young muscles and the spur of a young mind, alive and without much to answer for. How good it is.

I killed by first quail on the wing in the field just beyond Ole Man Yeatts's house on the left-hand side of the road leading to Bob

Harvey's store. The field was in wheat stubble. I was hunting with my father and Albert. We had borrowed a single-barreled gun for Albert from Dan Rakes, who was living with Aunt Minnie at Aunt Melia's place. It was an awkward piece that hurt his cheek when he fired and he didn't like it. I was carrying the .44 shotgun. Gyp and Rodney stood a covey of birds about the middle of the field. My father killed two on the rise. I picked out a bird and fired, and down it came. Albert had never killed a bird. I took great pleasure later in pointing that out to my father. That was after they had been dressed, mine included, for Albert to take to my Aunt Myrt in Roanoke with whom he was living while going to high school.

I grew up with farm animals, and we were surrounded by chickens, ducks, and turkeys. There were three hen houses, one at the barn, one in the yard of the old house, and one in the lower garden. Without chickens I hardly see how we would have got along. Their eggs contributed to our diet and to our pocket book. I remember barred rocks or domineckers, Rhode Island reds, brown leghorns, white leghorns, black Minorcas, bunties without the long tail feathers, and bantams. Customarily we raised chickens by setting clutches of eggs under the setting hens. Eighteen to twenty-one eggs were a clutch. When hatched the chicks were brought into the house and placed in a basket by the stove for a day or so, covered by an old sweater or some woolen piece. Afterwards we released them to the protection of their mothers' wings. In the summer there were chickens of every size and color running about the place. We would feed them on dough made from corn meal. When they were about half grown they began to eat grain. It was about then that we began to eat fried chicken, with marvelous gravy made by pouring off all but a little of the grease in which the floured chicken had been fried, mixing in some flour, and adding milk. On hot biscuits it was divine.

To awaken a little before day to the melody of crowing adult roosters and those claiming to be is sweet. It places one dutifully within an order of nature that admits no questioning. To hear the cackle of laying hens, the cluck of concerned mothers, the peeping of dependent chicks is a peaceful and civilizing experience. Today I awaken quite early, as old men do, and no rooster crows. I travel the highways and the byways, and no busy chickens are to be seen. They are all penned up in giant egg factories, seldom permitted the luxury of darkness, kept ever laying. I pity their poor lot. Never a rooster to minister to them. Poor psychotic fowls! In the old days they could steal a nest in some out-of-the-way place and perhaps raise a brood to bring home at the proper time, or lay their eggs in a remote corner of the haymow to be found by some exploring child. All of that has gone and some of the beauty and mystery of life with it. We raised turkeys to sell in the fall. My mother used the turkey money for many purposes—school books, shoes for active feet in winter, little luxuries like lemon drops or candy bars, a new dress, a new sweater, gifts for ten children at Christmas. The turkey-raising process went something like this:

Papa, holding sister Helen, and Mama beside him have gathered other important members of my family. Also standing are Aunt Elma Phlegar, Uncle Jud, my sisters Maude, Mary, and Annie, and Ida, an adopted child in the Phlegar family. In front are Aunt Nannie, my sister Virginia, Ethel Phlegar, and Dr. Bob Phlegar.

When the laying season came in late spring, the hens left for the woods, accompanied by the gobbler. My job was to watch them to their nests that we might take the eggs for safekeeping, to be later set under the mother hen or under chicken hens. At the proper time the hen would have her poults returned that she might raise them like wild things in the woods and fields. In the fall the mother hen would inevitably show up with maybe a dozen nearly grown young turkeys.

Some of my most exhilarating experiences of boyhood are bound up with turkey-watching. You had to be alert. You had to anticipate. You had to keep out of sight and try to outwit a turkey, the most wary of birds, half wild and intent upon grave business. On final extremity I have seen them rise and fly to a nest. Nearly always, though, I found the nest. I learned much about nature in these turkey-watching excursions. I learned of birds and their ways and calls, of bees and beetles, of red and black ants, of chipmunks with jaws full of black cherries, of the precarious balance of young squirrels, the mating antics of crows. I learned to love the smell of rotting logs and camp leaves, and the silence of the woods.

Once when I was absorbed in my duties I heard a great roaring in the sky, a strange mechanical noise. Looking into the sky I saw what I knew to be a plane, the first I had seen. Down in the meadow below me I saw Dr. Thurman run from his office calling out in his cleft-palate way: "Oh, Beulah, Beulah, come look! Come fast! Here comes an airplane!" I think it was the first plane that many of my neighbors ever saw in the sky, for there was much talk of it for days. A thing like a plane seen in a remote community is a marvelous, almost fearful experience. Even old men dream dreams when they should by the Biblical account be seeing visions. Remember, we were astraddle two centuries.

We had no geese. Why, I do not know, for we had kept geese in my grandmother's day. It may have been that on the eve of a new age we let some things go, like the gooseberry bushes, and the tame raspberries. We did have ducks, but ducks were principally for children. Their eggs were too strong. Their noise, though not so bad as guineas, was distracting. Then they were hard to bring to maturity. There were too many mud turtles that love young ducks, too many water snakes in the nearby creek. We had them, though. There is nothing so fluffy, so cunning, so lovable as tiny yellow ducklings. My sister Maude and I raised ducks, and we loved them. There was the immortal Yellow Jaw, my own who was taken by a turtle. There was Splayfoot, Creamy, Bo Peep, and a score more, all of whom had names, all of whom were a part of the family pattern. They followed the hen, drove her frantic with their love for water, warped her very soul. It was only after I was well along in life and got ducklings for my children that I learned that they give unhesitating loyalty to whoever first mothers them, duck, hen, man, or dog. There is something worthwhile to be learned from ducks.

I grew up among trees. They, too, were a part of our family life. They had names, especially the chestnut trees. Only the other day my brother Albert spoke of Josie. Josie was a great chestnut tree that bore nuts beyond her sisters and of greater size. She sprang from the ground like some tree goddess in the Trough Spring field woods. Old she was and deep were her roots and thick her bark. Then there were the walnut trees planted by my grandmother for each of her babies as they came along, planted by the lane leading to the milking gap. When I was young they were old but productive. My mother sold one of them for what seemed then the enormous sum of $500. I am told that the lumber from the tree eventually went to Japan for veneer. The children hulled the walnuts and spread them in the old kitchen loft to dry. Later they were cracked and sold for pocket money or used in the chocolate fudge that my sisters occasionally made. Apple trees we had too. There was the striped June tree that bore apples early in the summer, good for cooking, good for eating too. There was the Yellow Harvest, the Smokehouse, the Red June so welcome in June, the wonderfully flavored Maiden Blush that fried so well for breakfast, the Fallerwater, as large and plump and tender as a woman's breast, the Big Pippin, and a host of others from my grandfather's orchard. Trees were like people to me. They had a life of their own, they bloomed and bore, grew old and died.

In the fall the late-bearing apples were harvested. Those that were to be put in the cellar for winter use were picked. The others were shaken from the tree and brought in by the wagon loads to make apple butter. Apple butter was a staple in my community. I can still taste its tangy flavor on a hot biscuit, its soggy look and less appealing taste on a cold biscuit in a school lunch box. Much work paring and coring and quartering was done to prepare the great quantity that went into the huge copper kettle. Apple butter time was a gay time. Children and old people took turns stirring the boiling mass with a great wooden stirrer long enough to protect hands and faces from the intense heat of the fire. "Once around the pot and twice through the middle" were the words to a tune of one's own making. Hour after hour it went so until at last the red mass was ready for the crocks and cans. If put into crocks, my mother used to seal the top with paraffin. It kept well throughout the winter. By adding grape juice at a certain time in the cooking, one had a sharp-tasting grape butter that I especially liked.

Of all trees I loved the apple tree best, but the chestnut comes in a close second. In the days before the blight like a pest from Egypt laid low this great tree of the Alleghenies, the woods were full of chestnuts. From them came the delicious nuts, the rails for the fences, timber for building, acid for tanning. Many a child paid for his winter shoes and books for school with money gotten by selling chestnuts. I have seen Green Wood's back-room store filled nearly to the ceiling with chestnuts that he shipped away. Many's the time I listened at night to the wind and the rain of early fall, rejoicing at the thought of chestnuts on the ground under the great bare tree. I picked up as many as two gallons at a time and sold them for good money.

The hickories we loved too. I have a delicious memory of an event that came to climax in a hickory tree in the yard. My brother Albert and I were as close as he would let me be. I looked up to him and I tormented him when I could or paid him back for many a jab in the ribs when I was riding behind him on a horse. One day he got a letter from Libby Dalton, on whom he was very, very sweet. It came in a pink envelope. I saw it invitingly sticking from the hind pocket of his overalls. Of course I snatched it and ran. A merry chase I led him, down to the spring and through the meadow. I was losing the race fast when I saw before me a fresh cow pile and the hickory tree. Quickly I ran through the cow pile, pausing long enough to anoint my feet, and swung like an ape into the hickory tree. I climbed to the highest branches. Close behind me came panting Albert. Just as he looked up to grasp my ankle, I stepped full in his face a dung-covered foot, a stinking foot. Oh, I paid for it; but what a memory! I cherish it to this day. When the payment was over I could still taunt him—"What does it taste like, old buddy?"

Chapter Two

Houses, People, and Things

The family in which I was born was a kind of open-ended corporation. It was made up of father, mother, sons and daughters who constituted the first rank. The second rank was made up of uncles, aunts, nieces, nephews, first cousins. There was a third rank made up of more distant kinfolk like second and third cousins or even third cousins three times removed. All who were related had a recognized claim on the hospitality of the home. They came with and without notice, remained a day or a week, though in general Sunday was the great day for family visiting. I felt at home in the house of Aunt Elma or Cousin Lilah, or Cousin Will West. They and their children felt equally at ease in our house. Most of my extended family lived in the community, within walking distance. This kind of tribal arrangement gave children great security. I knew my place, what was expected of me, the limits of my freedom, what I ought to contribute, and when to speak and when to remain silent. It was only when I was visiting in town or at Roanoke that I felt the insecurity of a new environment. It seems to me that children today do not have the same security, the same freedom to come and go that was so typical of my growing up. Today I would probably be classified as underprivileged. If so, I never knew it. I did not own a bicycle, but who did? I had sturdy legs, occasionally the use of a horse, and on great occasion an opportunity to ride in a car. What more could be asked? Always there were the brook, the creeks, the river, the fields, the woods, sisters and brother, the warm cheer of the kitchen, the knowledge that I was a part of a family, the sense of being loved. As a result I grew up like a weed around the barn, vibrant and free.

I do not have many very early memories. I remember very dimly the birth of my sister Mary. I was about three at the time, and it seems to me that I can remember the displacement. It may be that I have no memory of this, for my mother periodically had babies, nine of them who yet live. I do remember distinctly being taken to the old Pizarro school as a tiny visitor. My cousin Ike Harvey was the teacher. I was shy and unhappy there. I did not know how to get out to go to the johnny house, how to ask. To my embarrassment, his, and my sister's, my bladder loosed its contents on the floor. On the way home we passed my Cousin Lilah's. She was on the porch of the store. She teased me about my wet pants, laughed, and gathered me to her in a great hug. I almost had another accident. She and her daughter Amelia were the bane of my early existence. When she came to visit I hid in the hen house.

I remember work and I remember play. It was the custom in my youth for boys at a very early age to go to the fields to work with their fathers. I loved this work at first. By the time I was nine years old I could hoe corn almost as well as a man, even bind wheat and shock hay. This was man's work, and it pleased me to do it, especially if I were praised for it. There was nothing so heady for me as praise and nothing so dismal as criticism. Like the boy, the man. As I grew older I longed for a rainy day in summer or the coming of Sunday, for it seems to me that I was constantly at work. It had its rewards, but oh, the joy of play!

Albert and I used to make flutter mills. By properly putting together two pieces of soft pine, a paddle wheel could be made which when placed in a split stick would make a miniature water wheel. Dam up the brook and put the paddles under the spillway, and the wheel would go merrily. I made little doll canoes out of birch bark for my sister Maude. These we would float with their cargoes of china-headed dolls down the creek.

Whistles we made by slipping the bark from a chestnut sprout at the proper season. Pop guns we made from elder. By pushing out the pith you had a barrel. Now fashion a plunger from a piece of hickory, chew up a wad of paper, push it to the end of the barrel, chew up another for the front end, push the one toward the other and "pop." Out comes the paper bullet with enough force to sting the skin through a blue denim shirt. Pop guns were carried to school to the vexation of the teacher and certain confiscation.

My early memory of our house, of the out-buildings, of the old log-bodied house in which my grandfather had lived are among the most distinct of my early memories. First there was the kitchen. Here the real living took place: The water we carried from the spring was brought into the kitchen; in winter, pails of milk bound for the spring house were first deposited in the kitchen; and in the coldest months the

The old log house built in 1796 of white oak logs under weather board.

family came together around the big wood-burning cook stove. With all the coming and going, it is a wonder that my mother got the cooking done. Yet amid disorder there was an underlying order. One did not get in another's way. My favorite resting place was the wood box nearly behind the stove. There is nothing so memorable as the smell of a country kitchen, from the rich aroma of frying ham or bacon to the subtler smell of ground coffee or the more acrid smell of wood smoke. To lie on the stove wood, smell the cooking, and anticipate the meal is an experience I would not forego. Did you ever smell the aroma of buckwheat batter? I have. Have you ever eaten buckwheat cakes covered with sausage and red gravy, with homemade butter and molasses? I have.

We often ate in the kitchen, especially in the winter. In the summer we gathered around the dining room table, sometimes twelve hungry mouths at a time. The kitchen was a room about fifteen feet by fourteen with a fireplace at one end and a cooking stove nearby with a pipe running into the chimney. Two doors led into this room, one from a front porch, one from the back porch. Behind the door from the front porch was a shelf that usually had on it a pail of spring water. By the wall next to the door to the back porch was the table. On one side, the one next the wall, was a bench on which the children sat. At the two ends and by the side were cane-bottom chairs made of maple, for the adults and older children. My father sat at the end of the table near the door. On the corner by him stood the highchair usually filled with a baby learning to eat and to behave. In my house there was always a baby in the highchair or one coming on. My father was a splendid disciplinarian. It came easy for him. He expected obedience and got it. For breakfast we always had hot biscuits baked the same morning by my mother. There was always butter and fried eggs or scrambled. Usually there was bacon, homemade, sliced, dipped in flour and fried, or a shoulder of meat. Nearly always she made both brown gravy and that staple of life, white gravy. Always we had molasses and apple butter, both homemade. On Sunday and occasions there was black-berry or grape jelly or preserved cherries or other fruit.

I have no certain memory of the midday meal; so often I was in school. Sunday dinners were a little special, with stewed chicken or chicken and dumplings. The ordinary midday meal was a big meal, though. Working men and children got hungry. This was the meal for cornbread and beans, green in the summer, dried in the winter. Meat was always served—usually some kind of pork, for we ate little beef when I grew up. I especially remember backbones and spareribs in the winter. I have a splendid memory of coming in with my father from hunting, and for short legs it had been a long day, to a wonderful pot of turnips and a bowl of backbones. This was the beginning of my fondness for turnips. By late winter the larder began to get depleted. It was, I realize now, a difficult time for both man and beast. The best had been consumed. The summer garden lay in the too-distant future. We made do pretty well. There was cabbage that had been put head down into the garden and covered with earth; there was the remnant of apples beginning to rot in the cellar. There were the canned blackberries and fruits still not used up. Always there was the potato, that life-saver and gift of the gods. Supper was the meal for potato soup and left-overs, for sweet potatoes baked in a dutch oven in the fireplace.

The living room had in it a collection of chairs, my mother's sewing machine, a chest of drawers with a bookcase on top of it, and the bed upon which my father and mother slept. The coziest place here was the fireplace. Here early in the morning before the light of day my father raked out the coals of yesterday's fire and kindled a new one. Fire began the day, fire ended it, fire made life in our house possible. Around that fire sat the family at night; around that fire the children dressed in the morning. Around that fire the fiddle was played and songs were sung; and conversation was kept well stoked. We were all children of the fire. Here our dreams were dreamed, here our hurts were mended, here was our comfort. In the blue dancing flames were the portents of our futures.

Downstairs there was also the parlor. It was heated by a stove. Here was some furniture that I was always ashamed of. It was made of cheap carved oak and covered with imitation leather. It never seemed to me to be authentic. It did not take a polish of use. Here, too, were the books of our house, of which we had a great many for our day. We were all readers. When the grey days came, when the winds persisted and the rains kept up the incessant chatter and drip on the roof, only the books lifted clouds, brought sunshine, stifled boredom, whispered promises, beckoned the spirit to take wing. On occasion the parlor could become an interesting place, but only when company came, and music was made, and conversation became animated and careless, or my sister Grace played the violin or my father the fiddle, or Kyle Weeks came with a love offering of fruit or candy and his great, roaring laugh. For a time that laugh was the hallmark of our going into and coming out of the parlor.

Upstairs were two bedrooms, and over the kitchen and dining room a garret that was later converted into two bedrooms. The two bedrooms were furnished each with a four-poster bed and a chest or chest of drawers. Along with a cane-bottomed chair or two it was enough. The beds were interesting. The mattresses were supported either by a network of cord or by wooden slats. On the cord was a tick filled with straw, and on that a feather bed. The same sufficed for the slatted bed. One difficulty with straw ticks was that they tended to attract bedbugs. Every so often we had to take down the bed, clean it thoroughly with kerosene, and refill the ticking with fresh straw. I never thought the beds were uncomfortable. They were beds and we were used to them. In winter the room was cold and the bed glacial. It was then that you needed a warm body to sleep with and I had my brother Albert or, when I was quite small, my sister Maude. There was, of course, no inside toilet or bathroom. Baths were taken in a tub on Saturday night in the kitchen. The toilet was the johnny house during the day and the chamber pot, or thunder mug, at night. Anyway youthful bladders hold a lot of water.

The garret was at once a place to sleep, a place to play, a storehouse, and a hideaway. I loved the garret. On rainy days the sound of rain on the roof was pleasant. Even on sunny days in winter it was comfortable from the sun on the roof. Only in summer was it uncomfortable.

Once Aunt Nanny, Uncle Jud's unmarried sister, came for a visit of a few days. She slept in the upstairs bedroom over the living room. She was old then and fearful, God fearing, Devil believing, a wonderful hand for spinning or crocheting, for tatting or growing petunias and sultanas. (For a long time I did not know what Aunt Nanny's sultana was. Albert misled me.) Maude and I were sleeping in the garret. The night was dark and stormy with sheet lightning playing across the sky and thunder shaking the window panes. Aunt Nanny went through her nightly ritual of preparing for bed. Maude and I lay low. As soon as the old woman was quietly cultivating sleep, I crept under her bed and by arching my back into the cords that held the tick, raised Aunt Nanny slowly in her bed six inches or so. Slowly I let the tick return to its former position. From Aunt Nanny there came the sound of a long drawn and quivering breath. She subsided. Again I raised the tick. This time there was a great and shrill cry: "Taz, Taz, come quick. There is someone under my bed!" That's when Maude and I lit out for the garret. Papa came upstairs to look around. There was nothing to be seen.

"Nanny," he said, "you're just imagining. There is nothing under your bed!" Maude and I quivered with suppressed laughter. "Go to sleep, Nanny," said my father, and made his way back to his own bed. There was no sleep for Nanny. She came in her night dress to the door of the garret.

"Maude," she pleaded, "come sleep with me for a while. I am all confused!"

Dutifully Maude climbed in the bed for a while. But soon she slipped out and returned with Papa's flashlight and began to snap it off and on about the room. Now my Aunt Nanny could not see well with her glasses off.

"Ah!" she said, "what a storm! I have never seen such lightning. Once down in Patrick County we had a great storm like this." Maude stayed quiet, flashing the light on and off. "Surely the devil is up and about this night. I believe the old Deil has been under my very bed." At this I rolled with laughter outside the door.

Somehow Aunt Nanny got through the night and so did Maude. Papa had a strange look on his face the next morning when he asked me, "What was happening upstairs last night?"

With all innocence I answered, "There was a bad storm."

Nearby, across the yard, were the house and the outhouses of my ancestors. There was the two-story, log-bodied dwelling house, at some more recent time covered with clapboard. Though once it had had more rooms, when I first knew it it was made up of a living room paneled with wide white pine boards with a great fireplace and a door leading into a remarkable attic or garret—the dining room or bedroom to suit the convenience of the occupant—containing another large fireplace. Adjacent was the log-bodied "old kitchen" where the cooking and most of the eating had formerly been done. When I knew it, it was used as a meat house where the salted pork was kept in great wooden boxes. It, too, had a room under the roof where we stored walnuts to dry or used for whatever came naturally. All of the fireplaces were provided with gear for cooking, for in the early days before the era of the cook stove all cooking was done in the fireplace. When these buildings were built is hard to say. Certainly they were there in 1812 and maybe before. In the yard was the log smokehouse, where meat had once been smoked, the hog pen for fattening a couple of pigs at a time, and the outdoor toilet, made of planks when I first remember it. While my grandparents lived, this log complex was their abode. It had come to the family through the West line. In the early part of the nineteenth century it must have been quite a pioneer establishment, marking its owner as more prosperous than the common run. At the foot of a declivity and a good hundred yards from the old house was the spring, bold and hand-shaped, providing winter and summer a stream of freestone water of great purity and clarity. I know of no bolder spring in my neighborhood. From this spring was carried to the house in pails every bit of water that we used. I would hesitate to estimate the number of gallons I have carried up the path from the spring. Here was the spring house. Here was the washing pot. Here was the churn. Here were the crocks of butter. Here were the staples of life.

These old houses made an impact on my early life. I am not yet ready to see them go into strange hands. They tied me to a family, to memories of the past. For me they were always inhabited by ghosts of the past. As boys in the summer Albert and I slept in the upstairs room of the old house. Occasionally as a little boy I slept there alone. To be alone in the old house—surrounded by grey shades of the past, startled by every creak and every sound of bird or animal—was to experience the pure agony of fear. To leave on this account for the security of my father's house was as a matter of pride unacceptable. Consequently, I learned to move toward danger, to rationalize my inordinate fears. For I was born fearful, imaginative, seeing or creating danger where there was none. I can even remember the fear I had of strange noises, especially those made by the threshing machine and the steam engine. In my early youth I finally learned to conquer fear,

Uncle Ike and Aunt Melia Martin prepare to attend church at Pine Creek.

so far as one of my temperament ever learns it. At least I learned not to give in. Once when I was very young I ate an apple that my brother gave me, from a tree of poisonous apples, or so he claimed. His word was law. I expected to be undone by the experience for at least a day. Gradually I learned.

The old houses and the stories my mother told about them always excited me. Many a time I looked for the bag of Spanish gold that was supposed to be hidden somewhere about the house. According to the story, one of my West forebears had a fine bag of gold coins. On his deathbed his wayward sons tried to get the gold from the old man. They even carried him to the smokehouse and fired rifles near him. He never revealed his secret if, indeed, he had one. After his death the boys—wicked men, rather—tore up the very hearthstones in their search. They never found the gold. My Uncle Ike Martin used to prepare by great concentration at bed-time to dream his way into the secret hiding place. He never did. If there was gold, it yet rests in its place. But what romance for a boy!

I did not grow up in a money economy. I have no idea just how much hard cash came into the hands of my father in a given year. It could not have been more than $1,500. I may be all wrong in placing the sum so high. There was the income from the surplus grain but there was little of this. What the family did not eat the animals and the poultry did. There was the sale of lambs but never more than ten or twelve. There was the money from the calves that were usually sold as veals. There was the income from hams and even shoulders of pork that were sold. There was money from eggs and butter, from chickens and turkeys. This was about the whole of it. Instead of money there was a living, not so crabbed or cramped as to stifle desire or imagination, not so scanty as to create the feeling of inferiority. The challenge was neither too great nor too small. It meant in my day, when the money economy was just beginning to see triumph, that every chick and child knew that his or her future depended on himself or herself, with a little help when it could be spared. In any event, the early death of my father further pointed in the direction of self-help for our brood.

In a typical year we would plant about ten to fifteen acres of corn, eight or ten acres of wheat, a field of oats, a field of buckwheat, red top, timothy, and clover for hay, perhaps some orchard grass. The corn was planted by a drill pulled by a single horse or by hand when we laid the ground off in cross rows so as to plough it both ways. Normally the corn was cultivated three times by ploughing with a double shovel or cultivator, hoed once or twice, and then laid by. The hoeing was man and boy work. As a boy of ten I could swing a professional hoe.

Once the ears began to harden, it was time to pull fodder. This was done by stripping the leaves from each stalk from the ear to the ground. When you had a small bundle stripped, it was tied with a blade or two and hung from the ear to wilt and cure. When properly cured the bundles were gathered, tied into larger bundles, and brought to the barn for the horses and cows to relish in winter.

Along about late September or even later we would cut tops. This was done with a sharp knife, the tops being the stalk above the ear. These were stacked in the field until such time as the stacks might be moved to the barn. This left the ears on the lower half of a stripped stalk which were pulled off by hand, pitched into convenient piles, and collected in one great pile behind the barn, or in it, for shucking. Another way of gathering corn was to cut it just above ground and shock it in the field. We used both ways. Corn shuckings were great occasions. Sometimes the liquor flowed. Often contests developed among the shuckers. It was sometimes a communal project, sometimes one for which wages were paid. Either way it was exciting to young boys and old men.

Wheat was planted in autumn, harvested in July. There were few reapers in my community. The land was high and sometimes hilly. The fields were small. Cooperative buying and using was virtually unknown. Wheat was cut with a cradle. The cradle was something like a scythe with fingers, four of them. A good cradler could cut a hundred dozen in a day—a dozen being a shock of twelve bundles. Behind the cradlers came the binders. At first I bound. The wheat lay in a perfectly even swath. One gathered up a bundle and, pulling from the end of heads a band, twisted it tight and tucked it under.

When I became older, sixteen or so, I began to cradle with the men. It was man's work. Think of swinging a seventeen pound cradle through thick wheat for ten hours a day! I used to carry water to the field of laboring men. I have seen Ike Davis, a colored man who was a great cradler, drink half a gallon of water at a time. I learned then that some men sweat and some don't. There was never a dry thread on a cradler who sweated. Those who did not sweat could not last as long.

After the wheat was cut and bound, it had to be shocked. It dried in the shock until stacking time came. Occasionally it was left in the shock until threshing time. Normally, though, the wheat was stacked to preserve it from the weather. We took our wheat from the shock to the stack by wagon with a special bed made for carrying hay and cut grain. One man pitched it from the ground to the wagon; another in the wagon placed it so as to build a stable load. At the stack the bundles were pitched down from the wagon to the stacker, who arranged them symmetrically around a pole. Once when I was twelve my father could not get anybody to help him. I worked two days pitching from the ground to the wagon and from the wagon to the stack. My father was full of sweet praise—my mother full of worry that I had worked too hard.

Along about late August the threshing machine came around. It went with a small crew from farm to farm, threshing grain. When I was very young the noise, the dust, and the whir of blades was maddeningly frightful to me. Later I came to look forward to the excitement of threshing time. The grain was pitched to the cutter, who cut the band and helped feed the grain into the maw of the machine. The straw was carried mechanically to the rick, where several men built the rick in a stable and secure way. My job was to hold sacks into which the grain was poured from the measurer as it came from the great screw of the machine. Threshing was the dirtiest and hottest work of the farm. It built huge appetites. Our table would be loaded with food—green beans from the garden, stewed corn, chicken, beef, pork, cabbage, and great pones of cornbread. It disappeared rapidly into hungry mouths. Once Charlie Glaspy got the cake mixed up with the cornbread. When my sister Grace said, "Mr. Glaspy, have some more beans!" he replied, "No, thank you. I will have some more of the yellow cornbread." For a time "pass me the yellow cornbread" became a favorite saying in the family.

When I was ten or twelve, I was at a threshing of my cousin Bob Harvey's wheat. There was a young man, twenty or so, by the name of Roy Nowlin, who was a member of the threshing crew. He was mischievous and even a little mean. To boot, he was probably a little liquored up. He seized me and rolled me over on the ground, threatening to put axle grease on my penis. Whether he did or not I don't remember. If he did, it did not act as fertilizer. My father was on the rick and could not see the indignity I was suffering. My cousin, little Bob Harvey, did. He was a stout man and a good one. He grabbed the

Nowlin man, threw him to the ground, exposed and greased him good. He won a friend. A threshing crew was a pretty earthy, hard-working, mean lot at times.

Rabbits young and old, caught in the ever-shrinking plot of wheat, at length had to make a run for it through the stubble. We boys would try to outrun the half-grown rabbits. Many a one I caught with my bare hands (after all, rabbits don't bite) and brought home for the skillet. There is hardly anything better than young fried rabbit to a Blue Ridge Mountain boy! I have known old, sedate cradlers to lay down their cradles and join the boys in the merry chase. My father would. He was like that.

Haying was hot work—shocking, hauling, pitching. It was dusty too. There is nothing, however, that has the aroma of newly cured timothy hay. It is aromatic. It is sexually stimulating. It has in its odor the sweetness of spring rain, the promise of a June day, the melancholy tinge of dying grass. No wonder that throughout history it is associated with wanton errancy, with erotic delights. I left the farm too early in life to test its subtle power, but I can understand it.

Nearly always at the end of a hot day in the field came a swim in the little river that ran not far from our house. Even if the river was too far for tired bodies, there was the nearby creek. With a piece of home-made lye soap and a rough towel a man or boy could get clean. I learned to swim quite early by following my father to the swimming hole. We shucked our clothes and tried the water. My father swam the breast stroke. It was that stroke that we all learned first. The river was not very deep but deep enough to swim in. Then there was always the White Rock Hole that was over a man's head, or the Sweeney Hole. I will digress now to tell you a story about Mr. Cannaday and the white rock.

One of the few places in the river near us where the water was consistently over a man's head was the White Rock Hole, named for a great boulder of flint rock that the water swirled against. This was a favorite swimming hole. It was very near the home of Amos Cannaday, a longtime friend of my family. Amos was a huge, hearty man who loved good land and on occasion good liquor. Once on a spree he dived into the water from the rock and disappeared. Loud was the lament. Diligent the search for the body. No Amos. His wife was notified. The children gathered by the river, hoping against hope. No Amos! What the half-pickled Amos had done was dive into the water, enter a vaulted ditch he had made for drainage, reemerge in the meadow some distance away and make his way to the house and to his bed, where he lay peacefully snoring while his wife and children wailed out their loss. The lost was found. The story had a happy ending for all except Amos. He is the same man who at another time had Dr. Thurman angry and speechless because his 1917 Ford would not move when he cranked her and pushed in the low gear. Amos, the whole 280 pounds of him, had a firm grip on the back end. He is the same man who used to say solemnly to my sister Maude, "Hello, Britches!" Unfortunately while I was still young he moved with his whole clan, including Irene at whose appearance I often blushed a beet red, to Pulaski County where he prospered and reputedly grew old and sedate.

Buttons and Britches reminds me of the time Albert hoodwinked Maude into taking off her floppy hat and bowing to Miriam Thurman. He said, "Maude, we are about to pass Dr. Thurman's. Miriam is in the yard. Remember how Papa always tells us to take off our hat and bow to ladies? Well, Miriam is a lady. Bow and take off your hat when we pass." Maude took him at face value. After all, he was the older brother. She took off the hat and bowed most respectfully as they passed. Whereupon Albert broke into great heehaws of laughter. Of course Maude was mortified as only young eleven-year-old girls can be. I am sure she threw road dust in his face. It would be like her.

Let me tell you about a typical day in the summer when blackberries were ripe.

We were accustomed to rise early in the summer months. There was much work to be done. First the cows were milked, and the milk was put away in the spring house. All of us milked at one time or another. I can't remember when I could not milk with both hands. Usually it was a grim task accompanied by little conversation except the inevitable "Back your leg" or "Saw, now, saw!" On occasion, though, it could be hilarious. To squirt a stream of milk in a brother's or sister's face was to start a battle of "free squirting." It usually ended in anger or in the cats being milked upon. Day by day they were there to get a mouthful of warm milk. After milking, the boys went with the men to the field to work, the girls to whatever task was open—washing clothes, preparing for midday dinner, sewing, or reading.

In the afternoons we picked blackberries. They were a staple, and nature furnished them free. Usually we picked in a field called the

Traveler, named, so I think, for the fine cold spring near the road where travelers stopped for a drink. We took two-gallon pails and smaller pails which we would fill and then empty into the larger ones. To find a shady spot near the woods where the briars grew tall and the berries large and juicy was a competitive enterprise. About the field you would hear the question, "Have you got your bottom covered?" usually followed by a laugh. Some afternoons we picked seven or eight gallons of berries. After processing they were placed in cans for the winter. The juice was squeezed out and jelly made. They were preserved. They were made into giant cobbler pies.

Maude and me after a morning of squirrel hunting.

When blackberries were not in season, grapes were. We picked the tame concords from the arbor in the middle of the old yard. We picked the wild fox grapes from the fences in the meadow or wherever they grew. From these, too, we made jelly, or preserved the juice for winter use. Then there were chinquapins by the thousands. Like the chestnuts, the chinquapins have almost gone. Why, I do not know. There were hazelnuts, black haws, red haws, and above all the delicious wild raspberries. All of these my brothers and sisters and I sought after and found.

My sister Maude and I had guidebooks for birds and wild flowers. All summer we would bird-watch until we could identify all of our birds, from the Baltimore oriole to the redstart and the vireo. At that time the Arm & Hammer Soda boxes contained cards with colored reproduction of the different birds. We were avid collectors of these cards. The wild flowers, too, gave us pleasure. We found the trailing arbutus, Indian paintbrush, and even the rare yellow wild orchids. There was much to see, much to learn, much to do. In the evenings we played the wild running games to take the spring out of young legs.

So it went in the dewy days of my early youth. There was work aplenty, play enough, food for hungry mouths, a mild discipline to keep everything in place, a sure security to strengthen young egos, castor oil for stomachs, stones to spit under for growing pains, bare feet for quick flight, fish in the creek, rabbits in the briar patch, squirrels in the trees, dreams in the head.

I have said that discipline was mild. I may have overstated the case. My father was a sensitive man, scholarly by temperament, and perhaps never cut out to be a farmer. He had a quick temper, usually well controlled. I remember an occasion, though, when discipline was wild and unrestrained. I had done something to sister Mary that infuriated my mother. She called it to the attention of my father. He took me to the wood shed for a whipping. I went. He whipped. I lay down on the floor of the shed and began to sing. He expected tears. He did not get them. He whipped harder and harder. I sang louder and louder. This continued until I was well stripped and until he realized what he was doing. He released me. I ran to the barn and nursed my sore back and sides until dark. Then I came to my room and crept into my bed. Some time thereafter I felt Papa getting in bed with me. I slid to my side, but he reached with his arms and held me close and told me how sorry he was that he had lost his temper, that he had whipped so hard. The tears that would not come from punishment came flooding for the love and kindness. I think I cried myself to sleep in my father's arms. Later on when he was so ill and I was so wayward and errant, I was a great burden to him, I believe. In age I have regretted at times the errancy of my youth, especially my mocking lightness that sometimes gave greater displeasure than heavy stubbornness.

We had plenty of kinsmen and some neighbors. Up the road towards Silverleaf about three quarters of a mile lived my Uncle Jud and Aunt Elma Phlegar, my father's sister. Uncle Jud and Aunt Elma were cousins. Uncle Jud was a small, meticulous man with a flowing mustache and a chronic stomach ache. As men went in my youth he was not strong physically, but he had a passion for order and discipline. His stove wood was always neatly stacked. Sometimes he was tyrannical and overbearing in his behavior to children and dogs. He was a staunch Missionary Baptist who wore a derby hat and a heavy gold watch chain to church. My Aunt Elma was my father's only sister when I was young, though there had been two others. She was patient, good-hearted, a good wife and a good cook who made the best grape butter I ever tasted. She had a way with children. I always listened for her praise. When she came in the summer I ran to get a cool bucket of water from the "sweet corner" of the spring. There were two sons in the family: Bob, who became a doctor, and Walter, a lawyer. I spent many a night with the Phlegars. There was in the upstairs back room a great stack of *Field and Stream* magazines going all the way back to 1909. I devoured them all. There I first read *Desert Gold* by Zane Grey, in serial. They were as much a part of my early life, the Phlegars, as my brothers and sisters. It was in Aunt Elma's garden that I first learned to love flowers. Eventually they moved to Tennessee to be near their son Bob, the doctor, but not before a strenuous bout with typhoid fever that nearly laid them low and did demolish the family of Cousin Jim Howery who lived across the road and used the same spring.

My great-grandmother Turner lived with her daughter Della, who married Jim Howery. They lived just across the road from the Phlegars. Aunt Della was my grandmother's youngest sister. Often we visited in this home. They had a foot-pedal pump organ that was a great delight. In this family there were my cousins Annabelle, Evelyn, and Marie, slightly older than I. Jim Howery was a stout, red-faced, pleasant man, who always had fat horses. When the family got typhoid fever from the spring water, within a week both Mr. Howery and Annabelle died. Their loss was keenly felt even by me. It left Aunt Della without a husband and a mainstay. It left us without Annabelle, who was sprightly and interesting. Nevertheless they got along very well as people do who have to. I loved their house with the quaint upstairs rooms and the smell of good food. Here Grandma Turner, the matriarch, lived. She sat by the fireplace in the kitchen and told me stories of her youth when wolves howled in the mountains and Andrew Jackson had not long been dead. She remembered pouring corn between the walls of the house to save it from the Yankees and hiding the colt in a sassafras thicket until the marauders went on. She remembered carrying a bantam hen up Runnet Bag, a pass in the mountains, when she was a little girl on her way home from a visit with a kinsman, and losing it when frightened by the white tail of a jumping deer. These were my people. Principally we visited kinsmen.

Up the Floyd Pike toward the county seat about half a mile away lived Cousin Bob Harvey and Cousin Lilah. They had a fine farm, a mill, a country store, the post office, Pizarro, Virginia, that was once Turtle Rock, an ice house, several barns and outbuildings, real silver plate, and a great family of handsome red-headed girls and some fine, soft-voiced boys. Many of them were grown and married when I was but a boy. I took pride in the relationship and visited as often as I dared to get some of Rhodie's fine cooking. My grandmother had raised Rhodie. She lived now with one family, now with another, of her adopted folks. I do remember counsin Bob Harvey's death and burial, the first in my memory, I think. When I came along Irving was in law school and Little Bob was running the store and farm as well as the post office. He was especially good to me. He was the one who rescued me at the threshing.

The Harveys were attractive, easy-mannered people. Underneath their affability, however, lay a strange streak of insecurity, of pessimism, of inability to face reality in critical situations. Too many of them left the world by their own hands. Whether this predisposition to self-destruction came from the Harvey or the Lancaster side, I cannot say. I can say that I am glad to have some tough Barnard genes to flirt around with, whatever else I may have inherited. The Barnards might laugh at themselves, but they never pitied themselves.

Further up the Floyd turnpike lived Uncle Green Wood, who had married my mother's sister Lillie. Uncle Green also ran a country store and farmed on the side. A keen competition went on between Wood's store and Harvey's store. Both men were good country merchants. Uncle Green had great pride and ambition. His schooling was scant, but he was the best-read man in our neighborhood and he valued an education. His son Hugh became a celebrated physician in Atlanta and dean of the Emory University medical school. Elizabeth, the second daughter of the family, was about my age. She, Maude, and I played together, planned together, and as children were very close. Aunt Lillie was a Barnard. She had a keen sense of humor and a dry wit that I recognized and respected as a child.

Off on the road to Meadow Creek and Tyler Turner's store near the top of the mountain lived Cousin Will West. My father had West blood, which he cherished. We always went to the West's at Easter. The food was good and the companionship of children in the house pleasing to a youngster. Cousin Will was the mail carrier and for a time, after George Redmond moved to Roanoke, carried our mail. Mail carriers were important people in my community. After all, they were paid hard money by the federal government and hard money was scarce and difficult to come by. I used to think that only mail carriers, store-keepers, bootleggers, and doctors had any. The West girls were spirited like their mother, who was a daughter of Cousin Sam Terry, who lost a leg at Gettysburg. They all were great riders and they rode the side saddle. To see one of them on an unruly horse on a frosty morning, plying the switch like a man, was good to see. One of the daughters, Irma, taught me in about the fifth grade at the old Pizarro school that is no more.

Before they moved to Roanoke the family that gave me more pleasure than any was that of George Redmond, who had married Maud Beckner, a relative of my mother. In the family there was Clarence, Elliott, Lynvall, and a daughter, Ora. Elliott was my constant companion and close buddy. Once when Papa and Mama were gone the boys came to visit us, or we them, I forget which. At any rate, Clarence brought a mason jar of white whiskey. We mixed it thick with brown sugar and all partook of it. Such a host of drunken boys you never saw. My brother Albert ran around on all fours like a dog, Clarence passed out under the swing, Elliott fell in the creek. I played possum—that is, I curled up like dead and I nearly was, but I could grin, I think.

I have said nothing of Ora. Even now it gives me a twinge to think of her whom I have not seen in fifty-five years. She was my first love. Don't think that a boy of nine or ten can't fall in love. I can testify. Never was there a girl with such thick, brown hair, such laughing eyes, such tawny skin. I adored her. I got palpitations of the heart when she was near. I blushed at the thought of her. When she moved away, it was the saddest day of my life. For several nights I could not sleep. I could not get her off my mind. Sometimes I went to the haymow and wept quietly. No. Don't think a young boy cannot suffer from the pangs of love. Never since have I ever in my life felt such blissful pain. Dearest Ora, you never knew the one who loved you most. Though, on the whole, I must say that I can love easy. It must be the result of my inoculation at so early an age.

These people were my kinsmen and neighbors. They were my early associates. There were others, like Dr. Dalton's family, but they lived in Floyd, six miles away. Sometimes, though, they came on Sunday and we visited back and forth. They were well-to-do, drove a Studebaker automobile when we went by horse and buggy, but they were our people, too, and the families were close. Dr. Dalton took out my tonsils. Papa took me to town behind him on the horse. In the doctor's office he held me in a vise-like grip, and Dr. Dalton extracted my tonsils without benefit of any kind of pain killer. Had it been a man, they would have given him whiskey. The experience was not too bad. I spent the night at the Daltons', and I remember the next day I fell off Heath Dalton's tricycle. It was the first I had ever tried to ride, and I had no thought of letting a little thing like the loss of tonsils keep me off that crazy three-wheeled thing. Maybe I spent two or three days, because at some point we chose sides and fought a fabulous apple battle in which we used the lids of lard cans for shields. My tonsillectomy did my singing voice no good, but it sure contributed to my entertainment.

All of this reminds me of the first cigarette I ever smoked. It happened like this. Uncle Albert came on a visit from Fayerdale, where he practiced medicine. He rolled his own Bull Durham. Albert sneaked a couple of bags with papers from his medical case or something. Then he and I went to Floyd with the horse and wagon to get some fertilizer for my father. Albert rolled a clumsy one and lit up on the way back home. As usual, he initiated me. I rolled a real humdinger and lit up. The first was not bad. I think it was the third that turned me green beneath my freckles. I spent the rest of the trip hanging over the side. Whether or not it made Albert sick I can't remember. He was probably an old hand at it. Anyhow, we got home that night with a load of fertilizer and a smoked-out boy.

By all of my people I was called Robert or Bob. I was red haired like my sister Mary—two among ten of that coloration. When I was quite young I deplored my red hair. I wondered why I could not have had a glossy black mane like my sister Maude, or brown like Albert. My father thought red hair lovely and becoming, and he taught me to take pride in what the Lord had given me. By the time I was ten or twelve I would not have traded manes with any boy or, for that matter, any girl. I learned that Thomas Jefferson had been red haired, that even Our Lord was pictured with rufous hair. Consequently I have always liked my nickname—Red or even Red Dog. It is a fact, though, that redheaded boys come in for more attention and teasing than others without this distinction. Once at Pine Creek church at an association of the Primitive Baptists, an acquaintance of my father, noticing me, said, "Taz, is that boy yourn?"

"Yes," replied my father, "he is mine."

"Waal, I'll tell you one thing. Put him on a stump and the woodpeckers would feed him."

So it went. But nothing dimmed my feeling that somehow it was a distinction to have red hair. I have tried to live up to my reputation, whatever it has been. I do believe, however, that it is a gross calumny to attribute a bad disposition and a fierce temper to redheads. To me it is a sure sign of energy and sensitivity and usually goes with an outgoing, good disposition. Like the patent medicine sold by the itinerant peddlers in the country, it will do everything except restore a lost reputation. Give me a red-haired boy with a freckled face, a sure smile, britches too big for him, and bare feet, and I will trade you any old black-headed or brown-haired for him, sight unseen, as the knife swappers used to say.

Chapter Three

Schools and My Early Education

S trangely enough, for a man whose life has been spent in education both high and low, I have few memories of my very early school days. I think I was a slow developer. Of reading I was fond from my earliest attempts, but I cannot for the life of me remember what it was like learning to read. The first books I remember are *Reynard, the Fox*, a child's story, and *Water Babies* by Kingsley. I remember no primer, no third reader, no book of geography or of mathematics. I went at the age of five or six to the Pizarro school. Here grades were taught from one through seven. Three teachers were available for the grades.

Our schoolhouse had three instructional rooms, so I cannot say that I ever went to a one-room schoolhouse. Each was heated by a stove that burned four-foot logs. They did a good job of heating the space if you could get close enough to the stove. In one corner of the room was a water bucket with a common dipper that distributed bountifully the common cold. Sometimes a water cooler was provided. Each child was supposed to provide his own drinking cup, but children easily lose them. Mine stayed lost. The water came from a spring nearby and was furnished by the bigger boys who were commissioned by the teacher to do this. Sometimes the water had a strange taste, but I would not go so far as to say that it had been tampered with. Billiard drinking had scarcely been heard of. The seats were the old fashioned kind, a folding seat and a desk with receptacle for books.

The teacher taught, helped, and supervised at least three grades at a time. She would start off, say, with fourth grade arithmetic. It was usually problem-solving at the blackboard. While this was underway she might hear a third grade child read aloud. When this was finished she would move to a geography class of the third grade. While some were reciting or being questioned, the rest were supposed to be studying. With a skilled teacher who insisted on good order the system was productive. At least students learned to read, to write, to figure. With a poor teacher who could not obtain order or command respect, the system was impossible. The subjects taught varied with the grade. At the lower levels, however, there was reading, writing, arithmetic, history, geography, and hygiene. From the last we were supposed to learn that the heart beat, the blood circulated, the hands were supposed to be kept clean and the teeth washed. The teachers that I remember always seemed to have good order in the classroom. There was very little whipping of children, some standing in the corner, some scolding. When a boy got too big for his britches or was guilty of a serious breach of the rules, he was sent home to be dealt with by his father. I was never sent home, and I was seldom reprimanded. I was clever at evading punishment and skilled at winning the favor of the teacher.

Every so often the school or teacher of a grade put on a play or provided a program for the entertainment of the parents. On occasion there were box suppers for the support of the school. The teachers, older schoolgirls, and young ladies in the community would prepare a box of food to be auctioned off to the highest bidder. The winner had the privilege of supping from the same box with the preparer. Sometimes the bidding was spirited, especially for the teacher's box. Invariably the teacher was an unmarried women, sometimes with great charm. Often there were two or three young men vying for the favors of the teacher. She boarded with a family in the community near the school.

I remember vividly one program in which I was supposed to be a robin and sing a song of springtime. My mother dressed me in a pair of blue trousers and a red sweater. My sweater had all red buttons except for one white. The one white button stood out like a belly button on a belly dancer. It was a subject of much embarrassment to me. On the night of the great delivery, I sang my song. It went something like this:

Through the air I dart
Singing as I fly
A merry song of springtime.
Hurrah, hurrah, for April skies,
Hurrah for May's bright sun.
I'll sing my lay through every day
Till summer's done.

My brother Albert, dadblame him, had inserted in the song a naughty word that rhymed with "dart" and sung it to me at the barn. When I got to the line "through the air I dart," in my trepidation I sang Albert's version instead of my own, or at least I thought I had, which is just as bad. There was much laughter and much applause. From the laughter I concluded I had made a fool of myself. My mother assured me that it was "real good," but I had my doubts. It made an impression on me, the whole episode, for you see I have remembered the song for more than half a century.

It is a great help to have in school a big brother or even a big sister. For a while Albert was in the same grade school with me. He was a very present help in trouble. When he left to go to West Virginia to work with a kinsman in a company store, I was left without protection. My sister Attaway was my teacher then, but she was mainly concerned with my wearing clean shirts and having my neck washed and my hair combed. Once she sent a note home by me asking that my shirt be changed. I took it home, but inserted underwear for shirt. My mother dutifully made me change my long-johns. Once when under great pressure in a fight with Ed Yeatts, a neighbor boy, my sister Maude came to my rescue with her book satchel. She laid about in a fierce way, her black eyes snapping. Ed Yeatts went to the ground from a blow to the head from a geography book. He ended up somewhere in Asia, I think.

By the time I had finished the first seven grades I had learned to read well and to like it. I knew something about arithmetic, though I had difficulty with written problems, especially those beginning, "If John can do a piece of work in five and a half days," etc. Fortunately, I had learned some grammar. I could parse a sentence and diagram it, if need be. I knew a little history, enough to lead me a little later into a love of biography. In those days the lives of great men were held up as examples to students. This seems no longer to be done. I believe it was a sound practice. It lifted horizons beyond the immediate and familiar. It sometimes stimulated ambition and motivated behavior. I wish it were more often done. At times I had visions of becoming governor of Virginia. I believed that any schoolboy by dint of hard work and good luck could advance to nearly any post. Even by schoolboys America was perceived as a place of unusual opportunity. The natural optimism of a people led them to inculcate in their children the vision of success that always accompanies the protestant work ethic.

At the end of my education in the Pizarro grade school there occurred one of those rare and fortunate happenings that open opportunity where little or none had existed. Just at this time there came to our community a most remarkable woman, Elizabeth Gwinn. Miss Gwinn was a great teacher and disciplinarian, and she had the ability to plan effectively and to inspire people to cooperate for the realization of her dream. She was sent by the Presbyterian synod to open a high school in what had formerly been a summer training school for mountain children. Churchmen of the area were concerned lest both religion and education languish in a very remote mountain county in Virginia. There was already in existence a schoolhouse of several rooms, the upper story of which served as living quarters for teachers and a few boarding students. In 1922 Cannaday School was opened for high school students. It was named for Amos Cannaday in gratitude for his gift of the site and a few acres of land. Almost immediately it generated great enthusiasm for learning in both parents and students. Miss Gwinn brought to her school well-trained teachers. Over it all she superimposed discipline and a spirituality that regenerated an entire community.

I entered the high school division in September 1922. My course of study consisted of algebra, Latin, English history, English composition, English literature, and ancient history. Overnight I changed from a lackadaisical pupil into an intense and eager scholar. To learn was fashionable. Learning carried with it prestige and praise. I began to stay up at night, studying long hours by my lamp. Though I did not earn the highest grade this first year, I came in second. Naturally my parents were delighted. All of the children of high-school age went to the Cannaday School—Mary, Annie, Virginia, Helen, and even John for a time.

Normally we walked the mile from our house to the school.

Sometimes we went by buggy in bad weather or Papa took us on the horses. The road to the school led down a rocky lane, past the old Barnard place, around a couple of curves, through a path in the woods down to a swinging bridge which spanned Little River, and up the steepest hill imaginable to the schoolhouse. Soon there were many conversions among both parents and students, and Presbyterianism flourished. It brought its usual virtues of faith and good works along with a desire for community improvement that goes well for those who know they are among the elect. All of us learned the Westminster Shorter Catechism by heart. For each page recited without error or hesitation there was a star. I still have my well-starred little book. We learned by heart and recited in unison many chapters from the Bible, both New Testament and Old. After all these years I can still recite from memory several great passages from the Bible. All of the children in school who had memorized passages from the Bible recited in unison. By the end of a school year each child would have stored up in his mind many noble passages. Almost imperceptibly this kind of exercise

I'm holding a hound pup named Ring.

contributed to the development of a religious outlook on life.

Quite early I became a favorite of Miss Gwinn. I think I first came to her notice in this way. I had been guilty of some offense in class. Perhaps it was pulling the bow from the hair of Myrtle Radford, who sat in the desk in front of me. Whatever it was, I was kept after school for punishment. Miss Gwinn put me to removing the rocks from a grass plot and pitching them into the gravel driveway that passed by the school building. I did this for about an hour, at the end of which she appeared to tell me to run on home. My punishment was at an end. "No," said I, "there is more work that needs doing." I began to hunt for the smallest stone to remove. I passed another hour in this way. Again she appeared and told me peremptorily to go home. "No," said I, "there is yet work to be done." I kept on. By this time it was growing late. In desperation she asked me to please go home. I kept on until my father rode up on a horse to find out what had happened. She told him that I was the hardest person to punish she had ever seen. He put me on the horse behind him and took me home. He could not quite understand my behavior, but I knew what I was about. I had won a victory of sorts. At any rate she knew who I was. Afterwards I noticed that she took pains to see that I was learning. Before long I was, I suppose, the apple of her eye. I was favored in every way like Joseph of the many-colored coat. It is a wonder that I was not spoiled beyond redemption by such attention, but strange to say, it just made me that much more charming. Ask any of my schoolmates. They will tell you.

During my third year at Cannaday School Papa died. For some time he had suffered from a strange and debilitating ailment that the local doctors were unable to diagnose. Finally he went with his nephew Bob Phlegar, the doctor, to the Johns Hopkins Hospital where they found that he had cancer. He returned home and prepared for the operation. Upon his return to the hospital he was operated upon and died. We were all numbed by the loss, my mother most of all. She was left with ten children, five of them far from grown and the last, John, just a baby. There was the farm; there was a remnant of Uncle Albert's war insurance; there was courage. There was hope and that was the whole of it. My mother took her courage between her teeth and, like the noble woman she was, hid her grief in her apron and made the best of it. Brother Albert, who was in school at the Virginia Polytechnic Institute, came home to help. He was about grown and help he did. Though I missed my father, having Albert home made the loss lighter. He and

I became finally great pals. We worked together, courted together, slept together on cold nights, and ended up more than brothers—friends.

I have splendid memories of my last two years in high school. Normally we walked. On bad days and in the winter I drove a buggy with the horse Kate in the shafts. I can still hear the sound of the buggy wheels on the sandy road and the clap of Kate's hooves. One rainy day when the river was out of its banks I had to send Mary and Annie to stand on the swinging bridge (Mary to hold my new mechanical pencil) while I attempted to ford the swollen stream. We pushed out into the river, Kate, the buggy, and I, with Kate snorting at the racing water. I drove her forward into the current. The swift water caught the buggy and began to sweep it down stream. Kate labored in plunging leaps, her feet now on bottom, now off. With luck she gained a foothold and, plunging and snorting, she drew me and the buggy to dry land. Glory be! Mary in her trepidation dropped my new pencil into the water. That's a woman for you!

This is not to say that women don't have spunk. All of my sisters were high spirited. Once Annie, looking down from the swinging bridge, saw a silver quarter in the river. "That quarter represents five candy bars," she said. She pulled up her skirts, waded into the water, and got that quarter. It was late November, too, and cold.

There was a teacher in Cannaday School by the name of Katheryn Hooper. She was lissome and willowy and needed courting. For a time she was Albert's one and only. There was in the school at the same time a bright lassie by the name of Marjorie Stringham. Marjorie was my girl for a long time. At least I thought so. One fine day in April, when March had waned and the gentle zephyrs crooned at our cheeks, Albert and I took Katheryn and Marjorie fishing. Can nature in her bounty bestow more upon man than a spring afternoon, flowing waters, green grass, and the racing pulse of young love? I doubt it. The stolen kisses, the touch of bodies as if by accident, the whispered promises, the chaste and restrained passion of golden moments—the full glory of it escapes me, but I can still remember. We caught fish too—horny heads, creek chubs, and the like—and ended the evening with a fish fry at the Sulphur Spring.

Shortly before this, I had graduated from knickerbockers to long pants. My first long pants were made by my mother from suits that Uncle Albert had once worn. She cut down the trousers to fit me and a fine fit they were. They were made from a grey, hard-finished material that lasted. The only thing about them that annoyed me was the creases. Instead of coming down the middle of the leg, these hankered for the side. In spite of our best efforts the creases were not just right, and creases are important even to grown men. I wore them with great aplomb, however. Annie Thompson, our neighbor, was the first person to see me in them outside the family. She will tell you that I moved from boyhood to manhood in a matter of moments with one pair of faulty creased pants. After that shaving was anticlimactic. The axe seemed lighter. Churning butter was for the women. That same winter I wore Uncle Albert's long underwear. It was a little big for me, since he was a six-foot-four giant, but it is really amazing what a boy of fifteen can wear in a becoming way if he wants to.

One of my early teachers was a young man by the name of Roland Rice. When he came to teach at Cannaday School he could not have been older than twenty. Since there was no room for him in the school itself, he lived at first in an abandoned house, run down and ramshackle, that had once housed the family of Henry Martin. He was a fine teacher and a good influence on young men. It was at his fireside that I ate the first wiener I ever saw. I had had plenty of country sausage, but a wiener was a new experience. At first I did not know whether to eat it or smoke it. One Easter he, Elliot Allen, and I rented an old Ford truck from Morton Turner and went camping to the Pinnacle of the Dan River and to the Buffalo, a high point in the Blue Ridge. We took plenty of food and plenty of patching for the tires. If I remember right, we patched inner tubes eighteen times before the trip was over. We pitched our tent in full view of the Pinnacle, climbed it, caught trout, fine natives, out of the swift, cold river at its base, and generally had a great time. I carried my father's .32 Smith & Wesson in a holster at my belt and felt myself a real mountain man. Mr. Rice was delighted with the countryside and the experience and so was I. We saw ruffed grouse in the roads, visited my great uncle Isom Barnard who lived nearby, ate well, and pleasured ourselves. Roland Rice was astonished to find a child who had never seen a banana. It was a remote area in the mountains and there were many children living there who knew not bananas and had never heard the song "Yes, we have none"; they knew many things, however, that other children had never heard of, like how to weave a coverlet and where the whip-poor-will makes her nest. Recently, I came across the name of Roland

Rice in *Who's Who in America.* I called him when I was in Annapolis for a meeting of the advisory board of the naval academy. He remembered the little girl who had never seen a banana and the boy who ate his first wiener at his fireplace.

There was no finer school in Virginia, I believe, than the Cannaday School. To excel in learning was to be the envy of every boy and girl in the school. I excelled. After I had got in wood for the stove and fireplace, after I had fed and milked, I hurried every evening to my own room to study. I lit my lamp and kept it burning until midnight. On the way to school the next morning I went over in my mind all that I had read or recited to myself some passage in Shakespeare that I had memorized. So addicted was I to study that my mother often scolded me for working too hard at books. By the end of my junior year I stood first in my class and won the scholarship medal that year, though I must say that I thought my friend Marjorie deserved it more than I. Being the favorite of a hard-driving woman like Elizabeth Gwinn did not hurt, either.

I did not spend all of my time with books. On occasion I hunted possums at night with Albert and my neighbor Leonard Peters. On one hunt the dogs treed a skunk in its den. We shoveled for it and got close enough to see the white markings on its back. "Get him with your hands!" cried Leonard. I got him along with a squirt of his scent, but I threw him to Leonard for his encouragement. Even after several washings my clothes smelled of skunk, especially when sitting near the stove that warmed the school room. The scent of polecat does not meld well with Tennyson's *Princess* even if it is being read aloud by a favorite teacher. It also affects one's popularity with young women.

One effect of the Cannaday School was to make a community out of a neighborhood. The school demanded and received the support of all whose children received its benefits. The building was heated by stoves, and stoves required much small wood. In the fall the farmers of the community would contribute a day or two to sawing and splitting wood for the stoves. On Sunday they came to Sunday school and church. It was expected. Sooner or later a man who had never given his relationship to God much thought began to think and, thinking, to prepare and eventually to join the church. So was God's work done, and the community became more alive, more law-abiding, more Christian. After only a short time community pride became manifest in better deportment, in more refined language, in greater inner satisfaction.

My last year in Cannaday School was the session of 1925-26. That year was both an ending and a beginning for me. I was sixteen, an age I had longed for. I had passed from boyhood to early manhood, and it had been a trying experience, for sometimes my imagination ran away with me and left me partly of this world, partly of another. I had left behind me the boils and the fall sores with which I had been from time to time afflicted. I had left behind, too, the vague unease that had troubled my life. I wore shoes instead of going barefoot. This was the mark of a man. I was highly respected by my teachers and most of my companions. I could shoot straight, wield a cradle, plough a field, harness a wild horse, and after a fashion hold my own in rough company. I had learned to hide weaknesses, to disguise fear, to keep quiet at the proper time. I had also learned that what happened to me was to be a matter of my own good luck and my own decisions. The year passed almost like a sleep in the night. I can remember few incidents. I do remember my two wild foxes and my dog Lead, and what pleasure the foxes gave me and what displeasure they gave Mama's chickens. I gave much thought to going away to college, but I scarcely knew how it was to work out. I believed that Miss Gwinn had something planned for me. From time to time she intimated that she did. My grades were excellent. There was little doubt that I would be valedictorian of my small class.

Near the end of my senior year Miss Gwinn called me into conference about what I should do the following year. I told her that I planned to get a job in a city that afforded a night college. She suggested to me that I must by all means go to Hampden-Sydney College. My cousin Hugh Wood had attended this college and I knew about it. She further told me that she intended to send me there. I objected, but I was secretly pleased. I told her that I could not pay her back for a long time. She said that she did not intend that I should ever pay her back. As it turned out I never did. It took me a long time to develop into a good, debt-paying citizen.

Chapter Four

College Years

In September of 1926, at seventeen, I entered Hampden-Sydney College. Since Cannaday School was not an accredited school, it was necessary for me to take entrance examinations. Because of this and my youth and inexperience, our minister R. Gamble See, who was himself a graduate of Hampden-Sydney, took me to be entered. We went by train to Farmville, Virginia. It was the first time I had ever been on a train, and one of the few I had ever seen. I watched closely and hid my nervousness as though I were an old hand at train travel. I shall never forget my first sight of the college. As we came by car around a curve in the highway there was a vast playing field where red-shirted youths were playing football. Further on, the red brick buildings began to appear.

Though the college was small, about three hundred students, to me it seemed very large and impressive. I was assigned a room in Cushing Hall and asked to appear for examinations the next day. I had no fear of the results. I knew myself to be well prepared. I was anxious about how I would be received by my new companions. I found my room, opened my trunk, and took out my things. My mentor had sent me to college with green and pink bed sheets. By the time I had got them fairly out, in came my roommate, James Crinkley of Blackstone, Virginia. He was a year older than I. We greeted each other as boys do, warmly, a little shyly. Soon some of his friends trooped in. They were overwhelmed by my green sheets. When I pulled out the banjo from my trunk, they demanded a tune. I sat down and played for them the "Fox Chase,"a rollicking tune in which the player tries to imitate the sound of the baying hounds and improvises appropriate words. I think this did it for me, for they appeared to forget the sheets, about which I was a little embarrassed. I had not known that pink and green sheets were not the perfect bed coverings for freshmen at college. Soon the word spread that there was a new boy in Cushing Hall with a banjo and pink bed sheets. That evening before supper there was scheduled a "taking in." What it amounted to was that the new boys lined up and the old men came down the line with paddles. I had not expected this.

I learned quickly that anything that set a boy apart, like red hair and pink bed sheets, spelled trouble. I immediately became "Red" fore and aft. Within moments I had learned a hard lesson but not well: Anonymity is the safer policy. Before many hours had passed I had learned to sound off for the "old men" when greeted. The answer was, "Freshman, Lancaster, Pizarro, Virginia. Here to serve the sophomores and upper classmen and study in the meantime." Every new man when challenged by an upperclassman gave this response. It had its uses. Before much time had passed one had heard many times the name and address of every new student. It did something, too, to blunt the egos of erstwhile prep school seniors. At least it was supposed to.

My first day in the college was a very busy one. I took five entrance examinations. On all of them I did satisfactorily. I was requested to take examinations for advanced standing in Latin and English. I took them and was granted advanced standing in two subjects. As it turned out this enabled me to complete the degree requirements in three years, a great saving in money and time, but it did eject me into the world before I had really begun to shave.

From the first day I loved being in college. There was the novelty of my environment, the boisterous company of youths my own age, the challenge of new minds. I studied hard, attended all meetings of my class, went to prayer meetings, said a few out loud, cultivated the friendship of boys on my floor and off, learned to drink Coca Cola with peanuts, and occasionally went into town, Farmville, to try my hand at shooting pool and watching the girls from the state college. Girl watching was a favorite pastime when I could bum a ride into town. I did all of this and saved my money, too—that first year, that is.

At this time Hampden-Sydney College was rather typical of church-related colleges. It was sternly Presbyterian. Even the YMCA was supposed to be afflicted with the virus of the new interpretation of the scriptures and hence suspect. The curriculum was as it had been for a long time. Great emphasis was placed on classical learning. Latin and Greek were the languages of a gentleman, to be preferred over French and Spanish. Those who came to the college for an education were supposed to be able to pay for what they got. There were few job opportunities and practically no scholarships. The students on the whole were a fairly homogeneous group, in that they represented the upper middle class of successful farmers, merchants, and professional men who came invariably from Virginia and especially Southside Virginia. The learning offered was broad rather than deep. About a third of the students came for learning, the rest for a college education. I do not disparage this approach to life, for as much was learned from association and conversation and companionship as from books. At any rate I had had a baptism in books before I entered.

The first year I learned a great deal. I learned how to dance after the fashion of the day, how to talk with young women, how to get along with young men, how to acquire prestige among my peers. My first and keenest disappointment came at the end of pledge week for the fraternities. I did not receive an invitation to join a fraternity. Before I came to college I had never heard, to my knowledge, of Greek letter fraternities. I learned to my chagrin that for some reason I was unacceptable. This knowledge did not frustrate me. I concluded that I had simply not had the proper letters of introduction and had been among my peers too short a time for them to know me. I was concerned, for at this time in small liberal arts colleges, fraternities were what clans were to Scotch highlanders. It so happened that when the first election of the freshman class was held to select a class representative to the honor council, I was elected by my classmates. Within a matter of hours I had received bids to two fraternities. Soon other groups felt me out. I was coy. It so happened that the one group that paid little attention to me were the Chi Phi's. I concluded that they were the best. Too, this group had a house in which some of the members roomed. By the spring of my first year I was a Chi Phi. I joined a clan of hard-drinking, fast-living brothers that first year. Many of them were to pay the academic price for their gallivanting and leave for the next year only a small band of more sober brethren to compete for the new crop.

During the first autumn the German club held dances in a hall near the Chi Phi house. From afar I listened to the music, watched the swaying figures for a while, and concluded that a man was a fool to be in his room with a book when others held girls in their arms. I borrowed a tuxedo, found an ill-fitting shirt, and joined the club. I had been to frolics and square dances in Floyd County, but I had never "round danced." Shortly after I entered the hall I spied a new friend of mine whom I liked. He saw me, brought his partner over to

I can be spotted at right in this dormitory scene in first passage in Cushing Hall at Hampden-Sydney.

introduce to me, and told me to go ahead and dance with her. Great God Almighty! I did. My partner was a tall, willowy girl who sized up the situation immediately. She volunteered to pilot me about for a spell. I said to her, "I can't dance a step, as you can see, but I sure enjoy holding you." We laughed together, and somehow it seemed to me that there was nothing much to dancing that a man with music in his soul couldn't master pretty quick. Unfortunately not all of the girls whom I broke took this enlightened view. I did have fun. At intermission we all crowded through the door for air and other diversions. The girl with whom I had been prancing—no, dancing—took my hands from her waist and placed them over her breast. The blood in my veins took such a surge that I stepped on the foot of a girl behind me. Somehow I got out the door into the air.

I knew college and the high life was for me. The great drawback was money. It's been the same for the greater part of my life. If I had been the son of a rich and indulgent father, I sure could have carved up a patrimony. As it was, after the thrill of the "openings" I returned to books and what ever else there was to use up my energy. I was seventeen and still growing.

Although Hampden-Sydney was run by stern Calvinistic scholars who opened the day properly with prayer and closed it the same way, the students, I soon learned, were not so godly. It was the era of Prohibition. Nevertheless there was a good bit of drinking of the forbidden brew, especially on weekends and at party time. About the college there were several purveyors of the white stuff. I was told that one could walk out into the woods to a proper stump, place a dollar and a half in the hole, walk away for a time, return and find in the hole of the same stump a pint of scholar's delight, the kind of stuff that would soon have you declining verbs and conjugating nouns. I was told that there was bath-tub gin available, but since I was a member of the student council it was all a matter of rumor that first year.

Each week movies were shown in McIlwaine Hall. I had seen few movies before going away to college. I missed never a one. To me there simply was no bad movie. Here I learned to respect Milton Sill, adore Vilma Banky, idolize Billie Dove. At Thanksgiving the college was in recess for a few days. I had taken my shotgun with me to school, and I had an opportunity to use it. All about Hampden-Sydney were grown up plantations. Tobacco had worn out the soil, and many formerly productive fields were grown up in pine and briar. I killed several quail without a dog but no turkey. There were wild turkeys about—Red Woodsworth killed one on Thanksgiving Day. I enjoyed the woods and especially the companionship of some local people I met. They were impressed by my marksmanship and cared not a whit about my scholarship.

In all of the clubs and fraternities hazing was practiced with great relish. It was customary for the initiate to prepare for this ordeal in the best way possible. Some students sewed into their pants rubber sponges to absorb the force of the paddle; some bought beefsteak for its absorptive qualities. The old men took turns with paddles, and the force of the blows depended on the character of the wielder. Near the end of my freshman year I was taken into the Seven and a Half Club. It was considered an honor but after the initiation I somehow doubted the significance of the distinction. I prepared in the usual way with padding. Even so, my rear was black and blue for a few days. The honor was great, no doubt. I can understand the virtue of being put to the test. I can even understand that the experience created a special bond among the brothers. I can't understand yet the mentality of the man who enjoys punishment for the pleasure it gives him. The practice has now all but ceased in most colleges. On the whole, I think its demise a good thing. There are occasions, though, when nothing is so efficacious as a few stinging blows. Words leave scars. Healthy blows are soon forgotten.

My first year at college was successful. I studied, made good grades, and enjoyed myself thoroughly. At the end of the academic year I went to Johnson City, Tennessee, where my Uncle Sam Barnard ran two Piggly Wiggly stores. I went to live with him and work in his store. He put me in charge of keeping the shelves stocked and after a time he permitted me to drive a Model T pickup to deliver groceries to good customers. I learned to drive the Model T without denting fenders, though I had some narrow escapes. I learned the lore of the back-kitchen boarding houses. I made the acquaintance of a few girls. I gained the friendship of the butcher, one Carrick Weatherby, who had a way with a knife, gin, and the ladies. When one of his favorites approached the meat counter, he might say, "Come on up, ladies. The smell of the body will make you dream of the finest beefsteak you have ever seen. Ham, Lamb, Sheep, and Ram! Take your pick." Strangely enough his antics never seemed to drive away customers. Even the most sour old maid would invariably reflect the Irish warmth of that crooked, Celtic smile. There is something about a butcher . . .

During that summer my brother Albert came to work in the stores. The two of us had fine times together. One Sunday we made a trip to a remote hotel along the Nollichucky River. We drank home brew, courted the girls, and ended up seining in the river. East Tennessee was Protestant but wet, and many a "bucket of blood" served up a potent brew. Unfortunately Albert invested a little money in the grocery business at an inopportune time. The stores failed. Albert lost his investment but soon found a job in the Franklin Guaranty Bank, which failed too in due course. It did give my brother some experience and a lasting appreciation of Tennessee Toms.

At the end of the summer I returned to Hampden-Sydney not much older or wiser or richer than when I left. Age and experience did not begin to mar the youthful carelessness of my approach to life. I grinned my way through "An Introduction to the Philosophy of the West," talked my way through *Beowulf,* laughed my way through Chaucer, cried through chemistry, back-seated my way through Latin 211, and studied my way through Bible. All the while I made good grades. My reputation carried me along after the will to win had languished. In a word or two, my sophomore year in college was a flop. Nobody seemed to know it but me. I did learn the back streets to Farmville State Teacher's College, how to appear older than I was, not to shoot pool for money, nor loan money to one poorer than myself.

At the beginning of my third year in college, I got out a catalog and figured that I could fulfill the requirements for graduation by the end of the third year, provided I scheduled six courses. So I did. My reputation for good grades had been established, and I encountered little difficulty except in mathematics. How I got through advanced algebra without opening the book more than a few times is a mystery. It shows the power that lies in starting off well—and, I suppose, that teachers are seldom aware of what their students are actually doing once a pattern or impression is created. That is why it is so difficult for a student who actually makes a change to see it noticed by the teacher.

My memory of my last year in college is hazy: I was so busy living that I had no time to reflect. That was the year I met Paula. Of all my loves she was the sweetest and the best. Her long brown hair had a fresh, sweet smell that has never gone from my mind. She was as natural, as shy, and as unpracticed in courtship as I. She made my last year a sort of hazy, rosy dream.

In any event I completed the course for the Bachelor of Arts degree, and when commencement came along I marched up to receive it. I was nineteen and as naive and curious as a young coon. My mother, Miss Gwinn, Attaway, and Albert came to my graduation. I was so busy with parties and goodbyes that I scarcely knew they were there except for Albert, who spent his time in the company of my fraternity brothers, some of whom took him for my younger brother who had grown a beard faster than I. I remained in Hampden-Sydney a day or two to gather together my things and came home by train, by bus, and by foot.

Yes, by foot. Many's the time I walked the three miles home from the road served by the bus to Roanoke. Those three miles could become a test of endurance. Christmas my senior year I had a devil of a time meeting the bus to Roanoke. I left at daylight riding Kate. The wind was blowing snow, and the mercury stood at ten below. I carried my suitcase in front of me on the saddle. One cannot ride easily with a buttoned overcoat nor carry to advantage a large suitcase on horseback. By the time I reached the top of the hill just above the poorhouse I was so cold and miserable that I thought of getting off and going in. I was to catch the bus, an old Packard car, at Jeff Wood's store, still a quarter of a mile away. I finally made the store with hands that were numb and fingertips white with cold. Just in time. The car was there. I hitched Kate to the post and made quick arrangements for someone to take her home. I got to Roanoke still cold and went to the Ponce de Leon Hotel to warm up before train time. It took some time in the warmth of the lobby to restore me. When I left home every member of my family was down with one of those stomach disorders that comes occasionally from eating tainted food. They recovered; so did I.

During my senior year I worried about what I would do after graduation. One Sunday afternoon I was reading the *Cosmopolitan* magazine. They carried a section advertising the merits of different preparatory schools, most of them military. I wrote three of them. Two responded. Of the two one was Gulf Coast Military Academy of Gulfport, Mississippi. They were interested. After further correspondence I was offered and accepted a position there as instructor at a salary of $1,400 per year, room and board. The school was far enough away to be attractive and offered the prospect of security. I was one of the few members of my class to have had a job upon graduation. In 1929 the bubble of prosperity had not burst, but, as I remember, pins were pricking. By October men would be leaping in despair from windows.

It may be well to take a look at the year 1929, the year I was graduated from college.

The year marks a turning point in the history of the nation. Never again were Americans to have the same faith in their economic system. Never again were we to exhibit that buoyant optimism that characterized pre–depression America. Never again were we to be so free from the overriding power of a centralized, bureaucratic government. The national budget in that year of grace was $3,831,735,661. Expenditures mounted to $3,794,745,192. The income tax on $10,000 was $101, on $5,000 only $28.13. The population of the country was 120 million. The population has increased by 75 percent, but the expenditures of the federal government have increased by over 300 percent. The budget has increased by more than 10,000 percent. Big Brother is listening now; then he had not been conceived.

There have been two momentous events in the history of my country. The first was the Civil War. In the course of that war we learned as a nation to do things on a vast scale: float loans, feed great armies, harness the economy for a cause. The war produced our first crop of millionaires and forever fixed on the nation a grasping, material-minded society, a kind of catch-as-catch-can lifestyle. It is possible that a southern victory might have produced a less materially minded, slower moving, more personal and less dehumanizing lifestyle, a style more like that which one experiences in Europe or at least used to. At any rate the Yankee dollar and the Yankee conscience won. The two always had an affinity and what they have done to us is all around us now.

The second event that changed forever the lifestyle of the nation was the Great Depression. Since that time we have had big government, big budgets, big politicians, and the little dollar bill. Since that time we have been led to expect on Wednesday what cannot be delivered until Friday, if ever. The belief that social problems can be solved by spending money and setting goals may easily be traced to that New Deal that I first voted for. By the defeat of expectations that were never really possible of realization, much frustration and bitterness has been generated.

I can't remember a great deal about the summer of 1929. I had finished college. I knew what I was going to do in the fall. I believe I worked on a new building that was being erected at Harris Cannaday School for twenty-five cents an hour. When I had accumulated a few dollars I probably quit work. I hope so. It seems to me I have been working for a hell of a long time now. Oh, I remember, I did make a trip to see a young lady in Farmville. Mama let me borrow the old Dodge automobile for the trip. Like all such visits it was filled with anticipation, happiness, and the sure and certain pleasure of young love. There is nothing like it in this world. If heaven is what they say it is, it must be something like being in love. Even the disappointments have a kind of sad, exhilarating, joyful coloration. Around the end of August, I left Floyd for Gulfport, Mississippi. I had packed my trunk with what I had in clothes, books, and bed gear. The green sheets accompanied me. My banjo I carried along as well as the fox horn which was a kind of symbol of my lifestyle. The Gulf Coast Military Academy was said to be very military, very strict. Its motto was "Send Us the Boy, We Will Return You the Man." As a consequence of my naïveté and my youthfulness, I traveled in uniform. I had bought a pair of pink cavalry pants with laced bottoms and a pair of knee-high boots that I adorned with my grandfather's Civil War spurs. I had acquired a military blouse with a Sam Brown belt. I topped it off with my Uncle Albert's World War I cap, a salty affair somewhat unlike what was actually being worn. I tell you, I was a military dude. I could not for the life of me do an about-face, but I had no need to. In my mind I was all front anyhow. I went first to Atlanta by train. The porter evidently thought me to be a young prince traveling incognito, for he was very patronizing. At any rate it seemed so, and I left him an appropriate tip. I must have been attractive for I noticed several people eyeing me with what I took to be approval. Unfortunately none of them was young and female.

I was met in Atlanta by my cousin Hugh Wood, who had shortly before my visit begun to practice his profession in Atlanta. Both he and his wife, Maria, were wonderful to me. Maria took me all over the biggest city I had ever seen and to Stone Mountain. I had discarded my uniform while there and put on civilian clothes so I melded with the environment. When it came time to take the train to Gulfport, however, I donned again my uniform. The trip was uneventful. Anyhow, by this time I had accustomed myself to train travel. I visited the smoker to listen to the stories of the traveling men. I even ventured to tell one myself. Somehow it seemed to lack point and evoked no laughter. It was about my first experience in storytelling. I learned something, though. It was to keep stories to myself. I have never been able to do it in such a way as to produce a neat and unexpected climax. No, I leave storytelling to my betters.

I reached Gulfport in the early afternoon. I left my gear in the station and went exploring. I had not gone far when I had my first look at the sea. To a mountain boy the sea is a picture in a book, a description in a poem, a painting. There is simply no way to describe to one who has never seen the ocean, its impossible immensity. I could not believe what I was seeing. There it was, stretching on and on and on. We all came from the water. The journey to the land took many millions of years. Even then I knew that we had once been sea beings. My eyes filled with tears, a great lump rose in my throat. I forgot for a moment where I was. I thought: "Once upon a time I swam in this." The sea has never become commonplace to me. I have never loved it as I love the great towering mountains, but it draws me and it at times frightens me. It is the great unfamiliar, the cradle of the earth, the snuffer-out of man's dreams. It is too changeable to be completely trusted. Now soft as the down of a young bird, now supremely violent with its roaring storms. Mountains are more trustworthy, less given to change. The sea is old, old, fickle, violent, faithless—and inviting.

Having satisfied myself with a long view of the Gulf, I made my way to Hotel Markham. Here I encountered a cadet of the academy who had not yet registered as a student. He easily guessed I was a new instructor at the academy. From the conversation I had with him I learned that Major Joseph Belka, the headmaster, was in the lobby of the hotel. He pointed him out and I introduced myself to him. He very kindly offered to take me the few miles up the coast to the academy. My first glimpse of the academy did not impress me favorably. The buildings were of brick, except for the administration building—one-story, barracks-like structures. The site was impressive, however. The academy faced the Gulf on a piece of high-lying land adjacent to the water. Major Belka showed me to my room and must have wondered at my youthful appearance. He told me that I would be rooming with another new instructor from Davidson College in North Carolina, William Archie by name.

I unpacked, hung my hunting horn on the wall, selected what looked like the best bed, and got ready for the evening meal. I noted the heavy atmosphere, the smell of the sea, the alien surroundings. At supper I had my first taste of shrimp in a kind of watery soup, very unpalatable I thought. I did not know that I would be destined to live on boarding school fare for many years of my life. Since I have always eaten what has been placed in front of me without complaint, I made a meal of it. After supper I returned to my room to find that Archie had showed up. He was a tall, well-built youth of about my age who had been a tackle on his college team. We hit it off well from the very beginning. It is remarkable how much better life is in the company of a friend. Everything that had been before grim and oppressive took on a kind of glow. We talked, laughed easily, and became as secure as a pair of bird dogs in a new kennel.

Within a week or so we had settled down to a kind of routine. We rose early to the call of the bugle, supervised the formation, saw that our charges were up and had their rooms clean and tidy before the morning meal. By eight we were ready for class. I had been assigned two classes of beginners' English and two classes in Latin. I shall never forget my early experiences as a teacher. I was twenty years old. A good many of my students in Latin were almost as old. The first few classes went well. Neither students nor teacher had too much confidence. Familiarity breeds contempt. During the first week I had trouble with discipline. Whenever I went to the board to explain or demonstrate I heard peculiar sounds, sometimes like the mooing of a calf, sometimes like the meow of a cat, then the quack of a duck. For a time I could not determine which student the sounds were coming from. I waited patiently until I had isolated the culprit. By this time the entire class was out of hand. I walked as briskly as I could toward the back corner of the room from which the sounds had come. Addressing myself to the student, I said, "I am here to teach, you are here to learn. I can't teach and you can't learn this way. As a favor, please stop what you are doing and let's get to work." All I got by way of reply was an insolent smirk. I went back to the board. Again I heard in an even louder voice the call of the cat. I wheeled in anger and stood over the offender.

He grinned at me like a possum, and I hit him across the face a hard slap. It took him by surprise. "My father doesn't hit me and no red-headed son of a bitch like you can do it." He attempted to get out of his seat. Fortunately he was sitting in a chair with a writing arm that somewhat impeded him. As he attempted to get to me I hit him again as hard as I could, right across his insolent mouth. He reeled back into his seat. Every time he attempted to get out I hit him, good, solid, open-handed blows. After a cuffing he began to cry. I led him to the door and flung him out. There was a splendid silence in the room. I returned to my explanations and had no trouble with students in the classroom.

This episode has an interesting sequel. Several years ago I went with a team of educators to inspect the air officers' school at Montgomery, Alabama. Soon after our arrival we were briefed on the curriculum of the school by a colonel in the air force. As soon as I saw him I knew him. He was the young student whom I had disciplined so long ago. He saw me immediately and recognized me. He stopped his dissertation at once and related to all of us his memory of the only time he had a whipping in school. Afterwards we fell upon each other's necks. "Captain Lancaster," says he, "let's go celebrate." We did.

My first year at Gulf Coast was an eventful year. I was my own man. I made money to spend. I was young. The coast was a free and exciting place. Afternoons and evenings were often free for visiting the hot spots in Biloxi and Gulfport. Every filling station and every joint seemed to afford a slot machine. My nickles and quarters burned my pockets. People were warm and friendly. Dates were easy to come by. Like a young prodigal I squandered my hard-earned money. Every day brought its own reward. I had no plans for the future. I knew more than my students, or at least I thought so, and that was enough. It was during the early fall of this year that I met Ernestine Desporte, who for good or ill was my wife these many years. It happened so.

On Sunday afternoons the corps of cadets were on parade—solemn, well disciplined, and formal. Customarily, visitors from the coast came to view the parade. Among the visitors were two young ladies who were driving a Chevrolet coupe. Phil Sprouse, a teacher at the academy, had taught the preceding year and knew a good many of the coast's young people. He summoned me to meet the two young ladies in the car. They were Audrey Spottswood and Tine Desporte. I remember well that Miss Desporte was wearing a purple hat such as young women then wore. I remember, too, that her hair was long, thick, and brown and that she was small and quick. Neither of us was overly impressed with the other. Some time later Bill Archie and I called for dates with Audrey and Tine. We were accepted. Tine could get her mother's car on occasion. Since Archie and I were without cars we dated them from time to time. It worked out well. We talked. We sang. We danced. Bill and I scrounged a meal whenever we could, and Mrs. Desporte set a splendid table. Tine danced as lightly as a maple leaf in a south breeze. She was impudent, strong-willed, filled with laughter. Before Christmas vacation had come, I was calling for dates quite often. Since she was engaged to be married and wore a ring, I considered myself in no danger. Thoughtless, artless boy! Nature has a way with young men and women in the springtime of life. But of that, more later.

During the Christmas vacation both Archie and I remained at the academy. Neither desired to return home, and neither could really afford it, though I do believe I would have saved money by leaving. I had never been to New Orleans. Christmas vacation gave me a great opportunity. Then even as now New Orleans was different. She projected an image of wicked charm, of indolence and grace, of memories of other races, of other and more joyous times. We took the bus to New Orleans. I remember the furtive bars, hidden away in back rooms. On Bourbon Street a hand quickly lifted my hat from my head.

"Come get your hat, redheaded boy."

I dared not go. "Let's get the hell out of here," I said to myself, and as I started to walk away the hat came sailing out.

"Go yo' way, redheaded boy. You too young."

Indeed I was too young, too self-conscious, too puritan, too much of a country boy and very glad of it.

Then as now the food in New Orleans was the best the nation had to offer. The smell of roasting coffee compounded with the aroma of the streets. To a young Virginia mountaineer this was high adventure, real living. It is a pity that we can't carry with us through life the reality of imagined sin, the satisfaction of heady, unquenched desire. To want is almost better than to have.

To a mountain boy from Virginia the coast was a strange but happy place. Here was none of the brooding contemplation of life, no predestination here. Life was to be lived. Sin scarcely knew itself in the mirror. Three times a day young people danced to Dixieland jazz in the hotel pavilions overlooking the water, in the mornings from eleven o'clock until twelve, in the afternoon from five until six, and in the evening from nine to twelve. The morning and afternoon dances were free. The fee for the nightly dance was, I believe, a dollar. Here the young kept the rhythm and glided around the floor with great style and energy. Even the old came to take their turn. The music was provided by various bands. Usually there was a black man who kept the time on a washboard with a silver dollar. My dancing improved.

Not only were the dances characteristic of the life of the people. So were the drink, the clothes, and the food. Here people had learned to accept the stranger for what he appeared to be. I suppose social stratification existed, but it was scarcely apparent to a casual observer—at least not at the dances or on the beaches. Many New Orleans people summered on the coast. It was easy to recognize the girls from that city. They dressed simply, usually in white. Sometimes their breaths bore the faint tinge of garlic. Always they were cool. They accepted men with a kind of gay but tolerant weariness.

The summer of 1930 was a great summer for me. It should have taught me something about life and living, but it did not. At the end of the school year Bill Archie and I bought a second-hand Model A Ford Runabout with a rumble seat and, pooling our money, we headed to California, following the Old Spanish Trail west. Through South Louisiana we meandered. Here too was a new life to be glanced at. I came to know this lovely and different area of the world later. Then I was most impressed with the many ferries, the slow-running rivers, the indolent grace of the people, and the white herons that stood so quietly by the canals engrossed in what kind of dreams I know not. From Lake Charles we headed toward South Texas and the Mexican border down to Del Rio. Until we hit the Mexican border I had never seen a real bar. Prohibition had clenched its fist around American throats, and bootleg seared our palates.

Our first real experience in a border town came at Juarez across the river from El Paso. A great sign hacked out on the side of the hill above the river advertised JIMMY O'BRIEN'S AMERICAN BAR. We headed for it. The town we found to be run-down and mangy. The streets were littered and dirty. The people were dispirited from poverty and disease—at least those we encountered. There were many bars in addition to Jimmy's. We drank fine Mexican beer and talked with the whores and barflies. I remember I was shocked by the pictures and by the girls. Everything was easy but everything seemed to have a price. Above the bar in one establishment was a picture of a very pregnant girl. Next to her was a deflated tire with a nail in it. The caption read, "A nail did this. Look what a screw can do." The town itself seemed to be in the same shape and condition as the tire.

The interlude in Juarez was brief for we were headed to California. The real reason for the trip, aside from our desire to see the country, was Bill Archie's wish to see a young woman whom he had met back in North Carolina. She was blonde and exciting, he said, and he cautioned me not to permit him to become engaged. I swore to remove him by guile or force in the event of danger of such an eventuality. This young woman was a private secretary to the musical director of RKO in Hollywood. Bill talked much of her as we made our way west in that faithful Ford.

In Deming, New Mexico, I had a very sobering experience. We spent the night in a tourist court on the outskirts of the town. For safety I put my wallet, containing my entire savings from the nine months of work, under the mattress of my bed. The next morning we left without it. I did not discover my loss until we had made the hundred miles to Lordsburg. I reached for my wallet to get the money for payment of a charge for gasoline and it was gone. I had about $400 in that wallet. We headed back for the tourist court at which we had spent the night. Fortunately the proprietor of the court did not run a tight operation. The bed had not been made and I recovered my money.

We finally made it to California. Our first stop was at San Diego, a beautiful city where the mountains nearly meet the great Pacific. The weather was clear, the great ocean roared at the beach, and our spirits rose like the gulls above the water. Since Bill was anxious to get to Hollywood, we soon headed north. When we arrived in Hollywood we were hard put to find a place we could afford to stay. One night we spent at a hotel, the next in the apartment of his girlfriend and her mother. I have forgotten her name, but she and her mother were good enough to put up with us for a few days. Things did not work out the way Bill expected. The memory of golden days in North Carolina had become overlaid with more recent experiences in California. The musical director was a demanding boss. Weekend plans with other girls had been made. We slept in a room which afforded a bed that fitted into the wall by day and came out furtively at night. It worked electrically, I believe. One night when Bill was deep in disappointed dreams, I pushed the lever, having first got out myself, and gave Bill a real shock of a different kind. Youthful disappointments are soon forgotten. Bill adjusted to the situation, and we decided to look for summer jobs. By the end of a few days our resources were melting away, what with lunches at the Brown Derby and dinners and dates. Money even then did not last in California.

We applied for chauffeuring jobs at the homes of stars, tried to sell lots in Capistrano, answered ads in the papers with no results. Each day our fare and expectancy became leaner and leaner. We found that even our car, which we had bought on the installment plan, could not be sold. When we were down to our last few dollars Bill borrowed thirty dollars from his kinsman in San Bernardino. I wired my brother Albert, who then had a job with the Franklin Guaranty Bank in Johnson City, Tennessee, for thirty dollars, and we decided to high-tail it back home where we knew people and felt secure.

In two nights and three days of steady driving, without benefit of so much as a night's sleep in bed, we made the trip from Los Angeles, California, to Alexandria, Louisiana. We drove and dozed by turns until, worn out with the journey, we made our beds on the courthouse green at lush Alexandria. When the next morning I was awakened by someone tugging at my arm, I looked into the bloated face of a fellow tramp who said to me, "Hey, fellow, have you got a comb?" I was sandy-eyed and used up but happy to be within distance, at least, of friends if not of relatives.

We headed for the Gulf coast knowing well that we could find a bed and perhaps food at the academy. Our only stop was in New Orleans, where I pawned the watch that had been a gift from my mother and Albert upon my graduation from college. I believe I got all of nine dollars for that watch. Gas and oil and hamburgers had almost exhausted the grubstake we started with in California.

Once back on the coast we spruced up at the academy and got dates with Tine and Audrey. It was soul-lifting to be back, to see Tine again. But both Bill and I knew we must head home. I borrowed thirteen dollars from Tine, and we got on the road to North Carolina and Virginia. That thirteen dollars sealed my fate.

Chapter Five

Marriage

In the autumn of 1930 I returned to the Gulf coast for another year at the academy. I was more mature as a teacher but less mature as a manling. I shaved, I taught my classes; I turned in my grades, but my mind was full of moonbeams and willow wands. I was skittish as a colt who shies at a stone, imagining it to be a coiled snake. I was in love. *In love* is a ravishing, a delicious, a mind-stretching state. Sleep is filled with fantasy, waking replete with dreams. We walk on the ground but advance step by step on clouds. I wasted my money on slot machines, knew not the name of responsibility, bought beyond my ability to pay, pondered in half moments the sure end of my folly. Every night I waited for the sound of the Chevrolet that would bring me Tine. Such a situation cannot go on forever, but it did. At least it lasted the whole academic year.

In May of 1931 I was informed by the superintendent of the academy that if I married there was no apartment available and no job. Tine and I took this as only the young can, without thought for the future. Sufficient unto the day is the joy thereof. By chance I met in the lobby of the Monteleone Hotel in New Orleans Colonel DuVal Cravens of Sewanee Military Academy. The conversation was one of those chance affairs that change the destiny of human beings. I told him of my difficulties. Both of us had reason to think rather unkindly of the superintendent of Gulf Coast Academy. At any rate he told me that Sewanee was thinking of opening a junior department for young boys in the seventh and eighth grades. He surmised that Tine and I might have just the qualifications to begin this enterprise. He would see. This gave us both some hope.

In the meantime we decided that we would visit Cumberland Law School in Lebanon, Tennessee. At this time this law school gave a one-year course in law and even a degree. Here also was situated Castle Heights Military Academy. Perhaps either or both of us might teach here, and I could prepare for the law. With this in mind we started out, Tine ostensibly to visit a friend in Memphis. The trip was eventful but to me too short. We arrived in Lebanon and had conversations at Castle

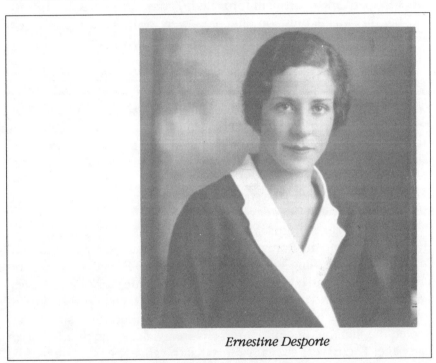

Ernestine Desporte

Heights. I enrolled in the law school. If worse came to worse Tine, who had money in the bank (when did she not?), was prepared to sacrifice her anchor to the windward for the uncertain future of a redheaded would-be lawyer with a sharp mind and an empty purse. Such is the trust of a female when marriage is the gauge. Things were looking up. We retraced our steps as far as Decatur, Alabama. Here we parted, Tine to Biloxi, I to Floyd County, Virginia.

Soon thereafter I had a call which I took on the old telephone hanging on the wall in the farmhouse, where it still hangs. Tine informed me with half the neighborhood listening that Colonel Cravens had visited her in Biloxi. His interest was real. Shortly after this conversation Colonel Cravens arranged for me to have a visit with S. L. Robinson, a teacher at Sewanee whom he trusted, in Christiansburg, Virginia, where he was visiting. Rob must have given him the good word. Anyhow we were both graduates of Hampden-Sydney. The upshot of it all was that within a short time we had a contract to start a junior school at Sewanee at a salary of $120 per month, board and apartment furnished. Today this seems like miserly pay but this was depression time. Few were so lucky as we. Anyhow just then we were very sure that two could really live more cheaply than one.

Now Tine was the daughter of Sophie Desporte and Sophie was a business woman of commanding presence. I had never spoken to her on the risky subject of marriage to Tine. She liked me, tolerated me around the house at late hours, occasionally banged her shoe on the floor for departing time, but in my opinion her plans did not include Tine's marriage to a school teacher with an uncertain future. She had to be informed. I ended by writing a queasy letter asking for her daughter's hand. Within the shortest time the response came. Tine had done her work well. She gave us her blessing.

We set a date in June. Much had to be done. Tine had to get dispensation from the Roman Bishop of Natchez to marry a Protestant. I had to buy a wedding suit. My car, the old 1929 Ford that Archie and I had purchased and taken to California, was a little weak in the knees. I traded for a brand new Ford coupe. Mama and the family had to be told. Mama was neither pleased nor disappointed. She simply accepted the fact that one of her ten children was getting married at an early age. There were so many of us that the adventures of the middle one could be taken like breakfast in the morning, natural. My little sisters and John, the youngest, accepted it, curious and shyly. Albert agreed to go with me and be my best man.

I started out about four o'clock in the afternoon a couple of days before the wedding to drive to Johnson City, Tennessee, where Albert worked for the Franklin Guaranty Bank. Since the car was new I had to break it in by slow driving. About twelve at night I made my way to the apartment he shared with two other bachelors. I was received with much raillery and some disbelief. I had $200 in my pocket, a new suit, much faith in the eternal goodness of life, a healthy appetite, and new wheels.

The day following my arrival in Tennessee Albert and I started out. I told him all I knew about my prospects. He was puzzled but loyal. We spent the night in a tourist home and about noon of the next day made our way to the Tivoli Hotel in Biloxi. Sophie was equal to the occasion. Whatever her inner feelings were, she welcomed us with hospitable grace. After she had looked Albert over I think she secretly wished Tine was marrying him rather than me. Tine and I were busy with plans. The bishop had grown balky about her marriage to a Protestant. Upon being told by Tine that if we were not to be married by a priest, we would surely seek out the Presbyterian minister, he consented. The Catholics know how to compromise at the right time. Albert had a great time. The coast was new to him, the girls were lovely, prohibition had not dried up available drink. Tine's friends rallied to his entertainment.

I had as yet been unable to buy a ring for the ceremony. We went to a jewelry shop and purchased for eighteen dollars a thin platinum band with three diamonds the size of medium-sized flyspecks. Anyhow the ring does not make the marriage. Furthermore we had a new car. That was something in 1931. So the day was set and Tine and I were married in proper order in the study of Father Somebody of the Society of Jesus. The whole affair is a little hazy in my mind after the passage of many years, some births, innumerable quarrels, and some thousands of breakfasts. So it is with marriage, an indispensable institution for keeping the trousers of society buttoned up.

I had never told Tine anything about my family. Sometimes I told her there were fourteen children, sometimes that I was an only spoiled child of a doting mother. When she asked Albert, he replied, "What did Rob tell you?" Her uncertainty gave me some pleasure, for I concluded that a woman who would marry a man with so little information about his family must be either in love or desperate. I preferred to believe the latter. You may imagine her surprise when she got her first letter from Mama saying, "I always wondered which of my ten children would be first to marry."

We took our honeymoon in the Monteleone Hotel at New Orleans. That was the day before air conditioning. The weather was hot, I was inexperienced but eager. Tine was a little sick at times, but we had our love to keep us—even warmer. One consolation was the delicious cherries we could buy at Solari's across the street; another was the cold shower. If the ring does not make the marriage, neither does the honeymoon, at least for an inexperienced youth and an untried maid. I remembered the picture I used to see in farmhouses in Floyd, the wedding picture. The wife was always sitting down in a chair with the husband behind the chair with his hand on her shoulder. The caption someone has said should be "She was too sore to stand up and he too weak to sit down."

After a few days of this we came back to Sophie in Biloxi, and we were both glad to be home. Now our plans were, or rather my plan was, to take Tine slowly to Floyd, visiting on the way my kinfolks in Tennessee. This we did, and it almost broke up our marriage before it had fairly started. My first stopping place was my cousin's, Dr. Bob Phlegar, a country doctor in Washburn, Tennessee. They received us with pure pleasure and hospitality. The trouble was that Bob was a fox hunter with a pack of Walker hounds. Nothing would do but we must go fox hunting—the men, that is. We took out the hounds and had several races. This was the East Tennessee brand of fox hunting by night and by spirits. In the ardor of the night and the chase we stayed out until daybreak. This was too much for a young wife, and rightly so. I should have been under the covers with the warm body of my wife. I nearly lost Tine. When I got back she had taken a walk down the railroad track and not to look for me. Early punctures are soon patched, but we decided that it was time to head for another road. This we did in a trip broken only by an overnight sleep in the apartment of my brother Albert in Johnson City. He did take us to a fancy restaurant near Linville, North Carolina, where I almost ordered the meal from the musical program. I was about to have Brahms on toast if Tine had not amended my order.

We got to Floyd. Now my mother lived on the farm I have described, six miles from the county seat. When we got to the top of the hill where the blackheart cherry tree used to be, my nine-year-old brother John was by the side of the road, returning perhaps from watching chipmunks stuff their jaws with cherries. John was beautiful then. The sight of his dear face, so young, so lovely, together with the uncertainty and the joy of being really home almost overcame me. Tears sprang to my eyes. I stopped the car and gathered him in, shy and embarrassed, and drove down the lane to Mama, Maude, Annie, Helen, Virginia, to the old house, the spring, the maple trees in the yard. Like the welcome of the sun on a day in March, they took Tine to their hearts, and she was a member of the family from that unforgettable moment.

John was especially delighted to see us and to have a new member of the family. He told me at once that he wanted to sleep with me. Mama did not tell him the facts of life, but she let him know that for him to sleep with me was entirely out of the question. Tine was willing, but I balked at the idea. Tine had never seen wheat growing, a cow milked, or a chicken plucked. She had brought long dresses, short dresses, and even an Empress Eugenie hat that was much in favor that summer. I should have prepared her for life on a farm in Floyd County, but I had so much on my mind that I never thought of it. We did spend a few days at a summer home on Bent Mountain owned by my cousin Lilah, but Maude went along to help cook. At that time we both knew how to scramble eggs and boil water. We visited for a night my mentor, Miss Gwinn, and we dressed for the occasion. Unfortunately the creek was up, the road was muddy and rutted, and we had a flat tire on the mile journey. I had to change it in my white linen suit. A farmer came along, one of the Radfords, I believe, and found me hard at work changing the tire.

"What are you doing there, Robert?" he said.

"I am fishing for bass," I answered out of frustration.

He shook his head in a solemn and uncritical way. "You are using the wrong bait."

A few of the neighbors came one night to give us a shivaree. They beat a few pans until we came out. A boy or two kissed the bride, and Dr. Thurman booed her. The Doctor was old and white-headed and cleft of palate, but he loved to boo the ladies. This act was accomplished by placing his head on their bosoms and wagging it about with never a bite. No telling the number of babies he had brought into the world and the number of women he had booed. All ten of us he delivered at the usual price of twenty-five dollars. Easy as peeling a grape, he always said. Another of his sayings in this context was "When the pear is ripe, it's easy plucked."

.

Chapter Six

Sewanee, Law Practice, and the War

About the middle of September 1931 Tine and I drove to Sewanee to take up our duties as developers of a junior department at the Sewanee Military Academy. We came by night. There were no street lights. A few lights from homes patterned their way through the dense foliage of campus trees. The moon from time to time, as it emerged from floating night clouds, revealed the presence of stone buildings. Where to go? Whom to ask? Quickly we decided to return a few miles to Monteagle, where we had seen a hotel. Solemnly, with little conversation, we made our way to Monteagle and spent the night in an unpretentious hotel. By night, at least, Sewanee was not what we had expected. Our spirits were low. My uncle Albert had graduated from the medical school at Sewanee. I suppose this had led me to expect more than I saw by night.

Fortunately the next day dawned bright and sparkling and clear as only a fair September day can be on the Mountain. With a hearty breakfast to lift youthful spirits that are naturally volatile, we returned to Sewanee to find what lay in store for us. To visit Sewanee today can give you no picture of what Sewanee was like in 1931. There was Walsh Hall and Breslin with its tower, the unfinished chapel, St. Luke's much as it is today, and four stone dormitories. The academy lay further west, a good walking distance from the center of the campus. We found our way to the academy. Colonel Cravens, our sponsor, was absent, but Major Clyde Fasick knew vaguely of our coming. No apartment had been prepared for us for we had not been expected for another day. We discovered that our apartment was to be two rooms in Quintard barracks on the second floor. There was no furniture immediately available, but in the quickest time a double bed, one of those iron bedsteads now in demand as antiques, was provided as well as a chest of drawers. Immediately across the hall was our living room–to-be. From somewhere a well-used wicker sofa was found along with a companion chair. The springs of the bed sagged but fortunately to the middle. We were in business. We had brought sheets, pillow cases, and a trunk full of gear; so we had a place to sleep and the beginnings of a living room. Meals were not to be served until the academy

opened a few days later. This was not too bad, because we had our first meal with Mrs. Wright, who served meals to such as us, and the meals were bounteous. The most disappointing aspect of the situation was the stark fact that there were no students in the junior school.

The next day Colonel Cravens returned. I had liked him from the start, and he never disappointed me. He explained that the depression had affected his plans, that there was the possibility of recruiting some little boys in Sewanee and perhaps one boarder from Chattanooga. We had a contract. It would be honored come hell or high water. We ought to begin immediately to solicit sons of local families. We did this. Within a short time we had nine students: Currin and John Gass, Billie Crockett, Frank Maner, Tino and Jim Johnson, Will Marsh Reece, and Charles Knickerbocker. Later a little boy from Chattanooga, Miller Smith, enrolled as the first boarder of the junior department. His parents have been our life-long friends; he was destined to lose his life in France in World War II.

The most satisfactory teaching I have ever done was with this group of little boys. They were in various grades, but this proved to be no obstacle. We gave them reading, writing, and arithmetic, and in addition French, Latin, and whatever else we thought they should have. They were required to memorize famous poems, read great books, and ever I held before them the examples of great men to fire their imaginations with the possibilities that life offers. I suppose that if I should say to any one of them today, "Hail to thee, blythe spirit," he would take up the poem and recite the rest of it.

This was a remarkable time in the history of Sewanee. The old lingered; memories of the beginnings still persisted. The honored dead were still remembered in the homes of the living. Henry Gass used to say that a group of people of eminent respectability lived together in cheerful poverty. Sewanee was small. The depression was beginning to do its work. Professors still thought nothing of teaching eighteen hours a week. Dr. William Knickerbocker, head of the English department, edited the *Sewanee Review,* taught full time, and still found time to teach graduate students in English in the afternoon.

Dr. Benjamin Finney was vice-chancellor. Though he was later to retire because of the financial plight of the university, he did not cause it; rather he was the victim of hard times. Never once did a faculty member fail to receive his check on time. He built the first stone dormitories that had been built in many years. Out of his own pocket he provided for students who came to graduation time without money to pay their bills. He was a good, grey man with a stylish mustache and a whispering voice destroyed by cancer.

Once he was in New York on a fund-raising trip. He went to a home where he had an appointment with the man of the house. He rang the bell and said to the lady who answered his ring, in his high, sibilant whisper, "Is your husband in?"

She replied in a whisper, "No, come in."

There was Dean George M. Baker whom another generation knew and loved. He was made dean, it was said, because he taught German and there were not enough German students to occupy his time fully. He was dean of the college, admissions officer, dean of students, chaperon of the parties, altogether a wise, resourceful man who knew student nature and tempered his rather strict discipline with paternal mercy. There was General James P. Jervey, professor of mathematics, a courtly gentleman and a retired officer of distinction. In the homes of all these people there was to be found generous hospitality and a grace and charm that have largely disappeared.

Perhaps the most talked-about, the most eccentric scholar of them all was Professor Sedley Ware, the one and only professor of history. He was a tall, stately man who reminded one of George Bernard Shaw. He was a dramatic teacher who read his papers and decorated them with spirited comments: "You boob!" "You think so, eh?" "What a historian you would make!"—all in red ink. He was a great admirer of the ladies. Once he was on an afternoon stroll with his mushroom basket on his arm when he encountered a sprightly nurse wheeling a baby carriage.

"Ah," said he, "what a beautiful baby!" all the while eyeing the nursemaid.

"Why, Dr. Ware," said she, "don't you know your own grandbaby?"

"How's a man to recognize his grandchild if they keep changing nurses?" he returned.

Of them all, however, the wisest, the gentlest, the best was Henry Gass, Rhodes scholar, lover of the classics, my early mentor, my friend.

Soon after we arrived in Sewanee we were invited to Colonel Cravens's for dinner. Both Tine and I dressed rather informally, I in a grey suit, she in a short dress. We were dismayed to find our host and hostess and the other guests in formal dinner dress. This was the day of large bridge parties. Without exception it was expected that guests dress formally. Though the dress was formal, the conversation was sprightly, relaxed, and even gay. I found that even scholarly people talked about other people, the weather, themselves, the latest happenings in a small village. Even so, more than in most places I knew, the conversation was about ideas, world events, and personages from the past.

Early we adjusted to a life regulated by bugle calls, filled with the hurry-scurry of student life in a dormitory. The corps of cadets marched in to meals, we before or after. Professors presided at student tables. Colored waiters served the food. It was good. It cost us not a cent. Our colleagues were friendly and helpful. My duties that first year were not too demanding. Tine and I were getting to know each other's weaknesses better and sometimes to make allowances. That two people can live together at all for the course of a lifetime is in itself a testimony to nature's power.

Soon after coming to Sewanee I discovered that the university still offered the master's degree. The only difficulty was to find a professor willing to offer the courses and supervise the research. A few students and would-be class members approached Dr. William Knickerbocker of the English department, whose son Charles we taught. He agreed to teach the courses, which were scheduled in the afternoons, when I was comparatively free of my own teaching. Within a short time after coming to Sewanee, I was enrolled as a graduate student in the College of Arts and Sciences.

The first class had only four students, and there was much writing and research as well as reading to be done. Dr. Knickerbocker was a learned man with a keen mind and deep learning. That first year we studied the Romantic period in English literature as well as Shakespeare. I enjoyed the work and the lively sessions with Dr. Knickerbocker. I continued this study for three years and in 1934 received the master's degree at the June commencement. Of the ten or so students who were at one time or another members of the group, only Major Fasick and I completed work for the degree. I wrote a dissertation that is somewhere in the university archives on *Fenimore Cooper, Critic of American Civilization.* Though Cooper is noted for his Leatherstocking novels, I thought his greatest contribution lay in his work as a social critic of the America of the 1830s. I especially liked his novel, *Satanstoe,* for its picture of life on the Hudson and his bitter revulsion at the political effects of Jacksonian democracy. Cooper was a firm believer of government by men who had a stake in society. Today I think there is much that is sound in the doctrine that property involves responsibility. I am sure that property rights is the matrix for the development of civil rights generally. Certainly it is historically true that out of property rights developed other rights of the individual.

The fall of the second year at Sewanee I was transferred to the senior department of the academy as instructor in English and history. Although I dreaded to leave my little boys, I welcomed the opportunity, because it meant more money and an opportunity to travel in the summer soliciting students. During the depression many private preparatory schools suffered a loss of students, as was to be expected. The South was then the home of many military academies. Consequently the rivalry for students was keen. Most academies responded by sending out in the summer their most persuasive teachers, who answered in person inquiries about the school and endeavored to steer them to the proper place—their own school.

During this period I occasionally visited my cousin Dr. Robert Phlegar in Washburn, Tennessee. He was a splendid country doctor and a hunter. While visiting him one spring, I had a wonderful and strange experience. The day was clear and cool, with little wind. I decided to climb Clinch Mountain, which rose above Dr. Phlegar's house. After a leisurely but demanding climb to the top, I lay down on one of the rocks that dotted the summit. Suddenly all was so peaceful, so quiet that I was carried away. Time flowed by me easily and silently. I became a part of all creation, of all being. My mind soared away into the clouds. How long I lay in this state I do not know. I came to and began to feel the breeze, to see the two vultures sailing the air streams above. The experience sobered me, remained with me a long time. For once, though, I experienced peace; perhaps I had a glimpse of heaven. The whole experience reminded me of Wordworth's *Intimations of Immortality.*

Dr. Finney, who was vice-chancellor when we came to Sewanee in 1931, was a widower and lived with his nephew Martin Johnson in a rambling frame house standing where Guerry Hall now stands. Martin Johnson was business manager of the university and a skilled builder. Whatever he built withstood the test of time. Both Johnson and Cannon Halls were constructed during his tenure.

Mr. Johnson loved to hunt. His special hunting companion was

Evert Myers, a long, tall drink of water with a perpetual cud in his jaw and an eye that took in much about him. After the end of hunting season Martin Johnson was accustomed for several years to give a game dinner for all the hunters in Sewanee. It was a grand dinner complete with preprandial warm-up. As one entered, on a table to the left of the door was a bucket of water and a demijohn of white liquor (Uncle Dunk Tate's best), glasses, and a dipper. You helped yourself. Of course this was during Prohibition. Modern readers will scarcely know what the word meant. It was somewhat risky to serve liquor even in Sewanee, but hunters are trustworthy in such matters.

The dinner was the creation of Matilda Johnson and her help. The Johnsons had a great inheritance of splendid old silver, and the table was magnificent with it. No flowers marred the beauty of the big mahogany table. The centerpiece was a great tray of brown quail piled in a mound of beauty. Perhaps a hundred birds had been baked like little hens, each nestled close to his brother, covey-like. On one end of the table was a Tennessee country ham, literally spoiling for attention. On the other end a mellow spiced round of beef, grinning a welcome. But first Christ's blessing on so superb a company and on so burdened a table. This was always said by Mr. Finney when he was present. In his husky whisper of a voice, he blessed food and diner alike and prepared the way for the appetite. The first course was always a bowl or a cup of clear soup. Then came the dinner. Bowls of scalloped oysters, dishes piled with sweet potatoes, tomato pudding, big stalks of celery, gravy boats waiting to be tipped, and of course the quail, the ham, the round. Whereas before the dinner talk hung heavy in the air with stories of missed shots, and wild dogs, and perfect stands, so soon as the men came to the table the only sound was of clicking forks. Occasionally, for the sake of civility only, a diner would voice a paean of praise for the ham or the gravy. Now and then the host himself would make a half-hearted sally at conversation. It did not work, though. Hearty appetites sharpened to cutting edge by mountain white moved into the fray. Then the dessert. None of your pumpkin pie, or creamy custards. Mr. Johnson knew what a fitting end of such a feast was. Lime sherbet prepared the way for the brandy and the coffee and the cigars and the talk. Town and gown, all hunters, tolerated no caste system at Martin Johnson's big supper. That's the way it was.

When we came to the academy the enrollment of boarding students had declined to around sixty-five. Financially the university and the academy were both in trouble. When financial trouble comes to an institution, sooner or later the head of the operation loses his place. It does not really matter that the cause lies not with him. I have seen it happen many times. So it happened to my dear friend Colonel Cravens. In his place as superintendent, Major General William R. Smith, a distinguished officer of the army and a former superintendent of West Point, was employed. Colonel Cravens remained as his assistant. General Smith was a man of imposing appearance and sound judgment. He realized that the problem of the academy was a problem of enrollment. He increased the number of those of us who traveled in the summer to solicit students. We were paid $100 per month, our travel expenses, and a bonus of $25 dollars per student who enrolled because of our solicitations.

As a result the academy began to rebuild its enrollment and to pay its way in the university corporation. This was a sound practice, and it continued until about the time of World War II, when recruitment travel was no longer as necessary.

For several years, as a matter of fact until I left Sewanee for an adventure in the law in 1938, I traveled each summer. At first I had only Mississippi for a territory. Later Louisiana, Texas, and Oklahoma were added to my domain. With the income from summer work, we who traveled added substantially to our income. I made from a thousand to fifteen hundred dollars each summer from this work. I learned much about people and geography. I also learned how to be at ease with strangers. During the depression those who could afford a preparatory education for their sons were, without many exceptions, well-to-do people. Invariably they were hospitable and often invited me to dinner. I found that if I were invited to dine we had a real chance of enrolling the student.

I learned to love South Louisiana. There are no pleasanter people in the world than the plantation people in that stretch of rich land between New Orleans and Lake Charles. They were more settled and contemplative than the people of the Mississippi Delta, who had their own charm but who were more nervous and restless, more given to the opportune splurge. I visited in many of the famous plantation houses from Parlange, Magnolia, to Shadows-on-the-Teche. I loved to visit with Mrs. Avery on Avery Island. She was old and wise and told me many stories of the people and the events of her lifetime. Here even then was the great salt mine and bird sanctuary. To see the egrets, the herons, and the birds of the marsh at close range, nesting, crying their evening calls, was an unforgettable experience.

I could stay at a hotel for two to two and a half dollars. Meals ran around two dollars a day. And what meals! It was impossible to find a place serving poor food. There was then a hotel at DeRidder that offered a lazy-susan dining table. It burgeoned with fine roasts, ham, oyster in season, fried chicken, and every vegetable that the land afforded. One could dine at this rich table for a dollar. Gasoline could be had for about twenty-five cents a gallon. I could travel all week for about sixty dollars. This was the day before air conditioning. It was hot. Hotel fans, whirring overhead, simply stirred the hot, humid air. Often I was awakened at night by the sweat that flooded my neck and pajama top. Cold baths did no good.

In 1933 our life changed. Ulysse was born. Since we spent the summer with headquarters in Biloxi, Tine felt more secure to have the baby there. She left by train from Decatur, Alabama, a week or so before I could get away. Then too we were uncertain about the exact time for the event, as is so often the case. I arrived and spent a few days in Biloxi. Still no baby. We decided that I ought to start traveling. I went to Shreveport for a few days and drove south to Baton Rouge. I was seated at supper with two soft-shell crabs on my plate when I was paged. Tine had called all over Louisiana and finally located me in Baton Rouge. She said the baby was on the way; the pains had started. I was so excited I left my dinner and headed for the car. I went through the little towns like a breeze. As I passed through Slidell, I heard the siren of a police motorcycle. I pulled to the side.

"Where do you think you're going?" was my greeting from the officer.

"Officer," I said, "my wife telephoned me a few minutes ago that the baby is coming."

"Is that a fact," he said.

"It's the truth," I replied.

"In that case I will give you an escort through town, but don't let me catch you coming through here at seventy miles an hour in the next nine months."

He escorted me to the city limits and I kept rolling.

When I reached Sophie's, Louella, the cook, told me that Tine was in the hospital. When I arrived the baby was on its way but slowly.

Champ and Tuck Gay, our friends from Ocean Springs, and Sophie were sitting by. I was permitted to see Tine. She looked all right to me. Well, in due time—and it was a long time—they called the new father to see his daughter. Ulysse was a thin, squirmy piece of pinkness with the faintest tinge of red hair. I was pleased to have a daughter then, and I still think that daughters are more to be desired than sons. For a week or so Tine remained in the hospital. When she finally came home, she was pinned tightly in a sheet and remained in bed for another two weeks. We employed a practical nurse to look after her and the little one. Ulysse was a good baby, no colic to speak of and hungry, hungry. This day and time the mother gets on her feet soon after the birth, but in those days the doctors believed that rest was the thing.

In time Tine was up and about. Ulysse was doing well, exercising her lungs, kicking her legs. In August I decided that we must take the baby to Floyd to show my mother. Mother and baby were uncomfortable on the long trip to Virginia. The first day we drove to Atlanta. We spent the night with my cousin Hugh Wood and his wife, Maria. I had a hard time finding my way to his house, but when we got there we had the warmest of greetings. That night Maria, who was a nurse, made a cradle for the baby in a dresser drawer in our room. We left the next morning and got home about four o'clock in the afternoon.

The whole family had been waiting impatiently for our coming. We took Ulysse immediately to Mama, who had had so many babies and loved them so well. We put her on the bed in the living room, and Ulysse smiled and chortled for them to their heart's delight. John didn't say anything about sleeping with the baby. As a matter of fact he was a little put out at all the attention given Ulysse. He had been Mama's youngest for a long time. It was cool in the mountains, and we all flourished for a week or so. Never did a baby have more attention than Ulysse got from my adoring family.

After our visit in Floyd we headed back to Sewanee. We wanted to arrive a little early in order to get everything arranged for the school year. Tine was continuing to teach. A nurse had to be found, a baby bed set up in our bedroom, and several other things attended to. We were fortunate in finding a splendid nurse for Ulysse. Mamie Taylor was a black woman of about fifty years, I would guess. She had raised her own, and she loved Ulysse from the beginning. Since she was by all odds the most beautiful of the few babies in Sewanee, Mamie took great pride in her baby. She would wheel her in a baby carriage to the chapel yard where the nurses with their charges gathered and let all and sundry know that hers was the sweetest and the best. Mamie Taylor raised Ulysse until she was five years old. She had a father and mother all right, but Mamie was her definite favorite.

Only once was Ulysse seriously ill. The illness developed from a cold. We gave the usual remedies, but she did not improve. Quite suddenly she began to swell up with gas. We called Dr. R. M. Kirby-Smith. He worked over her in the hospital for an hour or two. Then he called us aside and said, "If this were my baby I would take her to Vanderbilt Hospital in Nashville." He made arrangements for our admittance, and we sped on our way. Tine was holding Ulysse in her arms, and I was driving over icy roads at a frantic pace. During the trip the swelling began to subside, and we took hope. Upon examination by Dr. Overall in Vanderbilt Hospital, her illness was diagnosed as pneumonia. He really never believed that her stomach had ballooned as it had. She remained in the hospital for ten days. When I went to see her after the fourth day, she was sitting up in bed, her head a mass of tight red curls, the prettiest and sauciest baby in the whole city of Nashville. Soon she returned to Mamie and to her parents. Ulysse with all the attention she got was never a spoiled baby. From the first she saw things as they were. Actually Tine and I were so busy that we saw her but little during the day. She was with Mamie.

In the days when I travelled in summer solicitation, the state of Mississippi was like Gaul divided into three parts. There was the Mississippi coast with its French and Spanish background, vivacious, leisurely in its pace, frenetic in its politics, scornful of laws that interfered with living. It subsisted largely on income from fisheries, real estate, the piney woods in the back, and of course the tourist trade. Prohibition when it came made a dent but failed to tear away the conviction that good drink, like cold water, was the inheritance of its people. Catholicism was dominant among the older families and among the many southern Europeans who came to work in the shrimp and oyster packing plants.

Then there was the Mississippi Delta, the black land. Cotton was the staple. The black man was its handmaiden. I used to drive on gravel roads that passed through miles of cotton fields. Blacks and mules did the work, rising at dawn to work the rich land, answering, mule and man alike, to the welcome sound of the plantation bell that meant midday meal and short rest. There were the great plantations, owned by men who were well educated, aristocratic in their own way, responsible to their people and their land. There was a lesser breed, too, man on the move, sharp in practice, less cultivated in speech, wringing from their tenants and from their beasts all that the sun, the rain, and the soil would produce. It was a life that accustomed men to taking chances. They knew that the good year would be followed sooner or later by the bad year; so they made the best of the good year—in food, travel, and fun. The blacks were in a state of semi-peonage. Their sweat made the land rich; their condition gave birth to the "blues." In many ways they were free as only the very poor and the very rich can be, free and natural. Their voices, their recreation, their religion, their joys were as spontaneous as the flight of a sparrow. Often in contemplating their lot I envied them their spontaneity, their lack of inhibitions, their subtle subterfuge, their philosophic acceptance of life, their ability to make great joy out of little joy. The relationship of black and white was fixed. Each knew his place. Hence for many years the relationship was stable.

Between the delta and the coast was Mississippi proper. It dominated the politics of the state. It was a land similar to east Texas or middle Georgia. Small farms produced a hard living. Small farmers supported the cities like Hattiesburg and Meridian. It was a crabbed culture of a provincial people, hard-working with a Methodist or Baptist morality that kept the liquor in the barn instead of on the sideboard and voted for the spellbinder. Oases like Jackson existed, but they were the exception. Their style was their own, and it suited them. Life was generally hard, sin had its place and its punishment. These people weathered the depression better than most. They expected little, were accustomed to less, and took what came as a natural cross to be borne. Such a conditioning produced some good men and some cramped minds. I noticed that the lot of the black in middle Mississippi was hard, his life and status more precarious, his ignorance and squalor more obvious, his superstitions more compelling.

The students who attended the college in the thirties were a different breed from those whom we have today. They were representatives of the upper and upper middle class. To afford an education at Sewanee at a time when scholarships were few and hard to come by meant that the families from which they came could pay their fees.

They came for a college education. This education was, and was expected to be, more than merely an introduction to learning. Some came for two years, some for five. So long as they could pay their fees they were quite generally acceptable. The degree, though, was reserved for those who might earn it. Some of our most generous donors in later years were men who did not earn the degree but cherished the memory of those golden years at Sewanee. Emphasis was placed upon manners. The right clothes, the ability to converse easily, to feel at home in society.

Pre-World War II Sewanee was quite unlike Sewanee after the war. Before the war, memories of the past colored much that was said and done. There was ever in the background *The War.* Memories of the Old South still lingered.

The boarding house style of living produced attitudes toward life and ways of behaving for both men and women. Uncertainty of the future and poverty produced a pride that was easily offended. Students generally came from the Southeast. They came from plantations, from the professions, from business, and they could pay their way. There were no scholarships except for sons of clergymen and a few scholarships designed to honor a donor. Students made a group remarkably alike, sharing the same manners, the same attitudes.

The three balls of the Sewanee year offer us a portrait of the time. The best orchestras the nation afforded came for three-day stands: Kay Kyser, Jan Garber. There were afternoon tea dances, grand balls each night. Dean Baker and the traditional matrons chaperoned. There was a good deal of liquor consumed but never openly. Once in a while the dean would see a young man overflowing and send him home to his room for the night, but on the whole manners were genteel and the festivities well contained. The word *gentleman* was often used. Youths were expected to act like gentlemen and they generally did. I have not heard the expression "Sewanee gentleman" used lately. Once when I was dean and attending dinner at Gailor a food riot almost got under way. I moved to the loud speaker. I said, "Gentlemen, gentlemen! You are gentlemen, aren't you?" It was enough; the disorder subsided. A disorderly meal would never have occurred during the thirties. One reason was that Mrs. Eggleston, bless her soul, provided such good food at Magnolia that no one thought of complaining. Then there was a matron at most tables. Always gentle souls, they operated *in loco parentis,* darned socks, minded manners, discouraged drink, put up with much confusion, and loved their boys.

In 1934 I received the master's degree in English from Sewanee. It was a well-earned degree, and I have always been proud of being a regular alumnus of the university. Soon thereafter I enrolled in the Andrew Jackson University at Nashville to begin the study of law at night. I had always had a hankering to practice law. I was young and strong. I could teach five classes a day, take officer-in-charge duty, tend study hall in my turn, and still drive to Nashville two or three times each week to attend lectures on law at night. I did this regularly for nearly three years.

In 1937 I went to Roanoke, Virginia, to take the bar examination. I knew not what to expect. My legal education had been a kind of hand-to-mouth enterprise, or even better a catch-as-catch-can operation. I had learned from the lectures—they provided a guide and some regularity—but most of my legal learning came from my own reading of the hornbooks, like *Clark on Contracts*. I had gone thoroughly through a book of questions that had been asked in the previous years. I suppose this helped me as much as anything in preparing for the examination.

My brother Albert had an apartment in Roanoke which afforded me comfort. His being there lent me support. I knew that the mortality rate was high, and I rather expected to fail. After all, how could I expect to compete with those who had had the benefit of a formal study of law at prestigious universities? Each morning and afternoon we had three-hour written examinations. Strangely enough I felt that I knew the answers to nearly all of the questions. There were some about which I was dubious, but I made the most reasonable case I could, believing that law was a kind of crystallized common sense. After taking the examinations I returned to Biloxi to travel for the school and to rejoin Tine and Ulysse at Sophie's.

In July the list of those who had passed the bar was printed in the Roanoke *Times*. Someone in the family excitedly wrote me that my name appeared among those passing. It was a great feeling. Later I learned that I was among those in the upper ten percent with respect to grade. I think this was a real achievement, and it still gives me some pleasure to know that I did this on my own and at a real expense in human energy. For it was no small thing to teach full time in Sewanee Military Academy, with all the duties that entailed, and drive to

Nashville, a hundred miles away, to night classes in law and get up and go the next day. Later in the month of July I received official notification and the certificate authorizing me to practice in the state of Virginia.

In 1937 the Great Depression still held the people in its grip. Hope of better things was in the air, but only in the air. Of more importance was the fact that the shock had worn off. New beginnings were being made, and people had become accustomed to the prospects of hard times and had adjusted their vision accordingly. In such times it is difficult to go from making a living to more uncertain prospects. It was so with me. I had passed the bar, but the step toward finding a place to practice the profession was hard to take. We concluded that I had better stay at the academy for a year at least. My hope was that during that year I might find a firm that would employ me or a place where I might make a living with my scanty new knowledge of the law. Unfortunately the time that I could spare from teaching, Christmas and Easter vacations, was all too limited for the purpose of setting up a practice. Where to go and what to do were uppermost in my mind. By the end of the academic year I had not yet found a place, and my prospects seemed dismal. One who lives in this age of opportunity and wealth can hardly imagine the predicament that many people found themselves in.

Nevertheless at the end of May 1938 we packed our possessions and prepared for whatever lay ahead. Albert, who was in the warehouse business by that time, found a trucker who would come to Sewanee and for a modest amount—as I remember, $200—carry our things to Mama's where they could be stored in the old house where my grandfather had lived at Floyd. We packed the car with all it would hold, put the dogs Rod and Rip in the open two-wheeled trailer, and left Sewanee we thought for good one fine day in late May. Had I known what lay ahead I would probably have remained at Sewanee.

Once in Floyd I looked around for a suitable place to begin the practice of law. I was attracted to small towns for two reasons. First, few firms were employing lawyers with my training. Second, I felt that I could get ahead faster in a small town or county seat where I could become more easily known in a shorter time. Giles County attracted me. The county seat, Pearisburg, is a small place. Yet I was told that the bar was weak there and that a man might establish himself more easily there than elsewhere. I scouted the place, talked to lawyers there. They held out for me little promise. I might have settled there but for an unfortunate event. A man came to me with a case involving some small claim concerning an automobile. The claim he had was against a black. The case was tried before the local trial judge. I questioned the witnesses too severely. One of them I referred to in my argument as a "light colored Negro." His name was Louis, but I had forgotten his name in the excitement of my first case. This antagonized the blacks who were present. There were many blacks who, unemployed, lounged about the courthouse square and on the streets. Two days later driving my car I stopped for a red light. A black man standing on the curb yelled at me, "Get out of here, you white son of a bitch." Without thought I opened the door of my car and started for him. In those days these were fighting words. He was surprised and ran up the street.

I pursued him a short distance. Suddenly he stopped, picked up a rock, and threw it at me. It was a big rock and it narrowly missed my head. It did almost hit a baby in a carriage being wheeled by a young mother on the sidewalk. I ran back to my car and took from the glove compartment a .22 Woodsman. Fortunately a state trooper saw the whole thing. He came up, told me to put away the gun and get my car to the curb. He was very sympathetic. He said that he had been beaten up by a gang of blacks while attempting an arrest and had no love for the pack that lay about the courthouse. During the next week as I walked about from time to time blacks would say slurring things in soft voices that I could scarcely hear. The trooper came to see me and told me that sooner or later I would have trouble on some dark street. It seemed likely to me that I would end up shooting for my life and that I had made an unfortunate beginning in Giles County. I had no office. Housing was hard to find. I had been deterred by both chance and circumstance. I resolved to shake the dust of Pearisburg from my feet and try elsewhere. It was, however, with a feeling of guilt that I left. I feared some would say the blacks had run me out of town. In a sense they had.

I returned to Floyd and resolved to let time take care of my predicament. I found an office over the Blue Ridge Motor Company, set up my sign, and waited for clients. Tine found a job teaching in the school system. We rented a house with a big yard and garden. So we started.

My first client came to me while we were still living with Mama on the farm. He was a black by the name of Buck Minafee whose mother had once been accused by Papa of stealing our chickens. I have forgotten his trouble, but I will always remember what he told me. I was looking forward to the opportunity to impress the judge and the bar with my spirited defense at the first session of the court. Said Buck, "Mr. Lancaster, I was hopin' you would get this case put off. That would give me time to go to West Virginia, get a job in the mines. You see, by the next cou't I could afford a good lawyer."

The first few months were grim. A few clients strayed in. Waiting

I enjoy the moment with fellow attorney Kyle Weeks in the clerk's office of the Floyd County Courthouse.

is a game I have never played well. Now and then I got a case before Mr. Burwell, the trial justice. Fees were by modern standards pitifully low. The bar of Floyd afforded old and experienced lawyers. I was a Democrat in a ruggedly Republican county. Nevertheless we got along well. Expenses were low. I rented a house for twenty dollars a month and my offices for fifteen dollars. Food for a week cost no more than five or ten dollars. Those who have not lived during that time of deflation can scarcely believe food and lodging were once so low.

When the hunting season came along I was free to go. Chris Harmon and I laid low many a covey. My shooting improved. Rod and Rip became great quail dogs. Yet for Tine living in Floyd was more than grim. Sewanee had been bad enough, but Floyd was a nightmare. Fortunately she was busy teaching most of the day. We had a wonderful cook, Octavia, who looked after the house. Ulysse was in school. Things could have been worse, I thought.

At the end of the first year I had taken in fees $1,100 on my own. During the summer of my second year I resolved to run for commonwealth's attorney. The office had a secure salary and with it the further opportunity to engage in civil practice. I was at a disadvantage as a Democrat. Yet I was encouraged by the fact that my grandfather, Conner Barnard, had been elected county treasurer, and he was a Democrat. At this time, too, the county was split over the rise in the property tax necessitated by the cost of a new high school building. To get the nomination was easy. To be elected was another thing. I bought an old Ford that had seen its best days and started soliciting the people of the county. My goal was to visit every home and fireside in the whole county, and I believe I almost made it. It was great fun to me, I was constantly on the road. I visited the farmer at the plough, the wife at the milking gap, the merchant in his store. I made my plea and asked for their vote. When I could stay all night with a farmer, I did. When I could help with the milking, I did that. I went to Primitive Baptist associations, to Dunkard feasts, to Methodist revivals. I learned much about the people of this mountain county, and they got to at least know and recognize me.

Time and again I thought I had the election won, and I probably did. It is hard for people to resist the temptation to vote for a personable redheaded lawyer who is easy mannered and not put off by denial. The Republicans got scared. Their candidate was not popular at the moment due to the school issue. They were accustomed to winning, and they were led by the foremost lawyer of the county, the redoubtable Joe Proffitt.

Near the end of the campaign the Republicans published a public letter and appeal insinuating that I was a Mississippian and a foreigner. I determined to answer, but I think I chose the wrong way. I bought radio time and replied in a spirited speech that was heard, unfortunately, in Roanoke County but barely audible in Floyd. Nevertheless the fact that I had replied by that medium probably aided in spreading the truth that I was maligned by a leadership desperate and afraid that I would break the Republicans' hold on one of only two Republican counties in the state of Virginia.

I was defeated in the election by a total of sixty-four votes in a county that usually gave a Republican a two thousand majority. I learned later that the ballot box in one of the precincts was held out until the returns elsewhere were in, and then that box was used to count me out. I lost and perhaps it was for the best, for had I won I would no doubt have remained in the field of law. Thus my later life at Sewanee might never have been.

During the first summer after my removal from Sewanee to Floyd, Tine and Ulysse, my brother Albert, and I made a visit to the Gulf coast. We had a great time introducing Albert to the life of the coast. Once at the dice table he made so many passes that we were able to go on an overnight fishing trip to the islands. We went with the Gorenflo brothers, who were splendid fishermen and good companions. We spent the night aboard the boat and anchored near the Ship Island light. The mosquitoes were bad. They raised great welts on my brother Albert. We pretended they were small mosquitoes that a real fisherman would scarcely notice, but after he made a visit to the light house to escape we joined him. The next day was for the greater part of the day poor fishing, but the beer was good and the shrimp better. Toward evening we noticed the water boiling near the shore. We put ashore to investigate. Upon casting from the surf we found ourselves in a school of speckled trout. Big ones. Time after time each cast produced a fine trout. Albert had chosen to remain aboard, but upon seeing us hauling in so many fish, he leaped overboard and swam ashore. He arrived just in time to cast into the passing school. This is the only time I have ever seen such a school of trout passing a shore. I did once observe the mackerel migrating through the water between the coast and the islands, passing through by the millions for several days. They were easily caught. The sight of millions of fish feeding and throwing up bits and pieces of the prey with thousands of gulls flying overhead was a wonderfully savage yet natural sight.

We enjoyed the trip to the coast. Albert and I returned after a week, but Tine and Ulysse remained to spend most of the summer with Sophie. I was glad because she was never at home in Floyd. It was too little, too isolated, and too unfamiliar. My practice of insisting on spending Sundays at Mama's and my drinking habits did nothing to ease her pain. Floyd was a hard drinking place on weekends. Both Albert and I participated freely in lifting the glass. Nobody could feel the effects so quickly as I, and nobody suffered such remorse afterwards. I made it a rule to get up early the next morning and drive my body relentlessly regardless of how I felt. I have never passed out from drink, and I have never failed to get up and go regardless of my mental or physical state. I have thought myself capable of jumping ten-rail fences and flying off with the east wind.

My second year of practice in Floyd was a disaster. I took Jim Morgan as a partner into a business that could not support one lawyer. He was a true friend and an affable companion, but he brought no clients with him. When winter came we opened a second office at Hillsville, the county seat of a nearby county. There was little to be had in the way of practice there. What there was was monopolized by local lawyers who had been established for some time (in the case of two, for two generations). Something had to be done. It seemed to me that there was no future in what I was doing. I resolved to return to Sewanee where at least there was security.

Unfortunately there were no openings at the academy. General Smith did assure me that I could return the following year. Major Hayne Shumate was leaving the academy. He thought that he would like me to take the commandant's position. I returned to Floyd just in time to be with Sophie, who had come to Floyd to visit us and had brought with her Evelyn's son, Tommy, who was a year or two older than Ulysse. Ulysse was venturesome as a youngster. She and Tommy decided to do a bit of exploring. When I arrived home it was just discovered that Ulysse and Tommy were gone, not to be found. We hunted for them nearby without success. Finally we called the police. Shortly they were found on the road to Stuart about two miles from home headed the wrong way. Both children were surprised at our alarm. They were quite sure that the road they were on would soon take them home.

I had another year of law before me, so I resolved to move to another town. Judge John Draper of Pulaski, who was circuit judge of an adjoining county, had heard me defend a client while he was visiting Joe Proffitt in Floyd. He learned of my desire to make a move and suggested that I come to Pulaski to practice. He thought that he could help me in many ways. I moved to Pulaski.

We had some difficulty in finding a place to live. Finally we rented an apartment in the Fine Apartment Building on the fourth floor. I was able to rent an office of three rooms on the main street. Tine, who while we were in Floyd had given up teaching to do welfare work, was able to obtain a place in the welfare office in Pulaski.

I hung out my shingle, and from time to time clients came to my office. I had gained something of a reputation in the Western District Court of the United States for my spirited defense of a bootlegger from Floyd. The case against him was circumstantial and involved a path that led from his house to a still. I took the case to the jury. This was almost unprecedented. Usually the client pled guilty and threw himself on the mercy of the court. If he were not a habitual offender the judge usually placed the guilty person on probation with a suspended sentence. The judge well knew that it was hard for a mountaineer to make a living on a farm that slanted off at a forty-five degree angle. For years those who lived on the side of the mountain had taken their corn to market in liquid form. Since the case involved contradictory testimony and circumstantial evidence, I risked the jury trial. The jury brought in a verdict of not guilty. It was the first such verdict in a number of years and earned for me the interest and respect of the bootlegging community. They made good clients. They always paid cash. They were easy to please. This case brought me several others.

Though I did not get rich in that year in Pulaski, I did get enough cases to pay a stenographer to do half a day's work, and I held my head above water. Just at this time there was much activity in land sales. The Hercules Powder Company had decided to locate a powder plant at nearby Dublin. Much land had to be acquired, and I did a great deal of title work in connection with this project, making over $1,000 in about three months. Judge Draper helped by making available to me his records of land titles within the county.

Shortly before leaving Floyd I missed a great opportunity to stabilize my law practice. I learned that an assistant to the U. S. Attorney for the Western District would be appointed. Such an assistantship paid a good salary and left the incumbent free to do civil work. I immediately went to see my friend Murray Hooker, chairman of the Democratic party in the state. He called Harry Byrd, for whom I had done some work in his reelection campaign, and asked him to give me the place. He agreed. He did not make the appointment at once, however, and when he was ready to do it such political pressure had been generated in Roanoke for another man that he felt it politically necessary to appoint another lawyer. Had I received this appointment my whole life would have taken another course. Undoubtedly I would have remained in the law.

Judge John Draper was a great friend. I will always remember his interest in a young, impecunious lawyer. He was at this time in his seventies, but he occasionally went hunting with me and for a time kept my bird dogs Rod and Rip in a kennel in his back yard. He represented a great family in southwestern Virginia. The Drapers had come to Draper's Valley as pioneers in the 1700s. His grandfather carried a rifle at the great battle with the Indians at Point Pleasant. His great grandmother was Mary Draper, who was captured by the Indians and carried to Sandusky, Ohio, from which captivity she escaped and made her way home overland armed only with a knife and an axe. She joined her husband, who had long since given her up for dead, and raised a family of children at Draper's Valley. It is interesting to observe that occasionally the family was visited by an Indian warrior whose slave she had been. He had treated her kindly, and the family permitted him to visit out of gratitude for his kindness.

Now and then Judge Draper appointed me to defend a client who could not afford a lawyer. One of these cases was most dramatic and for me heartrending. A young man of about twenty years was accused of the murder of a young soldier of good family, home on leave from the air force, and of seriously wounding his companion. This young man whom I was to defend had led a checkered life. He was born in the local whorehouse. He had been brought up there by his mother, who eventually became the owner of the house. Time and again he had been before the court for petty crime. Twice he had served time in the state reformatory. His education had been neglected to the point he could scarcely write his name. On the night of the crime he had returned to his squalid home from a bout of beer drinking. He was in a drunken sleep when he was awakened by an inmate of the house, one Virgie Pate, who placed a single-barreled shotgun in his hands and said, "They are going to kill us all. They are rocking the house. Shoot out the window!" In his stupor, newly roused from the fumes of sleep, he took the gun and fired into a car parked by the house.

The soldiers had been denied admission to the house of ill repute. In their anger they had thrown rocks at the house, some of them large rocks that broke windows and endangered the inmates. The accused was arrested and placed in jail awaiting trial in a nearby county. This youth I was expected to defend.

The victim was very popular. That the slayer came out of the dregs of Pulaski society further inflamed the community against him. I believed that the extent and depth of feeling justified a trial outside the county, and I moved for a change of venue. This was denied. During the trial when I went from my office to the courthouse, I was followed by young friends of the slain man who greeted me with taunts of displeasure.

I decided to defend the case on the theory that the community was indirectly responsible for the crime by tolerating the conditions that gave birth to the crime. This was a mistake. In my summation to the jury, I pled for a verdict of second degree murder. Judge Draper in his instructions to the jury had left to them the decision on the evidence as to whether the crime was first or second degree. My line of defense was not effective. When I said at the end, "Let him who is without sin cast the first stone!" I merely invited an extreme penalty. The jury gave the poor boy forty years in the penitentiary. Not one of my better efforts! So much for crime and punishment.

During my last year in the practice of law Tine became pregnant. Until early summer she continued to work, which entailed much driving into the countryside, sometimes on muddy roads, and opening many gates to investigate people asking for help from the welfare office. When her time was near she went to Biloxi to have the baby. Tine always felt more secure in childbirth at her home. There she had the comfort of her mother and the assurance of good nursing for mother and baby. She left in May and Rachel was born in July.

By this time I had concluded my arrangements to return to Sewanee to teach again and become commandant of cadets. I was distressed at leaving the practice of law, for I was beginning to make a living. Each day I could see my practice expanding. Some months before this, however, I had agreed to return to Sewanee. At that time I could not visualize the progress in the law that I was to make. With war in Europe, the birth of a new baby, the prospect of our own involvement in the war, and the uncertainty of the future—the lure of greater family security led me to make once again a fateful decision.

The last few months in Pulaski were taken up in winding up my law practice. An old classmate and fraternity brother, Franklin Mason of

Kentucky, moved into the office with me and took the space that I did not need. Franklin was the nephew of Silas Mason of the Mason and Hanger Construction Company that had the contract to build the Hercules Powder plant in Dublin. He was engaged in selling lumber to the company. He was a great help to me during my last year in law practice. I had furniture to be packed and much to do. Tine had acquired an antique corner cupboard in Floyd that we had redone. It is a fine example of early craftsmanship which probably came out of the Lee family. We still have it, and it never fails to evoke admiration from antique lovers. We had by this time acquired several pieces that we did not desire to part with. I had to see to the packing of these articles and their removal to Tennessee.

Near the middle of July I went on a fishing trip with my brother Albert and some friends of his to Mobjack Bay. We caught fish, drank whiskey, and otherwise used ourselves up. On my return to the apartment in Pulaski I took a bath and prepared for bed. I had lost sleep and over-extended myself on the fishing trip. Just when I was settled between clean and cool sheets, I had a telephone call from Tine. The baby was on the way. I got out of bed, packed my bag, got into my car about midnight and started driving. By mid-morning of the next day I had passed through Chattanooga, but the need for sleep was becoming acute. I remained at the wheel until somewhere in southern Alabama I decided to stop and call Tine. I got Sophie on the telephone. She informed me that Tine was at the hospital and that I was the father of a baby girl. Both mother and baby were doing well. Upon learning this I stopped at a cheap hotel and went to bed. So I was not present at the great event that brought sweet Rachel into the world. At the birth of both my daughters I had done some fancy driving. In the case of Ulysse I arrived in time. With Rachel I was tardy, but I had raced the hour in one of the most grueling drives I have ever taken.

The next day I rose early and made my way more leisurely to Biloxi. When I first saw Rachel she was in a crib in her mother's room in the hospital. This was before the day when babies were at birth isolated in sanitized compartments. She was a wee bit of pink flesh still dewy from her journey into the world. Unlike Ulysse, who was a bald-headed baby, Rachel had rather long hair and a round head. Tine was well and saucy. We named the baby Evelyn Rachel. Nothing would do for me but that we should call her Rachel after my mother and the four other Rachels in my family, the first of whom was that Rachel

Cockerham who had kept house for Father Dickie Wood and ended up marrying the old man, his fourth wife. He is the same one who, being asked by his disappointed children "Why, Father?" replied, "I found a cabbage among the collards."

In September of 1941 I returned to Sewanee. I had Tine, Ulysse, and two-month-old Rachel. Since Hayne Shumate, the former commandant of cadets, had left to do graduate work, I was made commandant of cadets. At SMA the commandant of cadets was generally charged with internal and external discipline. This duty involved punishment for disobedience of regulations as well as the personal hygiene of the young students and the cleanliness of their quarters. We were assigned quarters in the Gladney House near Quintard Hall. This house afforded two apartments. We were upstairs over the apartment occupied by George Reynolds and his family. We had acquired some furniture while in Virginia, so we were able to furnish our quarters adequately. The house was old and drafty and cold in winter, but it was ours and it was home. The upper apartment had the advantage of a great attic in which there was a single furnished room. My salary was $2,600, board and lodging. We ate at the common mess hall in Quintard barracks. We did have a kitchen where we could occasionally cook for ourselves—a great convenience, for Rachel was a bottle-fed baby.

During the time that I was away at law practice in Virginia, Dr. Benjamin Finney had been replaced as vice-chancellor by Alexander Guerry, who had formerly been the dynamic and successful president of the University of Chattanooga. Dr. Guerry within a short time of his arrival on the Mountain had begun to put Sewanee affairs in order. By the time of my return the budget had been balanced, morale restored, buildings repaired, and a new spirit of confidence in the future created. Dr. Guerry sought authority from the trustees, obtained it, and used it to the profit and advantage of the university. Dr. Finney was the victim of the depression. It is to his everlasting credit that he held Sewanee together, paid salaries at a time when public institutions were using script, and labored long and hard for the university. He did lack the dynamism and the administrative skills of Guerry, who could take a dying cause and make it live.

Dr. Guerry ran the Mountain. No little thing was too mean for his attention, no great thing too big for him to tackle. He knew how to praise for a purpose and how to blame for a reason. He expected of all who worked with him the same kind of devotion he gave to the affairs of the university. By firmness, by example, by diligence, and by patience he acquired an ascendancy over the people and the affairs of the university that no other vice-chancellor has equalled. If a professor dismissed his class before the hour, Guerry might storm down the hall and demand the name of the professor. He insisted on temperance from both students and faculty. A group of us formed the Wimpey Club devoted to hamburgers and bridge. When he learned that whiskey was served, he demanded that the operation of the club be suspended. He thought it set a bad example for the students. Dr. Guerry thought everything with which he was connected was the best, even the Sewanee golf course. Once in an expansive mood he looked over the course with Gordon Clark, the athletic director. "Isn't this the most beautiful course in Tennessee?" the vice-chancellor said. "Look how it rolls. Look at the layout." Now the course was a glorified cow pasture. Gordon, provoked by the hyperbole, said, "Dr. Guerry, this is not a golf course. To have a golf course you must have greens, fairway, tees. We have none of these. This is not a golf course— this is a game park." Dr. Guerry turned away in disgust.

Shortly after my return to the academy General William R. Smith, superintendent of the academy, died. His death was a blow to us all. General Smith had brought to us a great name, a sense of security, as well as an experience with life and administration that related us to a larger world. His old-fashioned formality, his never-failing courtesy, his hospitality, and his vision for the academy did much to invigorate an institution that had suffered a loss of morale. Furthermore his departure meant a time of leaderless uncertainty for the academy. For a time Colonel Clyde Fasick acted in his place, but Colonel Fasick, for all of his energy and experience, lacked the personal attributes that are indispensable in a leader of men. Nevertheless the academy prospered. There were at this time at the academy a splendid faculty. There was George Reynolds, there was Samuel Robinson, there was Peter Garland, there was Robert Lancaster, and there was DuVal Cravens— rich in experience, all of them men who could attract students to Sewanee. Then there was the reality of war in Europe and the uncertainty about our own involvement that caused many parents to think of a military school for their sons.

Dr. Guerry always had a soft spot in his heart for the academy. He had first come to the attention of the academic world as headmaster of the Baylor School at Chattanooga. He understood the problems of a boarding school for boys. Soon he found for us a new superintendent in the person of General George R. Allin, recently retired from the army. General Allin was a fine businessman and a great administrator, but he lacked an understanding of secondary education, and he could never understand that the men who taught and lived at the academy were not in the army. He deplored our rather shabby uniforms, our easy informality, our lack of deference for authority. Shortly after his coming he instituted a class of instruction in military bearing and posture. Once he had me stand against a wall for observation.

"Lancaster," he said, "you are sway backed and your right shoulder is lower than the left."

"True," I said. "I carried heavy logs on my right shoulder as a boy and consequently it is lower."

"With exercise you can improve it," he said.

"I know," I responded, "but with all the work you want me to do, I don't think I will have time for it."

He finally gave me up as a hopeless case. Eventually he came to accept the fact that he was not dealing with subordinate soldiers, but it came hard for him. He did preside over the academy during the war years and the academy prospered. He even accumulated a surplus, a rare accomplishment in an academy superintendent.

In 1939 war had come to Europe. I think it is to the credit of Franklin Roosevelt that he saw before many of his countrymen did that the United States could not stand aside. In many ways he prepared the country to accept the inevitability of our involvement. Psychologically the country was prepared by what they heard on their radios and what they read and saw pictured in their newspapers. I can remember how disturbed I was by the pictures of the long lines of fleeing people being bombed by the German warplanes as they sought to escape on foot or by any means from the terror overhead. Dictatorship has no appeal for the American people, and the ravings and rantings of Hitler antagonized many Americans. Once for nearly an hour I listened to him by radio speak to his people in German, which I could not understand. In spite of his strident and sometimes volcanic tones, I could sense the magnetism of his hypnotic spell. First I think he became self-hypnotized and, becoming so, bound his hearers in the hypnotic trance. He had a tremendous power of evil.

In December of 1941 came Pearl Harbor. It came as a great shock to me and to most Americans. I was in the bedroom changing my clothes from my leaf-raking outfit when Tine burst in to say, "Turn on the radio quick. The Japanese have bombed Pearl Harbor!" We listened avidly for the next few hours, hardly daring to go to bed. A wave of anger rippled through America. When the extent of the damage became known there was shocked disbelief coupled with indignation. The country was stirred as it had never been before, by the treachery. We all shared the indignation, welcomed the rhetoric of our president, bent our minds to the question of our personal involvement. I longed to be an active part of the greatest national movement of my time. I think I sensed that the world would never be the same again.

One of the reasons I had left the practice of law was to return to a military school. Even in 1940 it was obvious that sooner or later we would take part in the struggle that at the time seemed to involve the freedom of the western world. I talked over with Tine the possibility of my going into some arm of the service. She saw no reason for me to be involved so actively. After all, I had a wife and two children, and there were enough young unmarried males to do the fighting. I understood her point of view but I wanted in. I had for many years had a hernia on my right side. Dr. Kirby-Smith advised me that I would have to have that repaired before I could become acceptable to the armed forces. So I remained on the sidelines of the great conflict for the time being.

In the fall of 1942 my brother John came to Sewanee to live with us and attend the university. I met him in Chattanooga early in the morning of one grey day. We had a room in the upstairs attic that I had fitted out as a kind of office. It just suited John. Ulysse, Rachel, and all of us were charmed by my brother John. He entered the university as a freshman that year; though he studied hard, he majored in golf. He soon saw there was more to a college education than books with glossy print. He learned a lot, joined the Phi Delta Theta fraternity, got to know my bird dogs real well, and on occasion learned to drive my car. At this time the college was in the war ferment. Young men were leaving to join the service. The air force had special appeal. Before long John decided to apply for training as an air cadet. I thought he would never master the mathematics of the training program, but I was wrong. He went through training that must have been most difficult for a country boy and before the war was out he was commissioned a second lieutenant in the air force. My brother Albert had in the meantime become an officer in the supply corps of the army. My sister Helen had become an officer in the nursing corps.

I stood it for a year. I traveled the summer of 1942 for the academy, principally in Texas and Louisiana. I traveled by train and by bus. The trains were grim. They were often filled with GIs on leave who were rowdy, undisciplined, and often drunk. The army police had all they could do to keep a semblance of order. Once I saw a lone captain on a train in Texas so badgered by the jibes and taunts of the traveling soldiers and sailors that he finally got off the train. There were no MPs immediately available, and he lacked the spirit that might have brought respect. A young lady took her virtue in her hands when she ventured to travel on some of the trains that were filled with men going and coming to the training camps. This was in the early years of the war. Later, I am told, discipline got much better. The military police force expanded, and most of the soldiers and sailors went out to where the bombs fell and the guns roared and chattered a language of their own.

While in New Orleans in 1942 I went by the Office of Naval Procurement to determine the possibilities of a commission in the naval reserve. I was examined and told that the only thing that would keep me from a commission was the hernia. I came home, and pretty soon Henry Kirby-Smith did a repair job. On my next trip to New Orleans I was accepted in the navy and soon commissioned as a lieutenant, junior grade. My age and experience probably justified a commission in the next highest rank, and if I had persisted in my efforts I believe I might have received it, but at the time I was impatient and my patriotism ran high.

My family accepted my decision with some lack of understanding, but everybody was going then. It was the thing to do. It had to be accepted, like death and taxes. So the women saw their men go off to war and did what was necessary under the circumstances.

It was by now the fall of 1943. The war was at its grimmest. The prospect of victory was in the air, but it was faint and like the promise of spring in early March. I arranged with the academy to be away. I was told by Dr. Guerry that my job would be waiting. General Allin took a dim view of my desire to be off a month before I left for training. His resentment ran even deeper, for he thought that as commandant I was reluctant to accept his orders. When the time came for me to leave for a little vacation before service, he pretended he needed me and forbade me to leave until Colonel Warner, who had recently come to the academy as a professor of history, returned from a physical examination incident to his retirement. I insisted that I had no obligation to remain longer. General Allin became very angry. In an angry voice he commanded me to stay.

"You will stay, Lancaster," he roared, "because I tell you to."

"General, you are not in the army now. I will go."

"Then you will never return to the academy," he said.

"I have already arranged with Dr. Guerry to return if I like when my service in the navy is over."

So you see that my leaving was a matter of some controversy.

I took Tine, Rachel, and Ulysse to Biloxi. With us went a young black girl, Jo Ada, who had been Rachel's nurse for some time. She lived in Sophie's home with the family for the duration. Incidentally, she never returned to Sewanee to live. She became a favorite pin-up girl at the black USO and married a well-to-do older man in Biloxi.

I enjoyed a short vacation on the coast, and one day in October I set out by train for Quonset Point, Rhode Island. I had bought my naval uniform in order to travel uniformed to Quonset Point. It gave me great pleasure to be in the uniform of the navy in the service of my country. The trip itself was uneventful except that it did give me a final time to consider what I had done and to worry a little about leaving my family to go off to war. I arrived in Quonset without mishap and was immediately assigned to duty. I found myself quartered in a barracks room along with fifty or so other naval officers. We slept in bunks. Each officer was assigned a bed and a small wardrobe with shelves for underwear, shirts, and the slim gear of an officer about to be indoctrinated. I immediately made the acquaintance of a young man from Pennsylvania who bunked beside me. He was more knowing than I since he had been aboard for all of a day before me. "Come," said he, "let us go up and badger the mate of the deck. He happens to be Henry Fonda." We went to the upper deck (the floor above). We found Fonda there. My friend Charlie Kunckle began to talk to Henry about his movie career. Fonda then was a celebrated star of westerns. I was a little embarrassed by Kunckle's temerity, but I was pleased to see the ease with which Fonda handled his inquisitor and to learn that we did have the famous Fonda in our company. He was a model officer, quiet, intelligent, and happy to be in the navy. Later in the session the Junior League of Providence gave a ball honoring my class. I was dancing with one of the "Providentials." She kept asking me about Fonda.

"Girl," I said, "you are dancing with a redheaded fox from the mountains of Virginia. Forget about Fonda."

"All right, Fox," she said, "just dance me over by him!"

I did. "Henry," I said, "bite this girl!" Whereupon he pretended to snarl and bit the girl on the shoulder.

I am sure she treasured that bite for many a month. I surrendered her, bitten, to another officer and went to the bar for a drink of courage. I did not see Fonda often. I knew him only casually. The last time I saw him was on the train to New York after we had completed our indoctrination. He was so anxious to be in the khaki working uniform of the navy that we had just become eligible to wear that he was changing his uniform on the train. I saw him years later in the motion picture *Mr. Roberts* in which he portrayed a naval officer. He played the part with the authenticity of an old hand and well he might.

I shall never forget the first evening at retreat. The evening was as cold as a New England evening can be. The sky was clear. Mackerel clouds draped the high ceiling of the heavens. The band played the national anthem. There we stood in ranks. It was as though all those men who stood there at attention were one man. Such a feeling of peaceful majesty came upon me that for a moment I was transported. I was no longer Robert Lancaster. I was one with all who were there. For a brief moment I became one with all men who fought upon the sea and in the air and on the land. The experience was ephemeral, but I have never forgotten its beauty. So it is, to escape from these corporeal bonds but for a few seconds. Chow, the eating of food, was an anticlimax. I immediately became hungry Robert Lancaster.

In 1943 I was thirty-four years of age. By that time a man has become an adult if he is ever to become one. Some persons never achieve that supposedly natural status. I think I must be one of those who are doomed to perennial childhood. At first like a child I did not take easily to indoctrination in the navy. The purpose of the training I could understand. It was obviously to break the pattern of accustomed life, to inculcate almost automatic obedience, to brain-wash in a shallow way. It was pathetic to see grown men patiently working to fold a shirt or a piece of underwear to the required standard, to labor for too long a time over the making of a bunk or the folding of a sheet. Once I failed to fold my sheet properly. A tiny piece of white could be seen under the bed. Such imperfections were called "Irish pennants."

"Lancaster, you have an Irish pennant showing," the inspecting officer said.

"Right, sir," I responded. "You see I am part Irish."

"That will be five demerits," he barked.

The next day at drill the same officer called out to me, "Lancaster, pull in your butt." I didn't know whether to pull in the butt of my rifle or to make an effort in another direction. We learned, though, and like young bird dogs we were broken.

One day soon after our arrival a young fellow by the name of Litkin was just behind me as we marched by the medics to get our shots, of which there were several. On either side a medic jabbed the needle into our arms. Litkin was upset and slow and got double doses in each arm. He had to go to the infirmary for a day or so, but soon he was out, doubly fortified against the ills of this world. I learned from this never to dawdle when passing a doctor with a needle in his hand.

Our course of study was well designed for the training, within a short time, of a naval officer. We studied the *Blue Jackets Manual*, learning about boats, signals including the Morse code, and all the information that could be crammed into the brain in a few short weeks. We drilled. We underwent very strenuous physical indoctrination that involved the obstacle course. Very difficult for me was the recognition of aircraft and ships of the navy. Recognition required that one identify the silhouette of a ship or plane in a tenth of a second as it was flashed upon a screen. The easiest course for me was the firing of side-arms and rifles. All my life I had used firearms. My brothers in arms were astonished at my proficiency. That I drilled well was proven by the fact that in the final contests I was in the last five of my company to be eliminated for making an error.

Time passed swiftly. We were busy every moment. It was a great relief to be able on the weekend to enjoy the privilege of the officers' club. There was gaiety and laughter, ten-cent drinks, and wonderful food. The every-day chow was not bad, though one did have to learn to enjoy beans for breakfast.

This naval training was hard on marriages. There were plenty of young women in Providence and nearby towns who were willing, even eager, to console young officers. Several members of my own company became so attached to new females that they permitted their marriages to lapse. The excitement of war, the freedom among the sexes, the loneliness and the change to a new life bred a kind of discontent with the ties of the past. I kept the pictures of Tine and Ulysse and Rachel in a prominent place in my locker. I wrote home regularly and received letters almost every day from one or the other. I looked forward to Christmas and my first leave, and before I knew it Christmas had come. I believe 1943 was the year Bing Crosby made "White Christmas" popular. In every tavern you could hear it and watch the change of expression on lonely faces.

I made it to Biloxi after a long train ride. In the short time I had been gone Rachel, who was two years old, had almost forgotten me. I came in the door. Ulysse ran to leap into my arms. Rachel looked, put her head down coyly, and burst into tears. Within a moment or two she was in my arms. My dear baby. That night she said, "Ulysse, I am going to sleep with Daddy." She went to bed with Tine and me but not for long. A returning soldier soon puts aside a sleeping child and returns to sterner duty. I have little memory of that little interlude. It must have been happy and gay. It was over in the flick of an eye and I was back in Quonset.

I told you that fifty or more men slept in the same room. Imagine the snores, the groans, the nightmares, the squeaking of beds, the quick trips to the john. I am a light sleeper. I soon began to suffer from tension and insomnia. I knew not why, but I simply could not sleep. Soon it began to take its toll of my nervous system. I had difficulty concentrating. At long last I went to the doctor. He gave me several tests, but he could not determine the cause of my indisposition. Some days passed almost as though I were in a dream. I continued to do my duty and very few knew that I suffered. I could not understand my situation. My pride prevented me from going again to the infirmary. This condition followed me for almost the entire time I was in the navy. One who has never undergone the struggle of such a disability can never understand it. I am ever thankful that I had the will and the courage to see it through. I worried about its effects upon my ability to do whatever I might be called upon to do. If I were sent to sea I worried lest my condition interfere with peak performance at a critical time.

When the day came for orders I was relieved that I had orders to remain in Quonset to attend Air Combat Intelligence School. This was a course of training that prepared one to gather and assess intelligence from combat. Each squadron of the naval air force was to have assigned such a person. I remember little of the training but I got through creditably. When the time came for orders I was ordered to a carrier in the fleet at sea, but almost immediately those orders were revoked, and I was among a group of ten who were ordered to attend another school to learn antisubmarine warfare. At this time the navy was just beginning to experiment with rockets in submarine warfare. The terrific toll taken by the German underwater craft was in 1944 the gravest problem confronting the allies. I learned much about antisubmarine warfare, including the use of sonobuoys and the new torpedoes that homed on sound. I especially liked the new rocket and spent much time in acquiring all of the knowledge available on this arm. I suppose it was due to this interest that I was ordered to Norfolk for further orders which was to be in rocket training.

Tine was able to join me in Norfolk for a few days. I had a cousin Amelia Harvey who lived in nearby Hampton, and I could leave BOQ and spend the night on occasion with Amelia. We did enjoy her—a big woman, jolly and clever. She was married to a Mr. Parker, an ugly man with a sweet disposition. One day Tine, Amelia, and I went out to look for clams. Amelia loved such expeditions. We found many clams with our feet. When Amelia had to get back in the rowboat, I would get my shoulder under her and roll her into the boat.

As we were returning home we came upon an old fisherman with a single front tooth and a sunny smile who was crabbing, running his pots. Tine and he got into a jolly conversation about the crabs on the Gulf coast, which he knew. As we were leaving he suddenly said, "By God, you see these crabs! I am going to give you every goddamned one of them! The fish as well!" We were entranced with him and especially with the crabs. Amelia said, "When we get home brag on Parker. He can make the best clam chowder on the Eastern Shore. But don't tell him where we got all of this." We returned and Parker made the best clam chowder I ever ate. We pretended we had found a fine hole in the bay where fish, clams, and crabs alike were to be had for the trouble of a boat ride. For the next day or two all the neighbors were out trying to find our hole. Amelia got a great deal of pleasure out of the episode.

While we were in Norfolk I had a trying experience. Tine and I went to a wet party at the officers' club. We returned by ferry to Amelia's late at night. I had received notice to report to the commanding officer for orders the next morning. Uniform was prescribed blues. I had left my black shoes in my room in BOQ. My whites, which I had worn to the party, were crumpled and soiled. When I awoke early the next morning in time to take the ferry from Hampton to Norfolk, I found that I had no black shoes. Parker's were too small for me. What to do? What to do? I hit upon a solution. I put on my white shoes and put over them a pair of black socks. I was foot conscious, but I had to improvise. On the ferry no one seemed to notice my strange feet. I reported for orders, made a muffled click of my heels when I saluted the admiral. Nobody took notice of my feet that seemed to me so obviously strange and embarrassing. I learned from the experience that people are interested in their own feet, not in the feet of another. It is quite generally true, at least among men, that clothes are seldom observed unless they are so strange as to be outlandish. The same principle carries over into many aspects of life including illness. One is seldom interested in the ills of another. Sufficient unto a man are his own troubles.

I had anticipated orders that would take me to a carrier or overseas. I was shocked to find that I was ordered to the Naval Air Station at Boca Chica, Florida, to help train squadrons in rocket fire. As it happened, Commander Reedy was then in charge of training certain aspects of a retraining program for naval air squadrons. He was good enough to allow me to accompany him by plane to Boca Chica. Tine and the children remained in Floyd to be with Mama for a while.

No sooner had I arrived than I was assigned to duty as officer in charge of night operations. At the time our planes were flying night training missions. My training had scarcely prepared me for such an immediate responsibility. Fortunately I had with me a chief to whom all the duties were routine. I confessed to him my trepidation. "Don't worry," he said, "all of you new officers are alike. I will tell you what to do." He did. I knew enough at least to trust the chief. I soon found out that those officers who built a close working relation with the chief got along very well. The relationship was a sensitive one, however. One had to keep the respect of such old hands by treading that thin line between authority and subservience. My experience in military school stood by me. Furthermore I learned my job quickly and soon felt confident of my ability to handle men and act intelligently when confronted with the many crises, some of them fraught with deadly consequences, that arise on any air base where men are flying.

Soon after I arrived in Boca Chica I began looking for quarters for my family. Key West had grown from a run-down and dying town of about twelve thousand to a town of fifty thousand. There were few houses or apartments to be found. The navy had not yet begun to build houses and apartments for married officers. I got to know a lady who ran the Old Island Realty Company. She knew of Sewanee, and she admired Bishop Frank Juhan of Florida. I called her each day for several weeks. At length, driven by my importunities, she called one day to say that she had found a house for me at 1402 Pine Street.

I went by after work to get the keys, having already told her I would take the house regardless of its condition. I proceeded to Pine Street, where I found myself before a two-storey house that looked all right from the outside. The street was not lighted, and I fumbled for the key, finally got the door unlocked, and entered. As I did I was struck on the head and shoulders by something furry and large. My blood froze. I believe I growled myself. With a swing of my arm I hurled the furry demon to the floor. I had no light. In the darkness I managed to strike a match. As I did a large, emaciated grey cat gave out a long yowl of woe and bolted through the open door. In all of my life I have never been so frightened as I was when I was received by that starving cat. She had been locked in since the former occupant had vacated nearly three weeks before my visit.

I explored by matchlight and never have I seen a house in such miserable disarray. A smell of long-mellowed cat dung pervaded the air. Old newspapers littered the floor. The kitchen smelled of decaying food. When I lit another match in the kitchen a dozen or more scorpions scuttled about with their tails menacing. I was dismayed. I had rented a lemon. I left and made my way in a somber and melancholy frame of mind back to my room in BOQ. It was Friday night. Everybody was out at the officers' club or on the town. No friendly poker game. No cheery conversation to dispel my gloom.

The next day I went back to the house on Pine Street. By day it was not quite so depressing. The smell was as bad, but the scorpions had retreated to their clammy holes. On the porch outside the kitchen I found gallons of poultry fat exuding its offensive odor. The officer who preceded me had obviously been an Israelite. Obviously, too, he had received orders in a hurry. Upstairs I found three fairly well equipped bedrooms. I could see that there was nothing about the house that soap and water and elbow grease would not cure.

The following weekend I took my rocket loading crew of ten able-bodied seamen to help me clean the house. They were ready, willing, and able—with the prospect of a keg of beer to move them forward. Within two hours you would not have known the house. It smelled of pine tar and shaving lotion. The floors were clean, the goose grease was gone, the scorpions had been frightened back to their dens in the yard. The chairs were cleaned, the cat even appeared and asked admission. I let her in for a time and found her to be a chummy, loving animal. If I could only get a day or two leave coupled with a weekend, I could have my wife and children with me. I knew Tine would like the lime tree in the yard and the sea almost at our door and the long sunny days.

I was granted leave for the purpose of getting my family settled. I hitched a ride on a PBY to the marine base at Cherry Point, North Carolina. I went by bus to Wilmington, where I spent the night in a room in a boarding house that accommodated four sleepers. The next morning I took a bus to Roanoke, Virginia, and from there went on to Floyd. I had sufficient gas coupons to make the trip back to Key West by car.

We left one fine morning for the drive to Key West. Rachel was only three years old and prone to car sickness. She managed bravely. We tried to keep her mind off her plight by playing games and telling stories. After we got out of the mountains her spirits rose and she enjoyed the trip. We stopped occasionally at historic places and interesting spots. One of our stops was an alligator farm. Rachel was appalled at the size of the gators. She screamed when the attendant put his hand into the monster's mouth and withdrew it just before the snap of powerful jaws. I thought it a foolish way to entertain the public. Ulysse observed that one day he would be a one-armed man.

Tine and the children liked the house. It took some more cleaning but shaped up to our comfort and needs. Ulysse was entered in school at the Convent of Saint Somebody (maybe Mary's). She soon made friends in the school and on our street. It was a street where things happened for children, of whom there were many—some Cuban, some Anglo-Saxon, some of uncertain ancestry. A family near us owned a great and fiery drake by the name of Rita. The children teased his unmercifully, but Rita held his own. Once I heard Rachel screaming on the porch. Rita had cornered her and had seized her by the soft baby skin on her belly. He was tugging and flogging with hard wings and the poor child was fighting and screaming. I drove him off, but he was so wary that I was never able to get in the solid lick on the head that

I wished for. The Pine Street Pirates, the name we gave to the throng of children that roamed our area, were a colorful bunch. We could trail them from our refrigerator by the trail of dropped food.

Next door lived a Cuban family that kept game chickens. The cocks roosted in trees near our window. We were often awakened by their crowing at four o'clock in the morning. I remonstrated in vain with my neighbor. He always observed that it was cock nature to crow. I finally solved my problem. When the roosters started their paean of homage to the coming dawn, I would rain small stones from my window onto his kitchen roof. One day he told me he had traded his chickens to a neighbor who raised cocks for the weekly cock fights.

We enjoyed the semitropical climate. We had palm trees in our yard, a lime tree in the back, and the Hall of Truth and Grace next door. The lime tree bloomed and bore at the same time. An old woman used to gather our limes before we could get them, until I turned Tine loose on her. The first few moments were obscured in verbal dust, but when the dust subsided she was making a strategic withdrawal. Clearly she had lost the battle. Key lime pie became a staple in our diet.

We all enjoyed the sea. On one side of us was the Gulf. On the other the Atlantic. We spent many hours wading with glass-bottomed buckets, watching the sea bottom below us. We all became shell collectors. Tine made a real hobby of it and put together a fine collection. One never knew what the sea would throw up. Sometimes the beach was covered with murex, the violet shells from which purple dye was made in ancient times. The water was warm. The sea was salty. Sometimes we went out after crawfish, the Florida lobster. They were plentiful and might be had by gigging. Once I set traps made of old oil drums in a recess holed out by one of the bulldozers at work on our rocket range. I baited it with old fish heads. Often the high tide brought crawfish into such places. The tide went down and left them there. The first time I pulled my trap I caught nine fine lobsters. On another occasion Tine and I were fishing in such a place. I noticed on the bottom the long tentacles of what must have been the grandfather of all lobsters. He had found a retreat in the rusting remains of an oil barrel. Each time I dropped bait he would come out to taste. At length he moved some distance from his den. Almost without thinking, I pulled off my clothes and dived down for him.

Now a crawfish can move backward perhaps faster than forward. He backed in a series of dashes into the shallows. I scooped him up and threw him on the bank and gave my Tarzan cry. We were near the highway and a car was coming. I ripped into my shorts and waved a greeting. That one crawfish made enough salad for a bridge party of two tables, and this is the God's truth or I hope I may die, as Homer Sweeny, a childhood acquaintance, used to say.

For Easter of that first year at Key West we gave the children little ducks. Normally ducks die soon from overhandling and too much attention. These were the exception. Pretty soon they grew feathers and became interested in the things that ducks like. Before the following Easter these two had become husband and wife, and wife had laid a clutch of eggs under the Hall of Truth and Grace. Rachel watched all of their doings and reported to me on Easter morning that she thought the mama duck was about to have little ones. Nothing would do but that I must crawl under that miserable Hall of Truth and Grace to investigate small noises. I risked my life to scorpions and coral snakes and pushed under. What a man will not do for a child! Sure enough, the eggs had pipped, hatched, and produced. Rachel stood by as I handed out that Easter morning an even dozen of downy, fluffy miracles of life. That made Easter. Even Tine was moved by little ducks, though she has been known to cannibalize adults of the species. Unfortunately we put them too soon in a basin of water to test their swimming ability. They swam beautifully, though some of them caught cold from the experience. Nevertheless we raised seven of that brood, and I got acquainted with more of my neighbors by way of duck presents.

When these ducks were in their early teens, a boy living near us became interested in ducks. Rachel scouted out the neighborhood after they had mysteriously disappeared and found where they were. She led me to their new home with a Cuban family. I too thought I recognized our own children. An old man was sitting on the porch. I approached and hailed him.

"Grandfather," I said, "we have lost our ducks. Have you seen them?"

"I ain't seen no ducks except our own right here in the yard."

"How long have you had these ducks?" I asked.

"Oh," he replied, "we've always raised ducks. Sometimes we have more than this."

"I think these are my ducks," I countered. "See how they come at my call."

"Why, mon, a young duck will come to anybody's call if there are children in the house," he said. About that time the suspect, a boy of perhaps twelve, came around the side of the house.

"Boy," I said, "I have come for my ducks. What are they doing here?"

"Oh, they followed me home from your house," he answered. "I was just about to try and bring them back."

"Boy," said the old man, "take them ducks back home." Then to me, "Mon, I was mistaken about them ducks. You know, one duck looks like another."

I agreed pleasantly and we took our ducks home. I wished later I had left them, for when we came to leave Key West we had a time finding a home for them. They finally ended up in a duck pen up the Keys, and who knows what fate was in store for them after that?

My work at the naval base was varied but interesting. We built a rocket range, installed a glide angle device for teaching pilots how to dive in such a way that the rocket's flight would obtain the proper angle for piercing the pressure hull of a submarine. For a time I was legal officer for the commander of the training unit. I liked standing by the captain at mast and giving whispered advice on punishment. For a time near the end of my service I was recreation officer as well. This was pleasant duty after VJ day, for I always had a fishing boat at my service along with a crew. The worst duty was service in the rocket hut, talking pilots into proper glides from the ground.

The rockets we first used were small training rockets. Later the squadrons were equipped with the three-inch rocket, a lethal weapon when well aimed. All of these rockets were propelled by a charge of ballastite extruded in cruciform shape and fired by an electric device. They were mounted under the wings of the plane and aimed by seaman's eye. Since there was sometimes a long wait in mosquito-infested swampland between flights, we often became bored with our work. Once to relieve the tedium we picked up small pieces of unfired ballastite which littered the range and stuffed a spent casing with the fuel. We laid a train of ballastite some distance and lighted. The rocket took off with a swoosh. Since it was not stabilized with fins, its flight was erratic. It turned in midair and headed for the rocket hut, missed by a fraction, rose in the air, and finally buried itself in the sea. We did not soon do this again. For several days I had visions of dead sailors and court martials.

Occasionally we lost a pilot who, diving low and at great speed, was unable to pull out of his dive. These losses always drew a pall of sorrow and apprehension over the base. Nearly always it seemed that losing one pilot, we were destined to lose three. Accidents and losses seemed to go in threes. We became, as are most sailors under critical losses, superstitious. The squadrons that came for training had always just returned from combat duty. They were filled with stories of the war, and brought to us, marooned stateside and far from the actual fighting, some of the color, albeit second-hand, of the real war. Pilots were a jaunty lot who took their chances without fear and gave no heed to the morrow. I never saw one who even though ill did not insist on flying his mission. My immediate superior was a fellow by the name of Connearny, a Boston Irishman of great charm. Once I flew with him from Boca Chica to Norfolk and thence to Quonset Point in a TBM to investigate a new rocket site. He flew a few feet above the waves most of the time we were over water. I pleaded with him to go higher. He simply hummed his Irish songs and went on as before. When we got to Norfolk he said, "Now you know what it's like." He was one of three of a squadron who had operated from the CVEs, little carriers, in the North Atlantic. The rest had gone down in the icy water to Davy Jones' locker.

I had only one bad experience that sent the water dripping from my body and gave me that pale, clammy look. We went out in a PV on a training mission to look for a submarine that was supposed to have been sighted in the area. The compass went haywire and we found ourselves lost in the Gulf in a PV bomber, a plane that was unstable on water. Our gas ran so low that all of us, including the pilot, became fearful. By chance the pilot picked up a radio beam, oriented himself, and set out high-tailing it for home. We made it with three minutes of gas to spare. I thought we deserved the Navy Cross for constancy under fire. Such an experience was commonplace to the real air dogs. They took it in stride, played their interminable game of acey deucey, and were always ready for the five o'clock opening of the club.

At Boca Chica there was a great deal of drinking after work hours. I think it has ever been so in time of war. We could fly to Cuba and be in Havana inside of thirty minutes. Often we flew in that crazy old lady of the sea, the PBY of the creaking wings. The best rum, Old Methusalem, sold for twelve dollars a case. We would fill up on free frozen daiquiris at Sloppy Joe's, take off with a cargo of rum, and be in Boca Chica in a few minutes. While one of us took a gift to the

Rocket crew in front of our PV Ventura bomber at Boca Chica in 1944. I'm second from the left.

customs officer in the hangar and plied him with conversation, the rest of us unloaded rum into a convenient truck and got the hell out of there. If the skipper knew (of course he did) he turned his eyes.

Once I flew over to Havana with a wild pilot friend who drank too many of those frozen pain killers. He had the duty that night and insisted on returning to Boca Chica. I remonstrated to no avail. I had my doubts, but like foolish men we got into the old seaplane. He started her engines and taxied out on the wrong runway. The tower screamed their warnings. The red lights flashed, but on he went. The plane took off, lost an engine at about five hundred feet and began to lose altitude. By this time we were off the runway and over water. Never did a man sober up so quickly. He bent to his work, and somehow, slowly, we began to gain a little altitude. He nursed her up to two thousand feet and heaved a great alcoholic sigh. "We can coast in from here," he said.

About this time, we began to anticipate the end of the war. Every sailor at Key West followed the landing on the Normandy beachhead and the Allied advance eastward with such anticipation that VE Day and the demise of Hitler were anticlimactic. The war with Japan went on, but we sensed that too was about to end.

There came one day the news about the dropping of strange new bombs on two Japanese cities. When I heard it I remember that I wept. Not many of my companions felt as I did. For me the world would

The Old Man of the Sea

never be the same. I knew in my mind and heart that a new and dangerous time lay ahead for mankind. I don't know how I knew, but I was profoundly saddened by the event. Most of my companions saw it as the end of the war and were glad. I was glad, too. I did not so much lament the dead Japanese. It was not a question of pity. I did not blame the president who had made the decision. My feelings and sadness had to do with the passing of an era. This was before the days of television and computers, which have changed the world, yet even then I sensed the coming of fear and unease. I belonged to the earth and the sea and the sky, and somehow these were in danger.

When the war came to an end everything began to unravel quickly at Key West. Pilots now flew to get in flight time. Squadrons disintegrated as men were discharged. There was a general contraction of the naval body. New jobs became available. A single officer might now inherit several jobs. Since I had no place awaiting me, I applied to remain in the navy for a few months. Men were needed; my request was granted.

I became once more legal officer and recreation officer. In the latter capacity I had under my command a number of recreation boats. They were fishing boats, if you will. Life was lovely. Almost every afternoon at four I would give orders for a boat with chow and beer aboard to be waiting for me at the pier. The fishing was good and leisurely. We caught every kind of fish in that part of the Gulf from Sand Key Light to Pigeon Key. Often we would anchor and fish the reefs. The water was so clear that you could pick out the yellowtail you wanted for supper. Tine enjoyed the fishing and the outing and so did the children. How lucky we were! Everything including the crew was free except the beer, and that cost ten cents a bottle. We lived in an apartment on the beach up from the Casa Marina Hotel, provided by the navy for thirty dollars a month. Soon all this would end.

Chapter Seven

Return to Sewanee

I n July of 1946 we left the navy and headed home. Sometime before that I had flown to Jacksonville and within a day had my release from the navy. I never once seriously considered trying to remain, though I honor the service and see many advantages to living such a life. I had left Sewanee to practice law. I had found the practice of law interesting but financially difficult. I thought of government service, of returning to the law, of returning to Sewanee where I had a job awaiting.

We packed up and headed for Sophie's house in Biloxi. The trip home was to be a tour of Florida, and it was. We saw the orange country. The trees were bowing with fruit. Just across the road the ground was littered with fall fruit. At one point I said, "Ulysse, when I stop the car, run under the wire fence and bring us some oranges." I stopped the car conveniently.

Ulysse said, "Daddy, you're making a thief of me."

"No," said I, "you are merely rescuing some oranges from the sun."

She ran quickly as a squirrel and brought us oranges. We were surprised at the price charged at roadside stands for a glass of orange juice. Ten cents! Horrible! This was before the day of canned or frozen concentrate, and ten cents would buy a beer.

We visited the Bok Tower and saw the famous Ringling Museum at Sarasota. We moved leisurely into northern Florida, shelled the beaches, and ate the good sea food that the coastal restaurants afforded.

We arrived in Biloxi to be greeted by Sophie, who always loved to see us, especially the children, of whom she was fond. We soon fell into the pattern of life on the coast—swimming, sailing, partying. During the month after our arrival, I had a bad time of it. I was nervous and despondent. To return to civilian life after the service was unsettling. I did not know what to do about my future. I took Rachel with me and went to Virginia for a visit. While I was there I visited Senator Byrd in Washington to see if he could help me with a place in the State Department. He was noncommittal. Many people from the armed services were suddenly in the job market. I thought of practicing law in Biloxi. I had an offer from Mr. Tonsmeir, who had formerly been with a friend of mine, Leslie Grant, who had become a judge. I talked to Sophie about living in one of her rental houses until I could become established. She thought this inadvisable. She felt that she needed the income from the house.

Tine and I always had difficulty talking about our future. Many of her friends were well settled by this time. To her, I am sure, I seemed indecisive and weak. For a while I seemed so to myself. That summer of my life was filled with frustration, unease, and insecurity. I believe few people knew it. I have always been one to keep my suffering to myself and let the world see a grimly smiling face. For me that is the best way in adversity. A little money would have solved my problem. I have never loved money, but I have recognized the power and the security of a sufficiency.

The easiest thing was to return to the military academy at Sewanee. This offered security, and finally I settled upon returning. Coupled with that decision was a decision to go for a doctorate and spend my life in the academic world, almost by default, for the need to provide security for my family was uppermost in my mind.

We returned to Sewanee in late August of 1946. General Allin was still superintendent of the academy. We had had our differences before I left for the navy. I had made special arrangements with Dr. Guerry, our vice-chancellor, for my return. Fortunately, too, the law provided that I should have my old job. When I left I had been commandant of cadets. The fact that I did not especially want this place back warmed the heart of General Allin.

He said to me once, "Lancaster, I have seen such a change in you as a result of your service in the navy."

"General," I replied, "I am just as I was, a little more experienced, perhaps. You have simply mellowed."

He smiled his iron smile and let it go at that. General Allin was a splendid administrator. He built up financial strength in the academy, fed his cadets potatoes for breakfast, went over every menu himself, and tutored backward cadets in his office, but he knew little about education in a liberal arts setting. He was a military man from the start, unpopular with both his inferiors and his superiors, but he did his job. He was very unlike the genial and popular General William R. Smith, who had been superintendent at the U. S. Military Academy before coming to Sewanee. General Smith set a fine table, reminisced about the old army, did magic tricks for the junior school students, and on occasion took the entire faculty to see the opening of the baseball season in Chattanooga. Well, men differ. Allin and I had always sparred. He thought I had little future. I thought he had little past and less civility. Nevertheless, we got on.

Colonel Craig Alderman, a gentleman and officer, upon his retirement from the army came to Sewanee. He was selected as commandant, and he made a splendid one. I taught five classes a day, helped with athletics in the afternoon, took my turn at holding night study hall when it came around for a week, served as officer of the day in my turn, and otherwise kept busy.

The first summer after my return I went back to soliciting students in the summer and bided my time. The next summer I started graduate work at the University of Michigan. I was well prepared, since I had a master's degree in English literature from Sewanee, training in the law, plus a period of military service.

In 1948 I received an unexpected call from Gulf Coast Military Academy. The leadership there was looking for a superintendent. I went to Gulfport to confer with the owner, Joe Milner, and as a result was offered the superintendency where I had started my teaching. I had doubts about attempting to run a family-owned academy, but I left with the option open. I had for some time wished to teach at the University of the South, in the Department of Political Science headed by Arthur Dugan. It was a two-man department then, and Mr. Minter, an instructor, was leaving to go elsewhere. I went to see Dr. Guerry to talk to him about my offer and about the prospects of joining the faculty at the college. A man with an offer elsewhere always gained stature with Dr. Guerry. He was enthusiastic about my coming to the college but insisted that I go ahead with my doctoral studies at Michigan. He immediately called Arthur Dugan, who was in North Carolina. Arthur was pleased to have me as his associate; so in a matter of moments the decision was made. Dr. Guerry was at the time very busy, and it was suggested that I see him later to work out the details. He was preparing to go to Knoxville on university business, and it was on that trip that he was stricken with a heart attack and died.

Dr. Guerry's loss was a great blow to Sewanee and southern education. He was a man of tremendous energy and splendid talents. He was a completely rational and persuasive man. He demanded the best of his subordinates and usually got it. Never before had Sewanee had the discipline that he demanded of students, nor has it since. He did not use liquor nor did he serve it in his home. He insisted that the members of his faculty live abstemious lives. If a class was dismissed ahead of the bell, you could bet that Dr. Guerry would ask why. Once I went to him about a raise in salary. When I left, it occurred to me that we had talked little about my needs and much about the needs of the university. I came away thinking that the future of the place hung upon my own work. I was pleased that my salary was not cut. Such was the charm and the enthusiasm of the man.

Dr. Guerry had one great failing. He wanted to do everything and supervise everything himself. He wore himself out doing just that in the service of Sewanee. He found the university floundering; he set it straight, balanced its budget, infused new life and enthusiasm into a sagging venture. In his work he had beside him a helpmate who supported him wholly and used her own energy and charm and family money to supplement what was lacking. Both Dr. Guerry and Mrs. Guerry were autocrats of a special kind, concerned, imaginative, hard-working, brooking little opposition.

Of the vice-chancellors I have known and worked for—and they are Ben Finney, Alex Guerry, Henry Gass, Boylston Green, Ned McCrady, Jeff Bennett, and Bob Ayres—Guerry was the ablest. He was a second founder. If this seems extravagant praise, remember that Guerry saved the university in the Great Depression, saw it through the war, and provided it with a vision of greatness in his last days. Even Happy Hollow, the living place of the black servants of the university, bloomed under his administration. He knew the black people by name. He encouraged them to clean up, plant flowers, whitewash fences. He supplied money for some of this from his own pocket, provided flower seed, and what is better, when he saw improvement he was quick to praise. Such a leader gets results.

I said before that the details of my position at the college had not been worked out before his sudden death. Henry Gass, my friend and mentor, became acting vice-chancellor after Dr. Guerry's death. The only record he could find was a notation on a tablet: "Lancaster, Asst. Professor, Salary $3,600 and a house." This was 1949; $3,600 and a house was slim pickings for a man forty years old. No wonder Tine wondered. I had made $4,000 the last year I practiced law in Pulaski, Virginia. Nevertheless I had bridged the great chasm which separated teachers at the academy from professors at the university. I had made the commitment to continue my education and get the doctorate. I was not satisfied, but we could live.

In the summer of 1949 I taught in summer school at the college. Tine and the children spent the summer in Highlands, North Carolina. Henceforth for some summers this was to be the way it was. At the end of the term I took off for Michigan and they to Highlands. The university had provided me with an old, run-down frame house, formerly belonging to Everette Myers. The furnace was creaky and smoky. One room upstairs was hot, another cold. There were two baths that ran water and worked after a fashion. In spite of these limitations, it was a happy home. Rachel remembers it as a happy place. So does Ulysse. We had fun, laughter, and tears in this house that is even now refurbished and occupied.

Here the five young rabbits were reared that Briel Keppler brought to me pink, unfurred, eyes unopened. We took them in; Rachel's Dydee Doll bottle filled with watered milk provided a first meal. I would poke the nipple into the bunny's mouth just behind the two front rabbit teeth. When the warm milk hit the tongue, the baby rabbit would give a sudden squeak of satisfaction, and chow was on. The children were beside themselves with excitement. Eventually the babies began to eat thin slivers of carrots, graduated to celery, and in no time at all were frisky and playing about the room, sniffing noses, leap frogging, leaping suddenly into a lap. When company came they ran to hide under an old armchair with all five white tails sticking up like tiny flags of cotton. They grew and prospered and eventually, when nearly grown, were taken to the woods for what we hoped would be a life of freedom with fun.

Here too was the home of the mouse we called Drowsy, who loved to bask by the fire, the mouse that came to such a tragic end. Our house was old and drafty. It was inhabited by an assortment of ants, cockroaches, and mice.

One evening about dark as I came in with a load of wood for the fireplace, Rachel motioned me to be quiet and pointed at the hearth. There sat a mouse, timid, fearful, yet loving the heat so much as to risk nearly all for it. Drowsy would watch us with beady eye until the warmth triumphed over watchfulness. Then her head would drop and nod for all the world like an old woman in her chair by the fire. For several nights Drowsy visited us. When she had her fill of warmth or there was too much movement, she crept silently away under the sofa.

One Saturday Tine decided to wash the cover of the couch in the washer. Unknown to her the mouse was gathered up in the folds and went with the cover into the suds. I heard a great outcry suddenly from Tine. She pointed. There in the suds was a struggling mouse. Tine feared no lion, ate burglars for breakfast, welcomed a quarrelsome dog with a snarl of her own. A mouse, though, sent her into high C. She pointed. I rescued the all but dead creature, wiped her carefully, and set her free to limp her way under the sofa. That night, however, when the fire glowed warm, out came Drowsy for her last nod. She sat in her accustomed place and slept the sleep of the blessed for a time and, as was her wont, crept away. I used to say that she blew tiny soap bubbles from her nostrils as she slept, but strictly speaking that is not true. Her end was sad. There came a another day when the cover of the sofa had to be washed. This time she endured the entire ordeal only to end up on the ironing table under the hand of my mouse-fearing wife. Rachel saw what was happening and screamed, "Mama, my mouse!" But that was indeed the end of Drowsy.

We always had animals around us. While I was still at the academy we had two pet squirrels for an entire winter. I found in September a tiny young squirrel that had fallen from a tree. Indeed it was too late in the year for a decent mother to have young. The mother must have been a sexy trollop to have found herself in such a predicament—and winter coming too. I took the little squirrel home, and again the Dydee Doll bottle made do. The next night at retreat I inspected the corps of cadets. On the shoulder of one of the boys was a young squirrel. I removed the young thing and put him in my pocket easily, appropriating what must have been a very desirable acquisition for a cadet. The two young animals flourished. They were male and female. Always the femalc was the bully. She was bigger, greedier, more demanding. They played like kittens. Indeed we had a kitten during their winter sojourn with us. Sometimes they would bait the kitten with their speed and suppleness. Often they would go to sleep under the folded cover at the foot of our bed. There they would lie flat on their backs for all the world like an old couple at their naps.

One evening we had a dinner party for Colonel and Mrs. Alderman, shortly after their arrival in Sewanee. The children were in the kitchen having their supper. As the Aldermans entered, one of the squirrels ran from the kitchen. Confused and frightened by the strangers, it took refuge by running up Dot's skirt. The look on her face was indescribable, a cross between surprise and anguish. She turned to Craig. "Do something!" His mouth opened twice without his making a sound. Just then out raced Ulysse from the kitchen. "Don't hurt my squirrel!" she cried. The scene ended with Tine taking Dot into the bedroom and extracting the squirrel. We had a great party. The decorum and restraint were broken.

The squirrels came to breakfast with the children, stuck their noses into orange juice, made themselves part of the family. In the spring we decided to turn them loose, introduce them to the trees and the out-of-doors. When I got on a ladder and put the female on the limb of a tree, she froze with terror. The height was too much for her. Her heart raced and her blood pressure must have skyrocketed.

Rachel and Ulysse in a Sewanee snow

Only gradually and slowly did both learn to climb and explore the tree. This goes to show that young squirrels must learn to climb and to live in the trees. The female very quickly adjusted to the new life, though even she returned each night to the screen door to let us know that she wanted in. The male was less adaptable. He hated trees, much preferring the comfort of the kitchen. The female after a time reverted to wild ways, but the brother continued to scold us for putting him out in the tree. Tine even built him a refuge in the tree. All to no avail; he continued to scratch on the screen. Eventually he disappeared. Whether he went off to live a life in the woods or whether he was snatched up by a hawk, we never knew.

My teaching experience began in the college summer school with a course in public administration. I knew little more than what I learned from reading a couple of texts. Arthur Dugan suggested that I use as a text the *Hoover Report*. This was the published conclusions and recommendations of the Hoover Committee for the Reformation of the Federal Government.

I had a large class made up of many veterans back from the war. Occasionally discipline was a problem, but not for long. I had a sure remedy for back seat sleepers. I called upon them to recite. Being unprepared they usually appeared ridiculous. Once I ordered a student, who suggested that prep school techniques were unworthy of a college professor, to leave class and return only when he was willing to accept the law of civility. It worked. After all, I had learned how to get discipline in a tough school. This introduction to college teaching during the summer was profitable. When the fall semester came, I had already been indoctrinated.

In some other respects I was not actually prepared to be a professor of political science. I knew it. I suppose my students knew it. I worked hard at learning American government and focused on the Constitution, the document and its interpretation by the Supreme Court. I tried to fill in the history necessary for understanding. It was a grim course and difficult to enliven with what wit I had. I was never able to find enough humorous stories to suit either me or the class.

I found it difficult to teach jurisprudence until I had taken several courses in political theory at Michigan. I learned that my approach to the law had to be theoretical and that jurisprudence is merely the philosophy of the law, starting with the most elementary jural postulates, like the importance of enforcing certain promises. If my students learned half as much as I learned, they did well. By teaching I was learning.

During my first year as a professor in the college, Henry Gass acted as vice-chancellor. The regents and a few other members of a selection committee looked for a successor to Dr. Guerry. Eventually they selected Boylston Green, who came to Sewanee from Emerson College in Boston. How he came to be selected I know not. The choice proved in the long run to have been a poor one.

Dr. Green was a man of charm and learning. He would have made a good professor of English in my opinion. For the job at hand he lacked courage, consistency, wisdom, and guile. Rather early he permitted certain faculty members to get the upper hand. Among them was Charles Harrison, whom he offended by refusing him a house that he had been promised. Mr. Green relied on the weak, distrusted the strong, spoke optimistically about an open administration while keeping it closed, and permitted himself finally to be tricked by a bishop in the chess game of campus politics. Near the end of his tenure in 1951, it was suggested that he write out and deliver to the regents his letter of resignation. Naturally, according to reason, the letter would not be accepted. The ensuing vote of confidence would re-establish authority and restore power. Poor Dr. Green did as he was asked and found to his consternation that his resignation was as eagerly snatched up as a piece of meat by a hungry dog. Dr. Green himself told me this story, so it must be true.

During this period I was a lowly assistant professor at the college without prestige and without authority or influence except what came of my having already been in the community for many years and from my knowledge of Sewanee people and Sewanee ways. I will always remember that the last official act of Boylston Green was to confirm in writing to me a year's leave of absence with a stipend of $600 to attend the University of Michigan to pursue the doctorate.

During my last winter at the academy Tine's mother, Sophie, died. She went out to water her flowers one cool evening in winter and dropped dead in her back yard. He body remained there until found the next morning. In the fall of 1947 a great hurricane had hit the Gulf coast. Though advised to leave her home on the beach, Sophie, who had seen the house sturdily built and had too little fear of the sea, had refused to leave. The water driven by a hurricane wind swept into her house. She fought to save her furniture, which floated around in three or four feet of water inside the house. She saved several pieces. The water made a great sucking exit from the house upon the change of the wind. The door was taken out and some cherished possessions swept into the Gulf. We have always believed that her struggle that night shortened her life.

Tine and the children and I went to Biloxi that Christmas. Sophie was extremely glad to see us. The hurricane had deposited under her house bottles from many bars on the beach. She ran off looters and managed to bring into the house a large number of bottles without labels. She was looking for me to help her identify the contents. This I heartily did during this last Christmas vacation in a great house with a great lady. We did notice that Sophie lacked her usual energy at times, though she continued to play golf, a game she dearly loved. The hurricane had swept away her car. She had not yet acquired a new one. Often she walked uptown several blocks for small groceries. She could easily have taken my car, but her independence was such that she seldom used it.

Upon learning of her mother's death Tine was stricken. She loved her mother dearly and respected her even more. We immediately left for the coast by car and arrived by nightfall. By this time Sophie was in her coffin in her own living room. The weather was bleak and colder than it had been for many years. It was so cold that Back Bay froze over, a thing that had not occurred in the memory of living people. Since Sophie was so well known in Biloxi, a town in which her father had lived for so many years and in which he owned so much land bought by gold from the California Gold Rush, many people came to pay their respects. All night people sat with the body. Sophie was buried in the family tomb in the vault along with her ancestors.

At her death she was the owner of several rental houses on the beach and on Delaunay Street, as well as considerable other property. She left no will; consequently what she had came to Evelyn and Tine. It provided Tine with some financial security which she desperately needed, a security I had not been able to provide.

The trip back to Sewanee almost proved to be our undoing. The weather was extremely cold. Snow had fallen in northern Alabama. Although the sun had melted most of the snow from the surface of the roads, there were areas where snow and ice remained. We were on our way to Huntsville on the trip home when suddenly, without warning, the car, moving at a speed of about fifty miles an hour, slipped on the icy surface and began to spin down the highway. Ulysse was in the back seat with baggage and a piece of furniture we were bringing home from Sophie's house. Tine and I were in the front seat with Rachel between us.

During the mad spin down the highway, Tine must have attempted to brace herself, and by chance her hand hit the lever that opened the front door. It flew open, and Rachel, who had no hand-hold, was thrown out of the car. Shortly before the car came to rest with its open door wedged into a road bank, Tine was thrown out as well. Fortunately there was a ditch by the road, otherwise the door would have crushed her against the bank. When the car came to rest my feet were outside and I was hanging onto the wheel.

The first thing I remember seeing was Rachel running down the highway a good thirty yards from the car, crying, "Daddy, Daddy, my leg is broken." She was using it to such advantage I knew that could not be true. Tine was picking herself out of the ditch. She, too, was moving. Ulysse in the back seat had suffered no bruises. We gathered in the chill afternoon to assess the extent of the injuries. Tine was bruised and sore but nothing broken that she was aware of. Rachel had a bruised knee. Ulysse and I had no injuries. The car appeared to be all right except for the door. I got in, started the engine, and was able to move it back on the road.

We decided to head for Sewanee. I used a piece of roadside wire to fasten the door. It was now about five in the afternoon. The weather was growing colder. At length we found a gasoline station open and learned that ahead the snow covered the roads. Nevertheless we continued instead of opting for a motel in Huntsville. It was as if the near disaster had nerved our wills for any ordeal. Up the road I learned that the highway from Chattanooga, by way of which city we had decided to travel, was closed. We decided to try to make it across Sand Mountain and come home by way of Stevenson, Alabama, and then Sherwood, in the valley a scant twelve miles from home. Necessarily we proceeded at a very slow pace.

The weather had become colder as night neared and on the mountain we ran into a snowstorm. The road was almost obliterated by the driven snow. We kept going, reached Stevenson. Through the night and the flying snow, barely discernible lights flickered weakly through the driven mist. A few miles out of Stevenson we came upon a car blocking the road. Two people huddled beside it. I stopped and greeted a young man and woman stranded in that lonely snow-swept road. They begged our help. They were on their way to a kinsman's house in Sherwood. Both were ill clothed. Both were grimy and unwashed. Our car was full. Nevertheless we wedged the girl into the back seat with Ulysse and Rachel and the furniture and took the young man into the front seat with us.

We managed to pass the stalled car and recover the road and start forward. The heater in the car hummed to its business. The wet and dank clothes of the man began to generate steam and smell, that unholy smell of dirt and poverty and an unwashed body. The woman in the back was carrying a .22 rifle. In the crowded space of the back seat she managed to hold it aslant so that its muzzle came just under Ulysse's chin. Each time it reached such a position Ulysse would push it aside with some vigor. It was almost as though our two rescued travelers were zombies. They grunted at questions, answered in monosyllables. The snow swirled down to be seen as it can only be revealed by the headlights of a car. On we prodded into the night. At length the snow began to diminish and the wind to cease its plaintive crying. The dim lights of Sherwood could be seen. With relief we relinquished our passengers into the snow and the night. We had stopped by the tawdry movie house that then perched by the roadside. I learned from two young men whom I questioned that no vehicle had gone up the mountain since early afternoon. There we were in Sherwood, within reach of our own beds, and the road an uncertain question.

One of the young men, upon discovering that we lived in Sewanee, volunteered that he would drive his jeep ahead of us and break road. He said that once he had been thrown from his motorcycle on that mountain and Dr. Henry Kirby-Smith had saved his life. The least he could do was come to our aid. He was joined by his companion, and the two of them began the ascent, breaking the road ahead. By this time the snow had stopped. The night was clearing. We made good progress until we reached the hairpin turn. There the jeep appeared to slip and slide, but with skill and determination the driver finally negotiated the turn. I came slowly behind him and made it as well. We reached the mountaintop.

From there on it was a breeze. We thanked our helpers and pulled into our yard seventeen hours after having left Biloxi, Mississippi. We were cold, hungry, some of us bruised, all of us weary to the bone, but we had made it. We were home. I quickly had the furnace going, and heat began to rise along with our spirits. We made a big pot of vegetable soup, ate, and rolled into bed. Oh, we were brave then, intrepid. Neither snow nor sleet bent our wills; but we were foolish.

Chapter Eight

Graduate Studies and Hunting Stories

In the late summer of 1951 we moved to Michigan. I had attended summer school there for a couple of summers. I had been granted leave of absence to spend a year working for my doctorate. I had met Dr. James K. Pollock, head of the Department of Political Science, at the Southern Political Science Association meeting in a previous year. He had awarded me a teaching fellowship at Michigan. With the salary from that, the proceeds from the GI Bill, and the $600 awarded me by the university, I thought I could make it. Ulysse was in Randolph-Macon College in Virginia. Rachel would go with us.

I had made friends in my summers at Michigan. Tine had accompanied me one summer and she, too, had cemented our friendship with Don and Betty Drummond. Don was a professor of history at Michigan. Betty was a big great-hearted blonde filled with beauty and goodness. She helped us find an apartment just across the street from where they lived, an unfurnished duplex owned by a widowed lady who lived above.

We arrived with our personal belongings and whatever we could bring in an overpacked car. Within days with the help of Betty we had bought or borrowed sufficient furniture to start us going. We had a bed for each of the two bedrooms, two second-hand dressers, a couch for the living room along with sufficient chairs, and a big desk that I bought from a woman who ran a junk shop, whom I got to know as a fine friend. As I remember it, we were comfortable, enjoyed the quick friendship of many people, and especially the friendship of Don and Betty Drummond.

The greatest strain fell on Rachel. She was removed from her home and friends. She was in a new school in a city that for her was large. At first she was sick at her stomach before leaving for school. Gradually she became accustomed to new people and new friends. She and I were very close. Some nights I slept with her for her greater security. We almost immediately started going to the Episcopal church together. After sunday school and church we were wont to go to the Blue Front, a corner drug store that was open after church, where I would buy a western and she a favorite comic book for catharsis. We both needed it—I for relief from the long hours in the stacks, she from the tension of school.

The black children sought her out. Black parents called Tine for pick-up duty for PTA meetings. Strange it was; because there seemed to be a feeling of understanding and empathy between us, who were from the South, stronger than that I felt with the midwesterners. I have often encountered it and credit it to the fact that the southern white has lived with blacks for long years. Blacks are better appreciated as people among those for whom they have done so much in the past.

Rachel with Queenie on the farm in Floyd

During Rachel's summer days with Mama, a wonderful strange event occurred. My mother had a single milk cow called Queenie, and Rachel became enchanted with Queenie. She followed the cow into the meadow; she tried to milk her; she stole vegetables from the garden to feed her. In the course of time, a strange relationship developed. The cow began to think Rachel was her calf. She mooed when Rachel left her and carried on as a cow deprived of a new calf. I have a picture of tiny Rachel lying asleep against the side of contented Queenie, who was chewing her cud. I have never heard before of this bonding between a cow and a human. It is a fine testimonial to the truth that all of God's creation are subtly related.

At Michigan my life was strenuous. I attended lectures once a week in American government. The lecture was given by a Virginia Ph.D., George Peek. He was a splendid lecturer, interesting, well prepared. The teaching fellows then took a section twice a week for discussion and quizzing. Each section had about twenty students. They were about like the students whom I had taught at Sewanee with the exception that there were girls in the class. This was my first experience with teaching girls. I liked it. They used, some of them, their feminine appeal whenever they thought they could in the most subtle ways to improve grades. They were never just students to me.

Women are more perceptive than men about human nature. They will inevitably recognize a man who innately admires and respects women. I was no sitting duck but occasionally I lit on the water.

Aside from attending seminars, I was forced to spend long hours in the stacks reading many books. I learned to read the first chapter in which an author usually states his thesis, skim through much, and read closely the last chapter in which conclusions are often given. This had to suffice for all courses except constitutional law. There the cases have to be read and understood if one is to do well. I was aided by the fact that I was much older than the average graduate student. I had a daughter in college. The younger graduate students accepted us whole-heartedly and willingly. The professors, knowing that I too was a professor in a reputable college, regarded me as something of a colleague. Actually it has been my experience that people in every station in life are willing to take you at face value until they learn differently.

In the fall when hunting season opened I drove one Saturday morning to the farm of a doctor from Detroit whom I had met at summer school at a picnic. He had told me to come to his farm to hunt when the season opened. I found there his son-in-law with a group of his friends about to go out for pheasant. They were annoyed at my coming. I explained my invitation and left. I drove around through farming country for some time. I came upon a farm with a barn near the road and a blue-tick hound tied in the barn. The farmer was feeding his stock. I got out and introduced myself.

"I noticed this hound. He looks so much like a Tennessee hound that I am curious to know if he came from there."

He was dumbfounded. "How did you know?" he asked. "I got that dog two years ago from a kennel near Columbia, Tennessee. He is one fine coon dog!"

This exchange started a conversation in the course of which I related to him my early morning experience. "Why," he said, "hunt all you please on my land. I jumped some pheasants in the corn field yesterday!" I accepted his invitation. I hunted all morning, and killed two cock birds and by mistake a hen. I plucked the hen in the corn field, and when I left I deposited by the door of his back porch, since the family was out, a fine cock pheasant in deep appreciation of his friendship and courtesy. I came home proud.

In the 1950s Michigan offered a splendid department of political science headed by Professor Pollock, who was a celebrated advisor to General Lucius Clay in Germany and a member of the Hoover Commission. There was Joseph Kallenbach in constitutional law, whose text on the presidency is still one of the best. Then there was a group of young scholars, many of whom went on to make reputations for themselves. It was an exciting place to be. There were no apparent feuds in the department. The faculty partied together and seemed to enjoy each other.

Later the department came to be dominated by the behaviorists, who expected to explain political behavior in terms of scientific analysis, often based upon dubious data, and filled texts with mathematical symbols hard to come by and harder to understand. What they often did was to put a pseudoscientific underpinning at the base of general conclusions that students of politics had long since arrived at by other means. I do not doubt that such data have a place and contribute to the discipline some knowledge. I do doubt that the methodology is exclusively relevant and productive. It has created a professional jargon that keeps the layman at arm's length. I suppose this is part of its purpose, for after all politics is a new discipline recently disentangled from political economy.

My own belief is that knowledge is a seamless garment. All knowledge is part of a whole. Physics is related to politics. When we break down the field of knowledge into many parts for purposes of mental digestion, we make it extremely difficult for minds to make the synthesis. Some chemists find it difficult to talk with other chemists, almost as difficult as to talk understandingly with a biochemist.

Soon after going to Michigan I decided to write my thesis on the jurisprudence of Judge Learned Hand. I was first attracted by the rhetoric and reason of his opinions, later by the man himself. In graduate school it is wise to determine early what you will research. It was especially necessary for me, intent as I was on doing quickly whatever was necessary to get the union card that declared to the world that you were at least a scholar, if no gentleman, and made promotion and advancement possible. By the 1950s the Ph.D. degree had become the *sine qua non* in the academic world. Its acquisition did not make me a better teacher. Perhaps it "froze the genial currents of my soul." It did give me standing and admitted me to a company signed and sealed with the authority of knowledge.

Very early in the year I was fortunate to meet a cousin of Martha Clark, Beverly Smith by name. He had a splendid farm near Detroit, a cabin in the Upper Peninsula, and a most productive Ford agency. He had graduated from Washington and Lee, had played quarterback on one of their teams, and had wandered north, coached, worked as a salesman, and done what came to hand to make a dollar. The story of how he got his start is interesting.

One day when he was selling cars for a Ford agent he noticed two old people, a man and his wife, in the heavy rain. He seized an umbrella at hand and, protecting them from the rain, brought them into the showroom. When the rain subsided he helped them to their car. When he returned to his office he was chided for his concern and accused of being what he was, "a damned Virginia gentleman." He took this banter in good spirits. Some time later he was astonished, and so was his employer, to get an order for 150 cars. The old gentleman whom he had shielded from the rain was a vice president of General Motors, one of whose jobs was to buy cars that the company gave to their selected executives. From that feat it was but a step to a coveted dealership near Detroit and money in the bank and cattle on the hill.

When I met him he already had it made. He liked me and invited me on occasion to hunt on his farm and to go to the Upper Peninsula for partridge and deer and trout from the Two Hearted River.

When deer season opened I was invited to join a party of hunters in the Upper Peninsula. I had bought for the occasion a red hunting coat and a .30-30 Winchester rifle. I was to meet Bev Smith at the ferry that crossed the lake to Upper Michigan at daylight. I left on a road that was covered with eight inches or so of hard packed snow. I had chains on my tires, but even so I was unaccustomed to driving on snow. At first I proceeded slowly, but soon I learned to keep up the pace.

It was a long drive from Ann Arbor. I had started at three in the morning. Many cars were headed in the same direction. I did not take into consideration the number of people that take to the woods in Michigan when deer season opens. When I at last got to the ferry there was a long line of cars ahead of me. Bev Smith would be hard to find. I decided to wait my turn and try to meet him on the other side. Fortunately I found him on the other side awaiting me.

I followed him until we disembarked for the hike in to the cabin, for the road did not lead there. We carried in our provisions and found several hunters who had come in the day before. A deer had appeared within shooting distance of the cabin, and one of the hunters had killed him for food and hung him some distance away in the woods where a warden would not likely find him. The cabin was warm and comfortable. A great old-fashioned wood-burning cook stove and a fireplace kept us warm. The companionship was hearty and hunter-like. Stories and banter were the order of the evening followed by a game of poker—the inevitable poker game.

The next morning we all went in different directions to hunt. About noon I returned to the cabin without having heard a shot or seen a deer. The weather was cold, snow seemed imminent. I ate a sandwich and returned to the woods. Soon snow began to fall in great moist flakes; this turned into sleet. About two o'clock I heard the snort of a deer. I found his tracks in the snow and began to follow without paying too much attention to where the tracks were leading me. From time to time I took compass bearings. Though the bearings told me the directions, I realized that I did not know in what direction the cabin lay.

By this time the afternoon was waning. The snow continued to fall. Far away I could hear a pack of wolves driving deer. It was the first time I had heard wolves and the sound filled me with apprehension. I determined to take a circular swing to see if I could find a path that I had been told ran in a westerly direction from the cabin. I did not find it. I was about to experience the panic of a man lost in the snow in a strange forest without landmarks. I sat down on a log to gather my wits. I was driven by intuition to go one way. My compass told me another. I put my gun by a tree that the iron might not interfere with the compass. It remained steady. My compass said, "Go east. Follow your footsteps. Back trail yourself. Always east."

I started out on the back trail. Soon my track was obliterated by the swirling snow. I held down my rising panic. Said I to myself, "I have matches. I can find an uprooted tree and build a lean-to. I am not far from camp. Morning will come. I can keep warm." As I was telling myself this, I walked into the water of a beaver dam and sank to me knees. I almost lost my rifle. I stumbled out, realizing that cold feet might freeze unless I could find either the path or a shelter. I continued to walk northward as I had been doing for some time, hoping to intersect a path that led eastward. By this time it was late afternoon. The gray day was closing in about me and night was at hand. Low in spirit, I suddenly heard what I thought was the firing of a rifle. I stopped and listened. Sure enough, there came to me faintly the sound of rifle fire patterned in three shots. I answered the fire in a pattern of two shots spaced thirty seconds apart.

I headed to the sound of firing like Kirby Smith at Manassas. Soon I did come to a discernible path in the snow. My heart lifted. I headed into the snow with a joyous heart. In time amid swirling snow and the sound of wolves after deer, I came to fire and friends. How joyous is the sound of human voices. How pleasing the glow of fire. Elemental things are best. To come home out of the storm, to feel the clasp of hands, to hear the joking banter of concerned companions, to stand steaming before the heat of a cook stove—is there anything better in the world?

As it happened, it was a good thing that a deer had been illegally killed and hid in the swamp. When morning came the snow was three feet deep. Nothing moved on that white sea of snow. The deer had gone to huddle together for defense in their yards, as they are called. Our meat was running low. Beverly Smith, a friend of his, and I went to bring out the deer. When we found the deer it was still hanging in the tree but an animal had chewed its head. Of course it was frozen stiff.

For some unknown reason men in the snow will sometimes quarrel. A quarrel broke out between Bev and his friend about, of all things, the proper way to get the deer the mile or so back to camp. So hot did the discussion become that it almost led to blows. I finally burst in with, "God dammit, if you are so all-fired eager, grab a hind leg of this buck and start pulling!" Each grabbed a leg and both were soon panting from the struggle to slide a deer through deep snow. At the proper time I relieved each and we managed to carry and pull the deer back to camp. It was three days before we could get out of the woods and back to civilization.

At that time the Upper Peninsula was remote and underpopulated. The remains of great logs six feet in diameter lay moldering away in the woods. The loggers had cut the big timber and floated it out to the lake when they could, but much remained that they had been unable to get to the water. A great, gashing waste it was. The early timber man had no respect for trees.

The winter passed but spring did not come. I learned that in Michigan there is scarcely any spring. The snow lies on the sides of the streets where it has been deposited by plows until early May. Suddenly summer comes! My studies prospered. Rachel became satisfied. There was art work for Tine, whose hands had to be ever busy. She did copper work, made silver jewelry, canvassed the antique shops, and kept busy, busy. By the end of the term I had completed most of the required work except for the dissertation, passed the language examinations in German and French, passed the preliminary examination. All that remained for the summer was a course in directed research and work on my thesis. Very quickly a year had passed and I was ready to return to Sewanee.

Chapter Nine

A Growing Vision

I returned to Sewanee from Michigan in 1952. The time at Michigan had been well spent. All that remained to be done on my pursuit of the Ph.D. was to write the dissertation on the jurisprudence of Learned Hand. At the time Learned Hand was not well known in academic places or by the public. Among the lawyers and judges of America he was well known and highly respected. He had twice missed being appointed to the Supreme Court on account of age. I had read many of his opinions, but much more investigation had to be done. I did it. I set for myself four pages of writing each day. Sometimes I missed my quota but nevertheless kept hammering away at my Remington portable. John Webb was writing his thesis at the same time. He lived near me, and I could hear his typewriter. We kept each other going. When my dissertation was completed, I had Charles Harrison read it and criticize my writing. He gave me much needed advice. I submitted it in 1953, defended it orally in the same year, and received my diploma in hand in 1954.

In the meantime I had built a house. Amelia Brooks, our lovely neighbor, had given us part of her lease. I saw that it had the possibilities of a view, and when we had cleared a place for the house and cut some trees on the bluff, we found ourselves with a fine vista overlooking Roark's Cove. We put $6,000 of Tine's money into the house. The rest I borrowed from the university at 4 percent interest for twenty years. In all, we built the house for $17,000, though later with some alterations and stone veneer we had invested about $20,000. We got a great deal of space for our money, but we sacrificed some adornments.

In 1953 I became dean of men at the college. Jim Grimes had been dean of men since the administration shuffle that came about with Vice-Chancellor Green's resignation. At that time Edward McCrady became acting vice-chancellor, Gaston Bruton, dean of administration, Charles Harrison, dean of the college, and Jim Grimes, dean of men. Grimes found that the handling of discipline was stressful and decided to give up the place. It was offered to me, and I took it. I had been commandant of cadets at the military academy, and I felt competent in disciplinary situations. Actually the job had evolved out of the keeping of records of class and chapel attendance. It was required that students attend class, though they were given a specific number of academic cuts. When they had used them in a subject they were removed from that class. By overcutting they might overcut themselves out of school.

A number of chapel attendances were required for both weekday and Sunday. If one came to graduation without the required number of chapel attendances, he did not graduate. I have sent students to every chapel service available in Sewanee on a given Sunday to enable them to graduate. There were as many as seven services available on the Mountain on Sunday.

I did not find being dean of men stressful. I was able to go home and leave my problems behind me until the next day. Of course there was no leaving all problems behind, because students get into more trouble by night than by day. Many are the times I have had to go to Jasper to get a student out of jail. Most of the cases were simply passed to the grand jury and indictments never brought. I had a good friend in Harry Templeton, the attorney general in my district. The charges were always petty, and a night in the Jasper jail was punishment enough. Of the jails I have known, the Jasper jail was second in filth and squalor only to the one in Key West.

Those were times before gays had come out of the closet. It was a policy at Sewanee to send offensive homosexuals home. A case came to the attention of the dean of men involving aggressive homosexuality by the misuse of a young cadet at Sewanee Military Academy. We acted quickly, and the offenders, having admitted their guilt, were quickly sent home. One of the offenders was a good student and friend of a senior professor. The professor was away at the time of the incident but his wife heard of it and came to my office to protest. I explained that the boys had confessed, that they were already on their way home. She continued to make demands until I finally said, "I have said all I can say. Now, will you please leave?" "No," she said, "I will not go." "Then you may have my office," I replied and left. I watched, and she remained in my office for fully twenty minutes. I expected I would be out of her good graces forever, but the next day I saw her at mail time,

I may have been asking David Boone, "Do you recall the hour of the morning?" Or perhaps a more scholarly question.

and she was as she had always been, civil and affable. She had taken the time to think about the affair.

Another time I was called by a professor occupying the house next to the Kappa Alpha house. His complaint was loud noise and boisterous conduct. I heard many such complaints, but since I had to dress, it seemed that I always arrived to find that all was quiet and peaceful. This time I put on a robe and got there quickly. As I appeared on the walk I heard a boy exclaim, "Here comes Red Dog!" By the time I entered the house all of the brothers had disappeared into the shrubbery or up trees. Tine's nephew Jack Thompson was president of KA that year. I went out and called, "Jack, bring your boys in!" They came out of the bushes and the trees very solemnly and quiet. I pretended great anger. I lectured them sternly about the complaints I had had of their conduct, all the while secretly amused by the situation. This was a long time ago. Think what it must be like to live next to the KAs with today's hard rock music.

I was glad to get out of that office and make way for John Webb. In 1957 I was made dean of the College of Arts and Sciences. It came about like this. At the general shake-up at the resignation of Boylston Green as vice-chancellor, McCrady became acting vice-chancellor, Charles Harrison dean of the college, and Gaston Bruton dean of administration. This was in 1951. By 1957 Charles was tired of the job; he loved teaching and his doctor advised that he go back to less stressful full-time teaching. He wanted me to succeed him. So he prepared the way for my full acceptance by the faculty. Of course, there were a few who did not want me to be dean for one reason or another. One of them was my departmental chairman, Arthur Dugan. He talked to me about it. He felt that the post should go to a more senior member like Stratton Buck. Nevertheless I had almost unanimous support in the faculty, and McCrady nominated me, and the regents accepted me as dean. I welcomed the responsibility and the salary increase. After all I had been on the Mountain and working for the corporation since 1931.

For the next twelve years I held that office; though in 1964 I went on a Fulbright lectureship to Korea; and from 1965 through 1967 I was acting director of development. I came to the development post in this way. The Ford Foundation made an offer to the university of $2,500,000 provided we could raise money to match it at the rate of three to one. An elaborate office was set up in Chattanooga, and a staff of professional money raisers from New York was employed to help. The co-chairmen of the enterprise were Cecil and Albert Woods of Chattanooga and New York respectively. By 1965 the undertaking was failing. I was in Korea when Bishop Juhan called me from Sewanee and asked that I come home immediately to work on the Ford campaign. Tine was somewhere in Asia traveling. I reached her in Hong Kong and told her of the situation. She returned to Seoul quickly, and we came home to Sewanee. I was given an office in Elliott Hall, the Sewanee headquarters of the campaign. Within a short time I made myself familiar with the development situation.

Bishop Frank Juhan, my friend and mentor, and Cecil Woods, president of Volunteer Life of Chattanooga, were both working hard to succeed with the campaign. They were old men at the time and were not coordinating their efforts effectively. I saw my first job was to develop quickly a coordinated effort. I was able to do this. New energy surged from these venerable men; many trips of solicitation were made; many challenges were accepted; and the undertaking that the professionals had already labeled a failure began to give promise of dramatic success. Since the deadline for matching the Ford grant was only a few months away, much had to be done quickly, and it was.

Within a single thirty-day period more than a million dollars came into the office. Sewanee's friends from everywhere began to make gifts and to pay off pledges. The success of it all was that we received over half a million dollars more than we expected.

Whether or not I was largely responsible for the outcome I cannot truthfully say. I do know that, after I entered the campaign, what was thought to be a failing enterprise began to pick up energy and speed. I was generally credited with being the man who brought success. The alumni voted a resolution thanking me for giving up a Fulbright grant to come back to Sewanee and shore up a weak campaign.

At the end of the campaign Bishop Juhan retired from the office of director of development, and I was asked to stay on and assume that responsibility. I agreed to become acting director of development, but I kept my office as dean of the college as an anchor to windward.

After one year I realized that I did not have the power and prestige to make the office what it should be. Any development officer must have complete access to the vice-chancellor and board of regents. However, my attendance at the board's deliberations would reflect on the authority of Gaston Bruton, the university's provost and vice-president, who did not sit with the regents. Vice-Chancellor McCrady decided not to invite me to the regents' meetings, but the chairman, Allen Kimball of Lake Charles, Louisiana, was of another mind. He saw the need for the director of development to counsel with the regents, and I would go to their meetings at his invitation. As the situation proved intolerable, I decided to go back to the deanship. For the following year or until Marcus Oliver was employed in that office, I was both dean of the college and *de facto* head of development. The office continued to provide record amounts of money for the university at the lowest administrative cost in recent history. The self-study of 1970 showed we raised money for the period during which I served at three cents per dollar.

When Bishop Juhan left the development office, he confided to me that if he lived long enough he hoped to raise the funds for a student union. After his death I talked to Cecil Woods about a memorial to the bishop; we agreed that we needed a student union and that it would be a fitting memorial to the bishop. I went to the regents with the proposition that we raise money for the purpose. The regents were not enthusiastic. Many thought that funds were needed for other purposes. I think I presented my case well. I spoke of our debt to the bishop and the need for the union. Finally it was agreed that I should form a committee for raising the necessary money. We began immediately to solicit funds. The enterprise had its ups and downs, but we reached our goal with the bequest of Niles Trammell of Miami, the first president of the National Broadcasting Company. It stands today in a fine location in the center of the campus, and it should meet our needs for many years if we limit our growth within reasonable proportions.

The other monument to my time in development is Rebel's Rest. It is the oldest house on the mountain, the house within which our new founding after the war occurred, the house that enshrines our most venerable traditions.

It is restored only because I persuaded the regents to allow me to raise the money for it without going to our established constituents. I did not observe their restrictions to the letter, but there it is. When I took over, the grounds were covered with kudzu, and the house itself was well on the way to decay. A plan of restoration was done by Edwin Keeble as a gift to the university. The restoration was done by our own workmen supervised by Carl Reid, a splendid builder. Much of our needs were supplied by gifts-in-kind such as tile for the bathrooms. The whole undertaking cost $55,000. In it we have a standing memorial to our founders and a reminder that we began in poverty but not despair.

All of this brings up my relations with Gaston Bruton, the university's provost. Suffice it to say we remained friends and co-workers for the good of Sewanee. I accepted the fact that he had the complete confidence of the vice-chancellor because he was necessary to the vice-chancellor's effectiveness. In all of my business with him, I found him to be supportive and friendly. Once I went to the vice-chancellor concerning a matter of salary structure for the coming year.

He called in Dr. Bruton, and we spoke of powers and responsibilities. Dr. McCrady admitted we did not need two deans of the college and asked us to work out our spheres of responsibility. We did. I was careful to recognize the authority of the provost. I was his dean; he was my provost.

In all of my activities, official and unofficial, I had the support of Bishop Frank Juhan. He was not only my bishop, he was my friend. He occupied a place of unparalleled respect at Sewanee. Not only was he acquainted with Sewanee's history and tradition, he revered and served them. Since he had the friendship and the support of Mrs. Alfred I. duPont, he could influence policy and provide financial support beyond any other person's ability. I remember one year when Mrs. duPont provided him with a discretionary fund of $150,000, tax free.

Bishop Juhan was a many-sided man. He was a churchman, loyal and faithful. He was a counselor without peer. Many were the calls made upon him for help in distress. He gave it. He was an avid hunter and sportsman. He had the friendship of men high and low. He knew everybody in the village. All kinds of men and women looked to him with admiration and respect. Sometimes he did not let his left hand know what the right was doing. Women admired him; men loved his company. He told a story well; he handled a gun expertly; he cast a fly accurately. His will was strong and well directed.

Sewanee owes to this man much for its present appearance, for he was instrumental in bringing into existence so many of the buildings that grace our campus. Of course, there were those who questioned his decisions, but even they respected his accomplishments. He was not universally popular in the church because he stood for the old-fashioned Anglicanism that Sewanee grew up with. Many of the new movements in the church he disliked. He saw them coming, and he was dubious. He was a prince of the church whose like I shall not see again.

I was dean of the college from 1957 to 1969. During those years the college grew in numbers, in academic excellence, and in reputation for producing students who won scholarships at many graduate schools. The production of Rhodes scholars and Fulbright grantees was remarkable. We brought to the college promising scholars, many of whom were athletically as well as academically competent. Both Gaston Bruton and I supported athletics and aided the coaches in bringing talented athletes to the college. Twice we had undefeated football seasons under Shirley Majors.

We instituted a lecture program that brought to the college outstanding speakers. We saw that both sides of any political question were presented during the year.

During the sixties a very real social revolution occurred in the United States. Blacks gained legal equality. The status of women improved. All of this was not accomplished without violence. Universities and colleges were not prepared for a revolution that often expressed itself in vulgarity and violence. Many great educational institutions gave in to unreasonable demands, and the failure of so many famous institutions to stand up for decency and right is a shameful page in our academic history.

Sewanee was small and family-like and escaped the worst in student disaffection and misbehavior. As dean of the college, I resisted unreasonable behavior. Once I was told by a friendly student that students were being provoked by a visitor from Berkeley and that very soon they would come to physically remove me from my office.

I said, "You tell them the first two or three who enter the door will be hurt and bad!" About that time Dr. McCrady, who had heard of the planned removal, asked me if I needed police help.

"No!" I said, "I would like to handle it my way."

About that time a football player whom I knew tapped on my window and said, "We have most of the team just outside. We will wipe them out if you want."

I was immensely cheered by this support. "Stand by," I said, "I don't think it will come to a fight."

It did not. Soon a messenger came from the students in Convocation Hall to ask me to come speak to the large group.

"No," I said, "You select six of your leaders, and I will meet them and talk in the Regents' Room," a smaller room, impressive, dignified, and formal.

They sent their representatives, and we met. Their gripe was that I had notified a member of the faculty of junior status that we would not employ him for the next term. They asked me why I had done this. My explanation was that the faculty member had acted irresponsibly by leaving his classes to attend a march in Washington. Then I told the students that firing and hiring were not their prerogatives. They disliked this blunt reply but soon students began to gather at outside windows and even push into the room. Fortunately they were generally my friends. We got the meeting going in a jocular and humorous vein, and the confrontation dissolved into laughter. It was, however, for me a grim encounter.

Before the sixties one heard much of Sewanee gentlemen. Students opened doors for ladies and rather prided themselves on their social poise. During the sixties we lost something we had prided ourselves in having. Manners declined; the Order of Gownsmen lost some of its leadership role; behavior became less attractive; and the drive toward equality eroded some of the emphasis on manners and social graces.

Twice during my deanship, I gave Founders' Day speeches. Both speeches were printed in pamphlet form and distributed. In both I extolled the values dear to our founders and deplored the loss of civility. I noted that equality and freedom are not synonymous ideas and that equality is not a natural byproduct of human relations. This was good old-time Sewanee gospel, but it was not popular among a great many who would in the name of equality and freedom destroy some of our most cherished values.

I have given literally hundreds of speeches to alumni groups, clubs, and graduating classes. Once I spoke to the graduates of the Sewanee Academy. I could never have given such a speech were I not a child of Sewanee. I quote it because it has an old-time Sewanee flavor:

"Most Worthy Vice-Chancellor, honorable and diligent headmaster, learned teachers, parents, guests, young men and women of the first class graduating from the Sewanee Academy and the 104th class to be graduated from this school of learning: I feel very deeply the significance of this occasion, for more than forty years ago I first came here to teach and my life has upon it the imprint of this place.

"I remember the words of the Psalmist, David, the King:

By the rivers of Babylon there we sat down,
Yea, we wept when we remembered Zion.
We hanged our harps upon the willows in the midst thereof.
For they that carried us away captive required of us a song;
And they that wasted us required of us mirth:
Saying, Sing us one of the songs of Zion.
How shall we sing the Lord's song in a strange land?
If I forget thee, O Jerusalem, let my right hand lose her cunning.

"Today I shall sing you a song of the people of the west. I shall remember briefly our inheritance. We shall be chastened, but we shall be glad.

"Long yesterdays ago God-intoxicated prophets taught us that we are the children of God; and if we are his children, we partake of his dignity and we are relieved by his grace. Western man holds his head higher because he is God's child. He seeks freedom and follows it because he is of worth. God gave him his spirit.

"Listen to David the King:

I ascend up into heaven, thou art there;
If I make my bed in hell, behold, thou art there.
If I take the wings of the morning,
and dwell in the uttermost parts of the sea,
even there, shall thy hand lead me.

"Long years ago a man by the name of Zeno taught on the porch of a temple. What he taught belongs to all men, but it is a priceless inheritance of western man. In a crumbling culture when the material and spiritual foundations of a splendid and sprightly people were dissolving, he taught men to be strong, to seek solace within themselves. From his teachings came the idea of human brotherhood. For all men were sparks of a divine fire, and that fire is the fire of reason. Because of him laws were softened, the burdens of slavery eased, the dream of freedom strengthened and Roman law lost its provincialism and became the support of an empire.

"Nearly 2,000 years ago Jesus of Galilee came into the world to teach men the meaning of life and the significance of death, to bring hope where before there was no hope, to steal from death the victory, to bring to a thirsty world a living fountain of love and finally to redeem men and give them a new life.

"Said he:

But I say unto you which hear, Love your enemies
do good to them that hate you. Be ye therefore
merciful as your Father also is merciful. Judge not
and ye shall not be judged. Condemn not and ye
shall not be condemned. Forgive and ye shall be
forgiven.

"And again:

In my Father's house are many mansions. If it
were not so I would have told you. I go to prepare
a place for you, and if I go to prepare a place for
you, I shall come again to receive you unto myself,
that where I am, there ye may be also.

"We call ourselves Christians in His name and in a poor and weak way remember his lessons. But from the great cathedral at Chartres, sacred to the blessed Virgin, to the chapel in the center of our own campus, the road is straight and the symbol is clear. Both are the way of the cross.

"Later but still many years ago, Martin Luther, a mere man but filled with the piety of faith and the courage of Christian soldier, nailed his theses on the church door at Wittenberg. He assailed a church corrupt and unfaithful, and he preached the doctrine of everyman his own priest. The unity of Christendom was destroyed, but piety and faith were reborn. In his way he helped disentangle the individual from the group to prepare the way for democracy with a greater freedom and a more pervasive equality of opportunity. Like Isaiah of old, his doctrine was the doctrine of individual worth and individual responsibility.

"As a result of spiritual turmoil sturdy Oliver Cromwell, citizen-soldier, won the battles of an English revolution that made possible the supremacy of power circled by law and gave to us finally the idea of popular sovereignty through representative government. Almost every provision in our own Bill of Rights is an echo of the great English bill—memories of stern times, monuments of old victories. Especially do I remember the maxim he would place over every church door: 'I beseech ye, by the bowels of Christ, bethink ye that ye may be wrong!'

"One last and looming figure I would resurrect to quicken our memories—John Locke, physician, philosopher. There is scarcely a page from our founders' books that does not reflect the influence of his mind. He taught that government is based upon agreement, inarticulate promises made; that they who hold power hold it in trust; that men ought not to become swallowed up by the state because they have retained for themselves the right to life, liberty, and property; that when the contract is broken by the sovereign he may be replaced by another more lawful.

"These memories I recall that we may weave together the strands in the rope of our inheritance. It is a thick rope and heavy with meaning. Of the many, I have recalled only a few, and I have said nothing of those millions who in their humble but sturdy lives have borne the burdens and kept faith in our inheritance: faith in Reason, the principle of quick intelligence; the dignity and worth of man as a free-willing child of God; the ultimate responsibility of men for their choices; the brotherhood of all men; the eternal worth of every individual for whom organizations and governments exist; power held in trust under law; progress over linear time; the principle of human equality—all men equal in the sense all coins are equal because they have upon them the insignia of authority; the redemption of the world by our Lord Jesus Christ.

"This is a mighty inheritance, rich and powerful. These propositions are not merely logical propositions that can remain secure detached from the faith that gave them birth. They can not find proper sustenance in a shallow and secular culture that begins to condition men to the belief that all things are relative; that one truth is as good as another; that what was true a hundred years ago is no longer true simply because time has passed; that nothing is true that cannot be empirically verified; that only the material world has relevance; and abundance the only measure of creativity; that children should be wards of the state rather than in the care of their parents.

"Yet there are those who in the name of our Christian heritage give lip service to ideas and systems that would destroy every strand in this value system of western man. Do not be carried away by those who would minimize your traditions. The world is complex; the forces of evil persuasive. Yet you are heirs of a magnificent accumulation of history-laden values. Though you may have the eye of a fish and the jaw of a primate, though you be the product of time spread thin with age, yet you are children of God. Your culture is carried not in your genes; it must be taught and it must be learned. Civilization is a thin crust, treat it gently lest you break through into the primeval mire. You, our children, are our only hope, our final faith.

In the atmosphere we breathe,
As buds grow red when snow storms flee,
From spring gathering up beneath

Whose mild wind shakes the elder brake,
And the wandering herdsmen know
That the white thorn soon will blow
Wisdom, Justice, Love, and Peace
When they struggle to increase
Are to us as soft winds be
To shepherd boys, the prophecy
Which begins and ends in thee.

"Men and women of tomorrow, you have listened to a child of yesterday. Be of good courage, lift up your hearts, hold fast to your inheritance. Go with God."

It was during my deanship that we admitted our first black students. It is true that I accepted our black students with some reluctance. I believed that we should admit students of all races who were prepared to meet our academic standards. However at Sewanee there is no city to provide companionship, and we would have too few black students for them to find happiness and security. I also felt that Sewanee was unsuited by history and temperament to make them happy. Once black students were here I did everything in my power to advance their happiness and to secure for them places in graduate schools. Our first blacks will testify to my energy and effort on their behalf.

I left the dean's office in 1969 by choice to return to full-time teaching. This was the first year that women students were admitted. I had opposed their coming on principle and in the belief that we should develop a separate woman's college. Once they came, I changed my mind. I found them more easily stimulated intellectually, harder working. Certainly they made the campus lovelier. The problems of housing, of discipline, and of provisions for athletics I never had to solve.

I think we made a great mistake in opening all dormitories at all hours to visiting. I would not have agreed to housing men and women students in the same dormitory. Too much freedom brings unnecessary stress and pain to young people. Choices are often dictated by peer pressure. As matters now stand there is a great deal of competition between the sexes. There is a noticeable trend toward segregation of the sexes. Men deny women students places at their tables at dinner.

Black students go with blacks and whites with white.

Full-time teaching permitted me to enjoy my students. When I was dean, I had little time to think about my classes. Between 1969 and my retirement in 1979, I ceased to lecture formally, choosing instead to have my students do most of the talking. To some extent this strategy forced students to read each day's assignment. The number who could not take part in discussions became noticeably smaller. Except in very large classes, I believe the lecture method of instruction is less productive than the discussion method. In any event, a teacher is forced to do a great deal of explaining, which is a less formal method of lecturing.

In February 1971 I received a letter from John H. Chafee, secretary of the Navy asking me to become a member of the Academic Advisory

Board of the Navy. The letter came as a surprise, and I still do not know who brought me to the attention of the secretary of the Navy. I speculated that it might have been Senator Howard Baker, for I had been one of his campaign managers in his successful race for the Senate.

The board was established in 1966 for advising the superintendent of the U. S. Naval Academy on academic matters. It has been credited by some with helping to adjust the curriculum to the era of fast-moving change in education. I was pleased to be a member of this board, and I accepted the invitation with some enthusiasm. The appointment was to be for two years, but I served an additional term.

During the time I was a member of the board, I found myself in the company of people of accomplishment and distinction from the navy and civilian life. There were members such as Admiral Robert Carney, former chief of naval operations; Admiral Isaac Kidd, Jr., supreme allied commander, Atlantic; John D. deButts, chairman of the board of AT&T; Thomas Boardman, editor of the *Cleveland Press*; presidents John Dickey and Arthur Hansen of Dartmouth and Purdue respectively; and other men of distinction and accomplishment.

It was a high-powered board and a board that could reach a consensus, if it could be attained, by a sort of general understanding. There is a tendency on such boards made up of several chiefs and no warriors to competitive talk and animated discussion. I observed that those who ran the naval academy knew quite well their problems and their wishes. Perhaps the board tended to produce a more balanced curriculum. I was of the opinion that a five year course of study would be more productive than the normal four years. There is now so much technical information required of a naval officer. It was pleasing to me to see that those who ran the academy were able and dedicated men who realized that the academy incorporated the attitudes and philosophy of both Athens and Sparta.

I was customarily met by a senior midshipman and chauffeur at the Dulles Airport and driven to Annapolis. I was most often the house guest of the dean of the academy, a civilian. We started with cocktails and dinner at the home of the superintendent, met for a working session next day, and left. Everything was tightly scheduled and well organized.

The dinner party with the superintendent and his wife was always interesting to me. Philippine servants moved about with well-trained silence and expertise. On the occasion of the first dinner in April of 1971, a servant brought me during the cocktail hour a miniature replica of the dinner table indicating where I was to sit. I had never seen this way of notification of seating arrangements before. I thought he was bringing me a strange arrangement of canapes. He noticed my confusion and with the utmost tact explained that what he had given to me was not to be eaten.

This reminded me of the time before we were married when Tine invited me to dine with her mother. They served artichokes, which I had never seen and surely had never eaten. Tine, suspecting I had never eaten artichoke, had conspired with her mother to wait me out to see how I would go about eating it. I ignored it, determined to wait to see how Sophie handled it. I waited her out, and when she finally set the example, I dipped the leaves in sauce and pulled them through my teeth like an accomplished artichoke eater. I always hated to lose face.

In 1974 I was granted a sabbatical semester to go to Oxford to do more reading and research in the field of English constitutional history. Through the efforts of Arthur Chitty, I exchanged houses, cars, and offices for the semester with Dennis Shaw, a professor of physics at Keble College. My experience was delightful. Shaw had a fine house with an adjoining orchard off Banbury Road. I had Professor Shaw's office and adjacent bed room as well as the services of his scout, who was forever bringing me tea. At the time we had an arrangement that permitted Sewanee students to attend Keble. There were five students from Sewanee in attendance for the semester I was there. Nearly all of them were football players at Sewanee who brought to Keble's rugby team new strength.

I never became adjusted to England's weather. Winters were mild enough, but the weather was fickle beyond belief. A single day might bring morning sun, succeeded by a cold wind and rain or sleet which might change in a few hours to frowning clouds. From March on, the promise of spring was in the air. Yet it was still only a promise in May when we left. We were still uncertain about the coming of summer.

Our English neighbors were friendly and helpful. The professors at Keble College were polite, uninterested, tolerant, and at times arrogant. Though I taught no students at Oxford, I met them occasionally at dinner. I had the privilege of dining at the High Table.

I used it only a few times. Always we assembled to have the pre-prandial preparation. The scotch was the best malt liquor Scotland afforded and strong. Some diners were "in their cups" before dinner. We were always formally dressed. The warden would lead us in like a line of nobles past the low tables where the students were served typical boarding-school fare. The High Table provided the best—five courses and both red and white wine. After dinner we repaired to the dessert room, assembling around a lovely table where port and Madeira circulated according to tradition, and the snuff box was sent on its way around the table. Afterwards those who could still navigate returned to the room where we had first assembled for more scotch and somewhat uneven conversation.

At one dinner I met a starchy dean who wanted to talk about "the last war." He engaged me in conversation and started off by saying, "Your man Patton was a real scoundrel and a poor general officer, wasn't he?" "No," I said, "he was a fast-moving, hard-hitting warrior with the same views about war as Stonewall Jackson. It was your man Montgomery who was the laggard in war." We went on from there. It ended by the old gentleman inviting me to have tea with him the coming week. I found the English to be like that. That is, they respected a sharp reply but would hound you if you appeared weak.

I had expected university lectures to be interesting. I found that most lecturers read their lectures in a monotone to slim audiences. The real work of education went on in the tutorials where students had to take responsibility for their own progress—a system that produced real scholars.

There is, I believe, no other place in the world where so much scholarly talent lives in close proximity to such a gloriously impressive landscape. It is an unforgettable sight to see from the rail cars returning from London to Oxford, that academic skyline with its spires and towers silhouetted against a pale sky. Nowhere are gardens and grounds so beautiful or flowers so well tended.

Class division is still to be seen in England. It appears in speech, manners, and behavior. England's elite class, though, has been open-ended. It could absorb ambitious, upward-pushing talent. This is what, I think, accounts for its long and, on the whole, productive life. An example of class consciousness appears in a little episode with our cleaning woman who came to us twice a week. I asked about her family. It appeared she had a son who worked at a bakery from which

I often bought cookies. I told her I would ask for him the next time I went to the shop. She suggested that he might be embarrassed if I asked for him by name. I did ask for him. He was a pink-faced lad, thoroughly embarrassed by being asked for and having to converse with a frightful American Ph.D.

Everywhere I have been, dress is important. In Iraq dress served to give notice of both tribe and ancestry. For instance, the Kurds wore fringed turbans that set them apart from Iraqi. I have always thought that dress and manner is an outward sign of an inner security or lack of it. When I was in London, I dressed for the city. When I went to Westminster Abbey, I was wearing a black overcoat and a homberg. Immediately one of the clerical attendants came to escort me and to ask what I wished to see. He asked me whether I was a senator. He seemed disappointed when I told him I was not but brightened perceptibly when I told him I was the dean of the University of the South, resident in Oxford. It is a shame that the revolution of the sixties made sloppiness of dress fashionable. It bespoke an inner sloppiness of spirit.

The highlight of my short semester in Oxford was Christ's Church's Easter service with the incomparable boys choir. I became at least for a time a better person for having heard them.

While we were in England we took a trip to Greece and some of the isles. We went with an English tour by air and bus. One place I had never visited was Epidaurus where the amphitheater is so well preserved. It is said of it that a whisper from the center stage can be heard on the highest and most distant seats. We decided to try it out. I was left at center stage to do the whispering. Instead, I was suddenly moved to recite the twelfth chapter of Ecclesiastes which begins with the famous line, "Remember now thy creator in the days of thy youth." I gave the chapter in my best manner and voice. All talk among the tourists ceased, Turk and Christian alike bowed their heads at these words from Holy Script. Tine was a little put out with me for showing off, but it was not that; a spirit moved me to speak.

On our return we flew into Gatwick. There the only transportation was by bus to London and by train to Oxford. It was far into the night when we arrived. A day before I had been striken by influenza. By plane time I was running a high fever; by the time we arrived in Oxford, I was quite weak. We had a long wait and a difficult time finding a cab, and when finally we reached home, I was reduced to going up the steps to my bedroom on all fours. For some days I was very ill. Tine called a doctor, who was kind and skillful. We tried to pay him for his visits, but he would accept no money. Even the drugs from the chemist were inexpensive. There is something to be said for socialized medicine.

Perhaps I was still weakened by this experience when we visited London for a few days and I had my purse stolen by a gang of pickpockets. We got on the underground at a station in the suburbs above ground. Tine entered the car and was seated. As I entered, I was accosted by one man who blocked my way asking directions, another seemed to be having a fit on the floor by me. The third expertly cut the bottom of the back pocket of my trousers and removed my wallet. All of this took place in the blink of an eye and as the car was about to leave. They all three made their escape as the doors were closing. Almost immediately I knew what had happened and reported it at the next station. I lost about sixty dollars in cash and all my credit cards. I immediately notified the credit card companies and the police. My Diner's Club Card was used once at a hotel in Stratford. My loss was limited to the cash and fifty dollars, a relatively light loss.

This encounter left me angry and shaken. I had been accosted, taken in, my purse stolen, my sense of self-sufficiency shattered, and I had not lifted a fist. At the time I was suffering from prostate difficulty. All of it together was almost too much. I was sitting in a chair in the hotel lobby waiting for bags before leaving, and suddenly I lost touch with reality. I did not know where I was or who I was with. Tine sensed my difficulty and got me on the train. Before we reached Oxford I was myself again and able to handle our baggage. Stress was telling me something. Soon thereafter we left Oxford for home, and I was glad to be on my way to Sewanee.

A few years passed uneventfully. My grandchildren grew. My daughters gave me pleasure. In the summers we went to the Rappahannock Cottage on the bay at Downing, where we fished and crabbed and enjoyed ourselves every summer. I bought the cottage soon after we returned in the summer of 1970 from a visit to Russia. It was situated on a high bank with a pier leading out into the water just across from Sharps Point but on the same side of the river. The opposite bank was about three miles across. I have never gone out for fish there without catching something—Norfolk spots, sea trout, croaker, stripes, or even something bigger.

Once I went out after a storm. The bay was like a mirror. I was fishing alone near the bank when I saw a great sea serpent or something in the water easily twenty feet long and swimming with a sinuous motion. To this day I know not what it was. I did not talk about it because such talk always seems suspect. I have thought it could have been two giant rays swimming in tandem. I don't know. There is a monster known as Chessie that haunts the Chesapeake Bay whom fisherman see, it is said, from time to time. The Bay has its memories and its stories like Loch Ness in Scotland.

In 1970 Tine and I joined a tour to Russia. We flew to Copenhagen and from there to Moscow. The people we found ourselves with were on the whole uninteresting, a strange and motley crew. One was an alcoholic who in his cups sometimes made advances to women and was accused of striking the mature daughter of a Jewish couple. Two or three of the travelers were Georgians from Russia returning to the homeland. Others were simply curious about Russia. The trip opened inauspiciously for me. Upon debarking from the plane, I saw in the airport a short distance away some men clothed in Mongolian clothes. I went closer to look at them. This drew the attention of a guard who in no friendly fashion headed me back to my group. This was typical of the treatment of our party during the trip. Intourist handled our going out and our coming in by bus or otherwise. One of our guides, an attractive blond who seemed friendly, was asked too many embarrassing questions by a persistent and untactful Puerto Rican school teacher of our group. Her replies were evidently too frankly spoken, for she was replaced the next day by a sour-faced older woman.

Once at lunch I left a little hand bag with my camera and hat on the stage for the orchestra which was near our table. The hat had been given me by Bishop Juhan, a $100 hat given him by the Winchester Hat Corporation. During the meal I noticed that my hat and bag had disappeared. I called the head waiter, and he in turn called his superior who told me that I should have checked my belongings and ended by making the point that "Russians don't steal."

"Oh," I said, "it is well known that Russians don't steal. All Americans know that. Some damn tourist has taken my camera!"

He sensed my irony, but what could he say when I agreed with him? The episode ended with his taking me to a closet where there were several dusty hats. Mine was not among them. One was a cap that looked like the one Stalin often wore.

Leningrad was an entirely different city. It had an Italian air and with its canals reminded me of Venice. The people seemed less somber and suspicious and the food was better. The glory of St. Petersburg is the Winter Palace, now the Hermitage Museum. It contains priceless treasures not only from Russia but from all the world. One could spend endless days there. Unfortunately, our time was limited. We did see the Summer Palace, with its fountains and the bed of Peter the Great— a bed long enough to accommodate his frame, Spartan-like in its simplicity. His long boots were still by the bed.

Our departure from Moscow was disconcerting. Somehow our ticket had been written in such a way as to preclude the payment to Russian Intourist of the Russian leg of the trip. When our group went to board the plane to Prague, we were not permitted to board and were told we would be on a flight to East Berlin. No way! Our travel director, a harried young man who knew his job, called the American embassy. After some hours of delay he was told the matter was straightened out. Still we were not permitted to board. The plane had been waiting four hours and our group was beginning to grumble. Finally I went to the desk and spoke to the flight officer.

"This matter has been settled between the American embassy and Intourist. I know you have been informed. If you don't put us aboard I will call my senator from Tennessee and there will be an international affair. You will be blamed by your government. You had better damn quick put us aboard."

The bluff worked. Within minutes we were aboard and on our way.

Unfortunately our alcoholic friend was by now drunk. He had to be poured on the plane, sputtering and cursing. The group appointed me his overseer. At Prague I almost had to carry him through customs. By this time I was worn out with him. As usual, when sober he was a pleasant man.

This chore was bad enough, but unfortunately when we reached Berlin the next day or so by bus, one of our impossible older members on the tour had refused to heed warnings and had eaten her fill of cherries bought at a roadside stand. She got deathly sick on the bus and was unable to control her bowels. Soon she was sobbing, smelling like a sewer, begging the driver to stop at a rest room. He like a stubborn German refused, saying there was no stop scheduled. I demanded that he stop and threatened suit against his company. He did soon stop, and it was my job, no one else being willing, to lead the poor woman to the lavatory. She left the trip in Berlin, for we did not see her any more. We had a quick trip to Warsaw and thence to West Germany and home.

Chapter Ten

Lectureship in Iraq

In the summer of 1954 I applied for and was granted a Fulbright lectureship to Iraq. Ulysse was just graduated from college; Rachel was a young girl of twelve; Tine was as always anxious to go. It seemed a good time to go adventuring. We sailed from New York on the *Cristoforo Columbo* for Naples, where we were to make connections with the *Enotria*, another Italian liner, for Alexandria. Tine and I shipped out cabin class, and the children went tourist, though this did not prevent them from sneaking up on occasion to visit the deck above.

The ship was crowded with Italians, some of whom were returning to Italy for the first time to show their kinsmen how they had prospered in America. We had never been on a ship of this class before. The food was good, the company exciting, the stateroom snug. One could escape from it all into the compartment when people and the sea became oppressive. The usual kind of entertainment prevailed: bars, food, dancing, movies, games, people. The sea does things to people aboard ship. The new environment, the sea, the motion of the ship have their impact. Some became seasick, others amorous, still others retreated into a kind of self-imposed isolation. I enjoyed it all. It was new. People are interesting.

Unfortunately the sea was rough for a part of the trip, and Rachel became deathly sick from the sea. I have never seen a child so sick.

Since I have never been seasick, it was hard for me to understand the depth of her misery. Ulysse comforted her, and after a time she began to revive. My own spirits revived with hers.

In due time we reached Naples, a ragged city on the most magnificent bay I have seen. Since I had the baggage of four people to look after and since I am by nature a villager and a little confused by the responsibility of travel, I have little memory of our arrival other than the chores of shepherding my flock, bag and baggage, to a hotel.

A marine friend of ours, Eph Kirby-Smith, and his family were stationed in Naples at the time. They were magnificently hospitable. Eph was a colonel in the marines and a big outgoing soldier usually followed about by children of the street who pursued him for his generosity, his size, and his way with children. We did the usual sight-seeing in Naples. One evening we were taken by the Kirby-Smiths to the officers' club. Eph was grand to Rachel and even had her dancing.

After a short stay in Naples we boarded the *Enotria* for Alexandria. This ship was small, cozy, and comfortable. The children could roam from one end of the ship to the other. Rachel was greatly taken by the fine horses that were being carried to Egypt. Every morning before breakfast I could find her with the horses.

Alexandria was a lovely city. We swam on a secluded beach, visited the museums, took a tour through King Farouk's palace, and enjoyed the difference. From Alexandria we went by train to Cairo to visit the Pyramids and see the sights. We were housed in a small hotel during an earthquake that set the building rocking. It was early morning. I had just shaved and was in the process of dressing. Tine, sensing the movement, called out to me, "Red, quit taking those exercises. The building is rocking!" The children, who had an adjoining room, were soon excitedly rushing in to tell us of the quake. We were all much amused at my starting an earthquake. Soon we were off to the Pyramids. I have seen three sights that left me speechless: one is the Acropolis at Athens, another the cathedral at Cologne, the third the Pyramids of Cairo. It seemed to me impossible that men could have put together such monuments to skill, sweat, human pride, and authority. Naturally we had to ride the camels. We all got aboard. One of our guides slipped a small, plastic green beetle into the hand of my wife and said, "I give you something green. Now give me something green." He got no green but perhaps a tinkle of silver.

Of all the sights to be seen in Cairo there is nothing like the great museum of antiquities. I had read of the glory and sophistication of Egyptian culture. They were only words. To see the treasures from the tomb of King Tutankahmen is enough to impress the mind with the significance of an ancient civilization. Better than a thousand words they told the story of organization and power, of priestly conservatism, of a kind of bee-hive human achievement that is still enigmatic and mysterious to any westerner.

In Cairo I left my passport in the hotel. Woe and damnation! It was sent for but I never expected to see it in time to take ship to Beirut. I fully expected our entire timetable to be disrupted beyond repair and well it might have been. The loss of a passport in Egypt is no small affair. It did arrive in time for me to clear for the ship, but again on ship it was misplaced. Tine was aboard, Ulysse and Rachel were aboard. There was I held up at the very gangplank by some mistake. Rachel was about to return to join me. Tine and Ulysse were waving a fond farewell when at last a truculent official waved me aboard. The precious document had been found.

The trip to Beirut was uneventful and short. In Beirut we were quartered for the first time in a plush first-class hotel. The food was good. The pool-side scenery magnificent. My females looked like poor fish compared to those bikini-clad females of the fleshpots of the Orient. It was our first sight of the bathing attire that was soon to become commonplace and render commonplace the female form. It is a fine attire for the beach walkers, but not so hot for the flat-chested girl, who dives quickly into the pool. The rich Arabs were having a field day at the watering places of Beirut. Later when I got to see what they were used to, I understood it. Though I must say that an Arab woman, veiled and mysterious as a dark night, has a freedom and charm of her own.

From Beirut we went by motor car furnished by our travel agent to the great Roman ruins at Baalbec. They are perhaps the best preserved ruins in the world. Here on the very outskirts of the Roman world were raised majestic and awe-inspiring temples to the Roman gods. Perhaps they were raised for the very purpose of striking with awe the barbarian on the frontier. Some of the temples are very well preserved; others are in various states of ruin; but altogether there is nothing in Rome itself that is so perfectly preserved from the ravages of man and time. The Temple of Zeus is almost perfectly preserved. In all we see the same egg design for adornment. Some of the columns were undoubtedly brought from Egypt and rolled many miles across the desert. One can see the quarry whence the massive stone blocks were cut. There is in the quarry a block so large that it defied the skill and power of the engineers to move it. It rests there today as if defying the power of man and the gods.

Along the coast are ruins of many famous castles that date back to the crusades. Others are testimonials to the enterprise and the seamanship of the Phoenicians. Not far away is the desert city of Palmyra from which the dusky Zenobia fled so many years ago. Unfortunately we did not make the tour to this city of an unfortunate but brave queen.

From Beirut we went overland by car to Damascus. The journey took us through several oasis villages that even then showed little sign of progress or change. The whole area seemed sleepy—restlessly and fitfully, as though disturbed by ugly dreams. So many battles, so much movement, so much blood spilling over the centuries, so much wasted energy seemed to have induced a somnolence above and beyond that induced by the sun and the wind.

Damascus! The oldest city in the world was in 1954 much as it had been through the ages. Time had passed her by in many ways since the Apostle Paul saw his Lord on the road. The cloth merchants still gave short measure; the food merchants still haggled with the buyers; for all I knew the girls were still as wantonly secretive and wise as when Abu Nawas went about in disguise with his friend Haroun, the Commander of the Faithful. This was our first taste of a city of the East, and it charmed our palates for more. Here we first saw the strange mixture of the very new and the very old that in 1954 seemed characteristic of so many Arab cities. Here we first encountered the suqs and bazaars. Wherever I went I never ceased to be captured by the life of these markets. They seemed to represent all that is most characteristic of mankind: greed, curiosity, organizational skill, ingenuity, expectancy, and comfort in close association. We loitered, bought only a little, ingested the sights, smells, and human flavor of an oriental market. We visited the street called Straight, saw the house from which the Apostle was lowered in a basket.

We had not long in this city, for here we were to start our journey across the desert by Nairn bus to our destination, Baghdad. At this time the only way one could travel from Damascus to Baghdad, short of air travel or by car, was by bus. For many years the Nairn brothers had run a bus line between the two cities. The bus we boarded was a dusty Mercedes-Benz. The road it was to travel was a winding trail across the sand. The journey took all night and a part of the next day. The air conditioning did little to cool the interior of this mechanical camel. Our companions were a motley mix: the poor desert dweller, the business-man intent upon a deal in Baghdad, a few hardy tourists, and four adventurous Americans.

About two in the morning a rest stop was made at a mangy village. The Turkish-type johns were steaming with misdirected excrement and redolent with the odor that is as old as man. Much better to have walked away a few yards and squatted in the desert like a native. We did not know this then. A Turkish toilet is a hole above a receptacle adorned on either side by foot places of metal splashed by the excreta of many hurried or careless users. We were scarcely impressed by the toilet facilities of this stop in the night. If this was typical of the harshness of life in Baghdad we were in for a shock.

We arrived in Baghdad one day in the month of September. There is no way to describe the heat of a September day in Baghdad. It smites you in the face. It strikes you on the head. It dries instantly the poor sweat that gathers upon your temples. On such a day we arrived at the Nairn bus station in the city of the Commander of the Faithful. We were met by an official of the Fulbright Commission and immediately hurried by taxi to our quarters, a house of two apartments on a side street a short distance from the American embassy. The fan was going; the house was comparatively cool. It consisted of a living room, a dining room, two bedrooms on the first floor and a bedroom above. The kitchen adjoined a garden and a slender courtyard. The house was furnished with rough but practical furniture such as one might expect in a third-rate American apartment. There was a refrigerator. There was Koshaba, our house boy, to meet us, all smiles, all excited, all-willing. Suddenly, in spite of the tiresome journey, in spite of the heat and the dust, our spirits rose. Here we were some thousands of miles from home in a strange place not like anything we had ever experienced. Life was to be lived.

In the next few days we were initiated into the facts of life in Iraq both by the commissioner and by the American colony. We were told what to expect and what not to do and how not to do it. We were introduced to the city. Baghdad was then a down-at-the-heels Arab city stretching nine miles along the Tigris River. It was filled with clamoring Arabs, mangy dogs, rich sheiks, and poor citizens. Camels and cars moved about the streets. Dusty flowers bravely fought the heat in well-designed parks. Everywhere there was the dust and the mauve buildings and the harsh noise of the Arab language. Here a butcher flayed a sheep and cast the offal in the ditch. Here a peddler of sour milk sold his fly-infested ware. Here a peddler with a pot made from an oil barrel dispensed his boiled turnips. Here a hairless dog moaned for someone to put him out of his misery. Here a soft touch of the hand of a beggar boy startled the stranger. We were strangers in a strange place. We were overpowered by the poverty, the carelessness, the dirt, the diseased and disfigured faces, the costumes, the impersonality of it all. It takes some time for an American to adjust to the harsh life, the vital differences between his and the Arab's cultures.

The Fulbright officials, members of the embassy staff, USIS people, and the entire American colony were very helpful in getting us settled. My teaching duties were at the College of Arts and Sciences, an institution belonging to but separate from the university. Actually the government, fearing the political consequences of concentrating students at a single place, had scattered the colleges. In the light of what later happened during the revolution, it appears to have been a wise move.

I taught only three classes. I had nine students in political theory, twenty or so in each of two sections of American government. Only a few of my students spoke and understood English. I knew no Arabic. Consequently my first few classes were a bedlam. When I lectured a great babble accompanied my efforts. It took me some time to adjust to the fact that those who understood were translating in stage whispers for their companions who had no idea of what I was saying. In a short time I learned to proceed sentence by sentence very slowly and wait for the inevitable explanation. This is difficult for a lecturer unless he prepares very carefully a written text. I tried using one of the English speaking students as an interpreter. It did not work. He became confused, which merely added to the confusion of the class. Eventually I became accustomed to a very slow, very elementary delivery.

My classes were made up of both young men and young women. Those students who attended the college were usually from privileged families. The girls had been carefully reared and virtually secluded from the company of all except members of the extended family and companions of the same sex. It was amusing and interesting to me to see them upon reaching the compound shed the black abbiah which covered them from head to foot and emerge like young butterflies in blouses and skirts like so many American bobby-soxers.

With my students at the College of Arts and Sciences in Bagdad

All of my students were very shy, especially the girls. They were diligent workers, however, and always friendly and even merry. I once spoke sternly to a girl, the daughter of a general in the Iraqi army, who was prone to carry on whispered conversation with a girl friend. She was so shocked by my severity that she ran weeping from the class. For a day or two she would come to class and sit with her hands over her face. She spoke English fluently so I asked her to remain a moment after class. I very gently inquired about her behavior and told her of my own difficulties with the language barrier. She forgave me immediately and freely and became an apt student. Later at a little supper that my class gave for me, she read a poem she had written which began with the line "Doctor Robert is like a red, red rose." All of my students, with the exception of two or three truculent revolutionaries, were kind, gentle, and warm in their relations with me. Time and again they would bring some sweetmeat that they had purchased on the street and, placing their hand over my eyes, say, "Open your mouth." Whereupon they would pop into my mouth some delicacy which sent me on sulphur pills for a week.

Iraq had once been an English dependency. Even when I was there, the English influence in the schools and in the country was dominant. The attitude toward the English was complex and baffling. While they seemed to think that everything English was superior, at the same time they despised themselves for thinking so and spoke bitterly of English hegemony. All Americans were rich, and I was undoubtedly the cousin of Burt Lancaster whom they had seen in the movies. Their ideas about America had been shaped by the cinema, which they attended in great numbers. We do not appear to best advantage from the movie image. I spent much time in trying to tell them what America was really like. Inevitably they always asked the question, "Would you allow your daughter to marry an Iraqi?" I always replied that my daughter was too young to marry, and that I thought husband and wife got along better when they came from the same cultural background. This was not the answer they wanted, but it sufficed.

The faculty at the college was a strange conglomeration. There were the English emigres who could make a much better salary in Iraq than at home. Some of them were capable, learned, and efficient. Others were the scum of the English teaching class, arrogant without cause, tending toward homosexuality, low-class people trying to ape their betters. There were Egyptians, Turks, and of course the Iraqi contingent who were perhaps better educated than any of the rest. Many of them spoke five languages and had had the advantage of university training in the best European and American universities. Many of them had been educated for a time at the American University at Beirut, whose influence for good in the Middle East was then unparalleled. I have often thought that had the United States spent as much money in establishing in the Middle East a great university as they spent improvidently upon misdirected aid, we should have built up such a fund of good will in the area among the decision-makers as to render the area impervious to Russian influence.

Some of the Iraqi professors whom I got to know led most unusual lives. One erudite and charming professor of geography came from a village near Basra. There he was chief, and there he had three wives. In Baghdad he was accompanied by a single wife. Here he appeared as a typical European in clothing, culture, and apparent interest. There he dressed in the native dress, smoked his hubblebubble, and directed the tillage of his land as did any other sheik. He reserved his greatest respect for the Bedui, the desert dwelling people of the black tent. They were the real representatives of Arab virtue. I found this to be a common view among both Arab intellectuals and even businessmen. The city incorporated no virtue. Tradition and religious conformity were kept in the purest state among the wanderers.

These black-tent people I at last came to know as well as any stranger residing in a new land for a short time can come to know people. It came about in an interesting way. I am a hunter. I love the fields and the forests and the birds and beasts who inhabit them, love to eat them on occasion too. I attended one day soon after my arrival in Baghdad an exhibition of athletic skill. We had brought William Anderson, the strong man from the recent Olympic games, to Baghdad on a good-will tour. He was showing Iraqi youths how to lift weights, though any burden-bearing Kurd from Raschid Street might have taught him something. Here I met a German wanderer who was presently teaching wrestling in a high school. He was a hunter and a mighty man who had escaped imprisonment in China and made his way afoot across the Hindu Kush. He invited me to go hunting for the big pigeons that live among the tall trees of the date groves.

The next morning I went by bus and by foot to his lodging, a rickety affair with sleeping bags for beds and barrels for chairs. We went on foot with our guns to the date groves and villages on the outskirts of the city. We found *taban*, the pigeon, in great numbers, but they were high flying and wary. We killed a few. About mid-afternoon we came to a village where we were greeted by the usual flock of village boys and mangy dogs. The boys swarmed all over me. I believe they would have taken my gun had not my friend Fritz called out to me to beat them off. This I did with a vengeance until they were satisfied that I was no easy meat. The boys told us of a field nearby where there were *darragh*, a fine bird about the size of a ruffed grouse. I killed one on the wing to the delight of the village boys. This led me into darragh hunting. My companion and I were eventually brought to the hut of the head man. He entertained us with the usual sour milk and cucumbers. The trip was pleasant and different, and I resolved to find out more about hunting in Iraq. I had secreted in my luggage a dismantled shotgun, which was not detected by customs agents. Shells I knew I could acquire at the embassy if nowhere else.

Each morning I walked from my house to the bus line a couple of hundred yards away. I took a bus for about six miles through the struggling city to the college. I finished my work by early afternoon. Usually I stopped at Raschid Street to mingle with the crowd and savor the street life of this principal thoroughfare. One afternoon I came upon a shop with guns displayed in the window. I went in and made the acquaintance of the proprietor, a young man of mingled antecedents by the name of Halkias, who sold everything from guns to refrigerating equipment. I observed that each time I visited I found sheiks from the villages. They talked and smoked as reticent as sober cowboys. They even rolled their own cigarettes. For a time they took no notice of me. After a few visits, however, Halkias told me that they had inquired about the redheaded foreigner. Since Halkias was probably selling guns to the tribes, they well may have been suspicious. He assured them that I was only an American professor interested in people and guns. Finally one of them conveyed through Halkias an invitation to visit his village. Arabs are both prideful and curious about foreigners, but if they accept you they do it sincerely and, according to their customs, will protect you with their lives if you happen to be their guest. I eagerly accepted an invitation to come with Halkias, who had a Land Rover, to hunt with the sheik and his brothers the following weekend.

Early one Friday morning Halkias came with his friend Leon, an Armenian giant who hunted with Feisal the king. We proceeded down the Tigris past the melancholy remains of Ctesiphon, that once splendid Sassanian city, to a village near the river. Here we were met by the sheik and his party, consisting principally of his brothers and some boys who were to carry the game. We began to hunt in a barley field near a date garden. In one patch of barley stubble we must have flushed twenty fine birds. The darragh is a fast-flying, gamey bird with fine white meat. The male bird sports a splendid black breast. I shot well. By forenoon Halkias, Leon, and I had killed forty or more of the fine birds. We stopped for lunch near a canal. The sheik spread his carpets and we feasted on lamb and saffron rice, the entire dish known as *cousi*, along with canned meat and some lovely sweet oranges which Leon had thoughtfully brought along. The morning and the scene were completely satisfying. The regular sound of the irrigation pumps, the distant sounds of village life, and the cooing of doves in the date trees carried far on the still air. In the distance on the opposite bank of the river a shepherd tended his flock of sheep and goats. This hunt was but the prelude to many excursions in which I had the opportunity at times of observing the life of the Bedouin, or *bedawi*, the desert dweller.

The Fulbright Commission was dedicated to making the stay of the grantees rewarding to both the visitor and the host country. In the first few weeks of our arrival they took us on several trips to see the nearby sights of interest. Early in our stay we went to Babylon, once the center of the earth, now the crumbling but still impressive ruins of ancient grandeur. Here the captive Hebrews wailed for their lost heritage. Here Alexander, the mighty conqueror, died his painful death. Here was a wonder of the world, the famous hanging gardens. Here was promulgated a famous code of laws. Now all was dusty death. There still remained about the place evidences of the rich carvings. Traces of streets spoke of former life. Much had been removed to Berlin by German archaeologists. What was left was enough to stimulate the imagination, enough to remind that change and dissolution alone are permanent. We took the usual pictures, made the usual banal remarks, but remembered.

About this time we made the acquaintance of Tewfiq Wahabbi, the Kurdish poet and scholar, once the minister of education in Iraq. He was a heroic figure among his people, and his house and garden were usually filled with visitors from his Kurdish tribesmen. It must have been trying for him and his family to have perpetually about him his unlettered folk. Nevertheless his hospitality was unfailing. He had been a member of the Company of Young Turks, for he had been sent to Istanbul at an early age to be educated for the army. He was a lieutenant in the company of which Kemal Pasha had been captain. His son, Seroush, took a liking to us and was often in our house. He longed to put in musical score the songs of his people. Later I secured his entrance into Sewanee. He remained only a few months, for he longed for his familiar surroundings.

One day Seroush came to invite Tine, Rachel, and me to go on a trip with him to his homeland in the mountainous Kurdish country. His father had permitted him to make the invitation and to use his Dodge sedan. It was an opportunity that we could not miss. I only wished that

Ulysse might have been with us, but she had not been happy in Iraq and had been allowed to return home to look for a job, which she could not find in Baghdad. We set out on our journey early one morning. I carried my shotgun, Seroush his revolver. We proceeded north by the road that for a distance beyond Ba'quba was paved. Soon, when we reached the desert, which begins where the water fails, the highway ends. Here were only the traces of a road in the sand. We were apprehensive, but Seroush assured us he knew the way across the desert to Erbil. Only occasionally we passed evidences of habitation. By early afternoon we came to Erbil, a most ancient city that sits high on its own debris, the accumulation of thousands of years. It rests on a great mound as if it had raised itself by its own bootstraps. Seroush would not permit us to so much as visit the city. His father had told him that tuberculosis was endemic there, and that we should in no case enter Erbil. Thus we missed the chance of visiting a city that some think to be the oldest site of continuous human habitation.

By mid-afternoon we came to a road and our faith in Seroush revived. Now and again we passed travelers, his own people. Each man rode a donkey. Each man had around his shoulder a belt of cartridges and on it a rifle.

"These are my people," Seroush said. "You see they always go armed."

Once he stopped to inquire directions from a fellow traveler. He was secure in his knowledge that every Kurd, however ignorant of some things, had heard the name Tewfiq Wahabbi. We reached the outskirts of Mosul and spent the night in a very clean and hospitable hotel run by the railway company. We spent little time in Mosul but instead visited briefly some archaeological remains and headed for Sulaimaniya in the mountains. Once we stopped to permit me to try a shot at a flock of *chuckka* that fled across the road. They were too fast for me.

Again we stopped to admire the sudden greenery of the mountains, much appreciated after so much heat and sand. Each went about natural calls that must be made from time to time. Rachel disappeared down the road a way. When Seroush returned he was dismayed that we had let her out of sight. He drew his revolver and went dashing off to find her. To his relief, she appeared around a bend in the road.

"Never, never," he said, "let her from your sight. We are in hostile country. Any fortunate tribesman might seize her and you would never see her again."

We understood then the extreme care he had taken with us and began to understand that we were in a different country.

The mountains of Iraq are like no mountains I have ever seen. The pressure of man and climate have denuded them of trees of any size. Instead of forestclad they are covered with low-growing shrubs or scrubby timber or are entirely bare of all covering. Here and there where the water flows in the valleys there are delightful villages inhabited by a tough, warrior-like people of independent minds and stout hearts. They have provided many great fighters for themselves and others. It may be remembered that Salah-al-Din himself, the opponent of Richard the Lion Hearted, was a Kurd. Even now, though divided and dispersed in four countries, they long for a state of their own and from time to time rise in bloody rebellion against their Iraqi oppressors.

We stopped at one such village. Its headman was an old friend of Seroush's father. The old man, spare and sour faced among his wives, greeted us with dignity and forbearance. He rolled cigarettes, placed them in a bowl of a long-stemmed pipe, and smoked away. We soon left the old man to resume our meanderings through these cool high places so unlike the land between the two rivers.

On our return journey we passed by the Assyrian villages in the hill country. These tribesmen are all that is left of the once mighty people who built the civilization and the great cities that now lie crumbling into dust. Their villages are fortified places because these people hold themselves apart and are ever ready to defend themselves. They have had to in the past, and they are all that is left, a dispirited, beleaguered people cast like foam on the high water of Muslim and Arab supremacy. Incidentally, Koshaba, our houseboy, was an Assyrian.

Our trip home was uneventful. We were content, though, to rest in the privacy of our own vine and fig tree. Home away from home is still home. Even the fox likes his hole in the ground.

Soon after our return I began to hunt in earnest. I lectured four days a week and hunted three. At times we hunted ducks and geese on the Tigris. Halkias, with whom I often went, knew an old Arab who owned a decrepit river craft powered by an inboard engine that he with much ingenuity kept going. We would rise long before day to make our way to the river near the great mosque at Acadamain. Even though we were early risers, the village women were up before us. Many a time we encountered them trotting with regular steps toward the market. Each woman had at least one and sometimes two trays of brass balanced on her head. On the tray was a jar of milk. Imagine the balance required to carry two trays and two jars, one above the other on the head, and carry it with never a drop spilled for three miles to market. I was told that the trays were balanced by pebbles. Maybe so, but imagine, if you can, the cadence of that movement of the legs from the hips with never a movement above.

We would put in the river before day. Always the mist like a grey pall shrouded the river. With the rising of the sun the mist would clear. The trick was to maneuver into or near a flock of ducks in the mist and shoot as the sun partially cleared away the fog. Sometimes it worked. Sometimes it did not. Another ploy was to run near the bank and suddenly shoot around the bend within range of a flock. Often we returned with twenty or thirty ducks or geese. The river Tigris is swift and at places shallow. Occasionally we would have to go overboard to pull the boat through the shallows.

Always the scenery was interesting—here a magnificent date garden, there an open field. Now and then shepherds with their black and white flocks came to the river to drink. Looking backward one could behold in the swirling mist the great golden domes of the famous mosque so revered by the Shiah sect of the Muslim people. Always and ever the irrigation pumps chugged as they brought water and life to the thirsty fields.

After several hours on the river we were ready for the Rover that met us some twenty or thirty miles downriver and brought us back to Baghdad.

Nowhere is the relationship between man and beast or fowl so intimate and natural as in the Arab world. I have seen men followed by geese leave the flock on the street to have their tea. The birds would wait or disport themselves in the canal until their leader returned. Then with a cluck and a wagging of tail feathers they would take up their places behind him and journey on. Sheep and goats look to the shepherd for advice as to the best grazing, and they run to him for protection when a stranger approaches. Young camels and young children grow up together. A colt is a member, a privileged member, of the family and lives in the tent. Only the dogs lead hard lives, neglected, abused, diseased, and dangerous as a pack of village boys.

The barley fields are an open invitation to the wild hogs. They do a lot of damage to crops and fields. Farmers are ever willing to put up with hunters who will deliver them from these pests. On occasion we hunted the wild hogs. Once we killed twelve of these dangerous, gamey pigs in a single morning. If we could get them transported to the Christian quarters of Baghdad, each pig would bring fifteen or twenty dollars. The Muslim detests pigs. It is even hard to persuade Muslim boys to pull the rope that would drag them to the Land Rover. The meat is firm and well flavored, better even than venison; much better than the mutton of the fat-tailed sheep that we were too often served.

On one hunt we jumped a number of hogs led by a great boar that must have weighed all of five hundred pounds. We all shot at the fast-moving pigs and wounded the big boar and a sow. There were in this area a group of Kurds with dogs. Their big black dogs brought the boar to bay. When I got to the scene I saw a savage spectacle. Three dogs

A successful boar hunt near Ctesiphon. My companions, who were attached to the Iraq military mission, and I are surrounded by a shiek and his brothers.

with eyes closed and jaws set were wrestling with the powerful boar, who was screaming with rage and pain. The Kurds in a frenzy of excitement were dancing about as wild as the dogs. Some of them were beating at the tusks with sticks. They did not give way to me nor did I insist, but after the pig was killed they extracted the curved teeth, called off their vicious dogs and went their way like so many wild Indians.

On the same day I had my first close-up encounter with a wild boar. Colonel Powell, the American officer with whom I was hunting, ran out of ammunition for his big rifle and was hunting with a .22, a dangerous practice. He jumped a big boar and shot it with the small rifle. The boar, wounded and angry, headed down a path in the reeds towards me. I heard him coming. I was shooting a twelve gauge with ball. In an instant and before I could properly aim, he was upon me. I leaped backwards into the reeds by the path. He took one slash at me and roared on. I shot the pig five times at close range, aiming behind the shoulder, but he did not drop. As hunting etiquette demands, we trailed the pig for several hundred yards by the blood and pieces of bone he was shedding. Still we did not get him. Evidently he went to water and sank. I am convinced that wounded pigs are dangerous. Natives have known them to lie in wait for the opportunity for vengeance. I do believe, though, that a running pig will keep to the path. If the hunter can avoid him in the narrow passage, he will go his way.

One of the most interesting trips I took turned out to be a fiasco, so far as concerned the hunting, but an experience that few westerners ever had. I went in the midwinter, if winter it may be called, in the company of the minister of the interior and the counsellor of the embassy to visit a sheik of some importance who lived a few miles beyond Najaf, the sacred burial city. We were met by the sheik and two of his brothers at a chia house near a canal. After the usual amenities and several tiny cups of sweet tea, we embarked in an old Studebaker belonging to the man and made our way in the late evening to the banks of a larger canal that flowed near the sheik's village. Since I was in the company of important people, every amenity and courtesy was observed. Just before we reached the canal, two darragh flew across the dirt road and lit nearby. I got out my gun and proceeded to walk them up. I killed both birds, to the delight of the sheik, who had never seen flying birds killed. He appeared to be much impressed. I later learned my reward. At the canal we crossed in a boat covered with splendid carpets. On the other side we were surprised to see that we were to walk through a lane of tribesmen, every other man holding a Coleman lantern to light our way to the *diwan*, a communal building for entertainment, meetings of headsmen, and such purposes.

Our host took us immediately to his own house. It was a large structure fashioned of mud brick and roofed with a mattress of reeds. His living room was large and furnished with Western furniture, all arranged about the walls. There were no carpets on his floor. They were being used at the time for another purpose. Upon our arrival we were immediately provided with a choice of several whiskies and brandies. The Arab loves to ply his Western guests with liquor and watch their behavior with a superior air. He poured me a full water glass of scotch. I sipped it, and when he was not watching I discreetly poured most of it into a plant that decorated his room. As soon as he believed us to be mellow, he introduced an orchestra and three Saluba dancing girls.

The orchestra was composed of a piper who played a reed instrument similar to a shepherd's pipe, a reboba player who had mastered the one-string fiddle of the desert, and another musician who was alternately a drummer and a timbrelist. The musicians played their wailing music and the dancing girls danced. They were clad in a single black garment that reached from neck to ankles. Even the arms were covered to the wrists, but they danced with hands and bodies in a remarkably graceful and attractive fashion.

Arabs are not supposed to drink alcohol, but the richest and most powerful of them sometimes risk offending the holy law. The sheik's brother did. He became much annoyed by the attention one of the girls whom we had labeled Minnie Mouse was paying to the westerners. Suddenly he reached out an arm, seized the girl by her wrist, and twisted her to the floor. Immediately his brothers spoke to him in harsh Arabic, and he released the girl and left. The sheik was much humiliated by the action of his brother. After that evening we did not see the sheik's brother again.

After a spell of dancing and some more whiskey, his servants brought in tins of Western food: salmon, sardines, potted meats, caviar, all kinds of Western delicacies. I thought this was our evening meal and consequently ate more than I would have had I known what was coming. For in a short time he invited us to accompany him to the diwan. This particular diwan was very impressive. A great thatched roof was supported by massive columns of woven and plaited reeds. Each column was at least two feet in diameter. The walls were constructed of sheets of woven palm fronds. The whole area covered by the roof was the size of a large church.

We entered this impressive building to behold a sight that I will never forget. Arranged around the walls were his tribesmen, perhaps three hundred of them. Every tenth man held a lantern. The entire floor was covered by carpets and the carpets covered with every variety of Arab food. I was told that he had more than six hundred dishes on the carpets. In the midst of all this food were eight serving boys. Places were arranged for about fifty guests. Before each place was a roast lamb, pale-eyed and leering from a great pile of saffron rice and roasted bustard. Fifty lambs and fifty bustards!

As was the custom, the sheik served his guests with his own hands to start the banquet. He first served the minister and then, scooping out the eye of the sheep and a piece of brain attached, he extended it to me. I solemnly took it in my right hand and ate it. It tasted a bit like brains and eggs. This was a great honor to be served the eye and all. I had impressed the sheik with my marksmanship.

We ate of many dishes, drank bitter coffee in the tiny thimble-like cups. All the while the tribesmen stood like so many frozen men. We ate, and during our meal from time to time serving boys brought ewers of water and towels for our hands. Once we had eaten, the sheik's brother served him. The brothers ate. The headsmen ate. The women ate. The children ate. The dogs growled over the bones, and what was left went into the canal to feed the fishes. The marvelous thing about the whole banquet was that each person considered himself both host and guest. This was not the sheik's affair. It was the village's affair. All were hosts; all were guests. This was a tribal offering and celebration, and it was a very happy occasion.

After dinner everything else was anticlimax. We returned to the orchestra and to the dancing. I was weary and went to bed, but all night the orchestra played. Sleeping fitfully, I could hear from time to time the harsh, high-pitched voices of villagers at play. When I arose in the morning I found that my door had been guarded all night by a tribesman armed with a Lee-Enfield rifle. Such is the hospitality of Sheik Ibrahim of the Green Turban. I encountered him again on the streets of Baghdad. He recognized me and came in a sort of huffing pace to greet me with the fraternal kiss upon each cheek. Having received me as a brother, he and his tribe would have guarded me in case of need to the last gasp. Such are the Arabs of the desert.

With spring approaching Tine and I determined to make a trip by bus to Persia, modern-day Iran. We boarded the bus in Baghdad for the long thirty-six-hour trip to Teheran, the beautiful city at the foot of the Elburz mountains. We were the only Americans on the trip, though there were a New Zealand couple and a couple of Frenchmen. The rest of the company were Iranian pilgrims returning from trips to the great Shiah shrines at Kerbela and Najaf. They were a colorful group with their long blue garments and the Iranian kufiah. Several children were aboard. All were extremely shy and scarcely dared look at two foreigners from the West. The children took refuge beneath the skirts of their mothers and peeped out with shy but observant eyes. The first part of the trip was dusty and uneventful. The tenor of things changed after a rather remarkable incident.

As we were passing through a village, a young village boy ran across the road and was struck by the bus and sent rolling into the dust by the roadside. Along with the driver I went immediately to his aid. I felt of his body and concluded that he at least had the breath knocked out of him. As I rolled up his skirt-like covering, he opened his eyes. The sight of a redheaded foreign devil bending over him sent the adrenalin flowing. With a bound he sprang to his feet and raced away more frightened than hurt. When we returned to the bus the atmosphere had changed. The Iranians, much impressed with my desire to help a stricken youth, bowed at me and made little clucking sounds of appreciation. From then until our journey's end they accepted us as members of the company. When lunchtime came they shyly offered food which we dared not eat. We had brought boiled eggs, cans of juice and bread, for we knew by then the danger from native food.

After some hours of travel we came into Kurdish country and passed through several villages. We stopped for gas at one of them. It was April. Willow trees were beginning to green with the first touch of spring. The villages were drab, but the villagers were a sight to see. The men swarthy and masculine with their turbans with fringe falling around fine faces. The women more colorfully dressed than their Iraqui neighbors. Almost every woman wore a necklace of gold coins and bracelets of gold. It is the custom of these people to put their wealth into gold. The women wear it at all times. If disaster strikes or they have to make a run for it in their incessant feuds and fights with the Arabs, they can the more easily carry their wealth with them. They are a proud and admirable people, some of them as wild looking and as uncivilized as American Indians of the West a century ago.

The road to Teheran passes through high mountainous country. The way is very narrow and steep and at times very frightening. As we safely negotiated sharp turns with the blue sky too nearly beneath us, the Muslims would sing out in unison verses of the Koran. I decided to imitate them in their long drawn-out, high pitched wails. They were not offended. On the contrary, they seemed to be much pleased by my attempts, for I did it all with a very straight face. In the midst of these turns and twists of the road we came by the famous Bisitoon Rock, on which is carved in cuneiform and Aramaic the list of victories and the hymns of praise to a great Persian king. By concluding that both inscriptions contained the same language, scholars learned to read the ancient Babylonian script. The driver permitted me to get out and inspect this historic monument to the past and to the ingenuity of persistent scholars.

Of course there were no rest rooms for the convenience of travelers. At intervals the driver did stop to permit the calls of nature to be answered. Right welcome they were. The women moved to one side of the bus, the men to the other, and without self-consciousness and with grave decorum each relieved himself of nature's burden. I found this natural attitude, so devoid of prudery, very admirable and of course very necessary.

Around evening of the first day the bus stopped to admit aboard a remarkable man. Big he was with a great belly, a fierce black beard, and merry eyes. On his head he wore a red conical cap and about his ample body a black gown tied around where the waist might have been by a golden colored rope. He was a dervish and a Sufi, dedicated not to the black arts but to spreading the news of the joy of life. He seated himself across from Tine and me, looked us over carefully, and bowed and smiled. There sat behind us a poor woman with a worm of a baby that smelled to high heaven. The bus fairly reeked from the stink of this little bit of life that had been carried for many hours without diaper change. The Sufi could not endure this torment for long. Soon he drew from within his garment a vial of perfume. With slow care he anointed his beard, his hair and his wrists with this attar of roses. Then with an ingratiating bow he extended the vial to me.

I went carefully through the same ceremony. With a nod toward Tine he insisted that she partake of his blessing. She did. I handed the bottle back. With a bow he handed it to the woman with the smelly babe. She got the message. She anointed herself and at the very next stop cleaned her odorous offspring. The whole company of passengers were obligated to this spreader of happiness. At length he began to sing in the high-pitched, wailing notes of sons of the desert. He got off after a time at a small village. As he left he bowed deeply and then smiled his sunlit smile. We were sorry to see him go.

We traveled all night, sleeping or dozing as we could, and when morning came we found ourselves nearing a great mountain. At the foot of it lay the city of Teheran, and by nine o'clock we pulled into the bus station of this attractive city. We soon cleared customs and made our way to the hotel where a room had been reserved for us by the embassy in Baghdad. Our room was comfortably furnished and very welcome after so long and so wearying a ride. We immediately bathed and had a delightful breakfast of fine Persian melons followed by bacon and eggs. After breakfast we returned for a short nap to replenish our energy after our journey. We awoke around noon to begin the exploration of this civilized and sophisticated city. A far cry it was from the harsh sounds and ragged life of Baghdad, though even here there were the same smells and some of the same drabness that seems to characterize Eastern cities.

We found Teheran to be an interesting city, with many fine suqs and broad tree-lined avenues. People were better dressed. Here Western dress actually prevailed. We were fortunate in being in the city at a time when the magnificent Peacock throne was on exhibition. This is the famous throne of the Moghul emperors of India that was taken in the sack of Delhi in 1739 by the famous Persian soldier Nadir Shah and transported to Persia. It was valued by Tavernier, who saw it while it was still in the possession of the Moghul emperors, at six million pounds. One can believe it, for it is studded with diamonds and other precious stones, some of them the size of peach seeds.

We had heard while we were in Baghdad of the beauty and wealth of the fabled city Isphahan. We determined to visit it and were able to arrange a flight. Upon our arrival we sought out and found a room in a comfortable hotel and immediately began to tour. Isphahan is a splendid and beautiful city that has preserved much of the atmosphere of the Middle Ages. It is a city filled with splendid mosques and a center of Muslim religious learning. Never have I seen such beautiful tile work nor so many mosques in a single place. The people are hospitable and pleasant. We were there for No Ruz, the Persian New Year. At night the streets were filled with people carrying on their heads gifts for their friends in trays lit by a single candle.

The city is a city of flowers. So great is their concern for beauty that even the meat hanging in the butcher shops is adorned with the petals of flowers to hide the unsightly. The gardens are magnificent and well tended by henna-haired and bearded gardeners. Persian roses are without peer and, unlike our tea roses, they have retained the true fragrance. We found many delightful pastry shops filled for the New Year with pastries of the most unusual designs.

Here is the famous rug factory where the Isphahani rugs are made. The factory itself is a small place but big enough to accommodate the twenty or so young girls who tie the knots. These girls range in age from ten to fourteen. Their hands are small and their fingers nimble. Here they work for ten hours each day for a pittance. It was quite cold when we were there, and the poor children were blue with cold. Tine grew tearful at the sight of these tiny, cold children laboring so cheerfully. The rug under construction was nearly finished. For almost a year they had worked on it. No wonder that these rugs are vastly expensive. Seldom are they exported, for rich Persians can buy the whole production. Indeed as a matter of pride they prefer to keep them in Persia.

Here, too, is the famous bazaar running underground with many a twist and turn for almost a mile. There is nothing like it that I have seen, not even the bazaars and suqs of Istanbul. Here almost everything that the East affords is made and offered for sale. We bought several yards of hand-stamped cloth material that we later used for draperies in our dining room. I saw here workmen fashioning spigots from lumps of metal, using hammers and files. I saw here too a pit in which a camel turns a mill for grinding grain. The camel is brought in young and never sees the light of day again.

Here is the famous polo field of Shah Jehan. The game itself is original to Persia. Here too is one of his famous palaces. One of the rooms has a ceiling made for receiving many-shaped glass bottles of various colors. The bottles are gone but their cradles are still to be seen. The palace itself is the epitome of luxury. The world has not known such luxurious living since the days of Shah Jehan, nor can a westerner appreciate its exquisite refinements.

The inhabitants today favor Western dress. No longer do the mullahs and seminarians wear the great wide-brimmed hats that once set them apart. When Pahlevi Shah, the famous father of the late Shah, determined to put his people in Western dress, the mullahs and students resisted fiercely. They did not intend to give up their hats. Because no one could touch these people, when they walked down the street ordinary folk were driven from the walkway. The wily Shah had all of the harlots of the city dressed and hatted in the same way as these keepers of the faith. Seeing their customs so profaned, the mullahs gave in.

Our return flight to Teheran was nerve-racking. To begin with, the plane was hours late in arriving from Dahran. When it did arrive it was crowded. Many of the seats were occupied by manacled prisoners being transported by air to Teheran. We did manage to get aboard, though had we known what was in store for us we would certainly have postponed our flight. At the time, the air field at Teheran was without lights. Since the plane was late, to arrive before darkness was all but impossible. To complicate the problem, we lost an engine and ran into severe weather that filled the plane with the stench of air-sick passengers. I realized we were in for it, but I hesitated to tell Tine. Of course, she was not dumb and soon realized our danger. We lost altitude, flew between mountain peaks, and at last over the white desert so near to the ground as to be able almost to discern the camel tracks. We arrived at Teheran after dark. Fortunately the runway was outlined by torches that had been quickly improvised. Our pilot made a beautiful landing. We heard people thanking him for bringing the plane in safely. Perhaps we had never been so close to death. Who knows? Sometimes she lurks at our elbow, and we are unaware.

From Teheran we had to make the bus trip back to Baghdad. We dreaded the hard journey, but we were prepared for it this time. Our driver was much concerned for the comfort of his American passengers. Unknown to us he had persuaded the other passengers to break the journey by spending a night at a small town. As soon as darkness came on he stopped at the town and informed us and the New Zealand couple that we could find rooms at the hotel. There was a small hotel some distance away, and we were taken there by taxi. Our hosts were kind and considerate and prepared for us a meal of sorts. We immediately went to bed.

We had arranged for the taxi to pick us up at seven in the morning. We awoke, breakfasted, and were ready on time. No taxi appeared. Our driver had told us to be at the bus without fail at seven-thirty. Seven-thirty came and went and no taxi. We were frantic. At last we took up our bags and began the long walk to the bus. We were greatly fearful lest we be left in this godforsaken place. The New Zealander suffered from a heart ailment. He began to breathe hard and his wife was beside herself with anxiety. I took his bag along with my own and a small one of Tine's and ploughed ahead, hoping that we were on the proper street. After a long walk we saw to our relief the bus with the passengers anxiously awaiting us. Our friend from New Zealand made it pantingly and we hustled aboard. By nightfall, after a harrowing experience getting through customs at the Iraqui border, we made it safely to Baghdad and were let off within a hundred yards of our home. *Salaam Aleikum!*

In the spring the Fulbright Commission took all of the grantees on a trip to the north. We went by train. It was a pleasant trip. The weather was beginning to turn toward summer. We passed through the desert carpeted with flowers. They spring up by the millions, have their brief day in the sun, and quickly die. There is no way of picturing the beauty of the desert in spring. For miles it stretches, a mass of blue flowers. At a stop I disembarked and noticed the remains of an aqueduct. In ancient times water was brought in stone ducts under the desert floor for many miles to provide water and life to desert stations now long gone.

We made our headquarters in Mosul across the Tigris from the site of Nineveh. From the air I am told one can make out on the ground below the outlines of former streets and even buildings. From ground level one could never imagine that once here was a city, the heart of an impressive civilization. So do time and the elements work a mighty magic. Mosul is another drab city on the Tigris. The mosques are not so impressive nor the people so sprightly as those in Baghdad. The Kurds are seen here in greater numbers, and they are a dour and sullen though brave race.

One day we traveled to the ruins of Nimrud. Here is the great ziggurat, or mound, in which Professor Mallowan, the husband of Agatha Christie, has been digging for many years. Here it was that the first great stone lions and the first evidences of the Assyrian people were found. Professor Mallowan was good enough to lecture to the assembled group about the history of the place and his own work. I remembered that Xenophon had marched with what was left of the intrepid ten thousand by the walls of what was then a city. I had visited the place before when Seroush took us to the Kurdish country. At that time no work was in progress. The houseboy of Professor Mallowan, noticing that I had gathered broken pieces of shards, had given me a fine brick bearing in cuneiform a memorial to Assernasirbal, the king who ruled nine hundred years before Christ. At Christmas time I had among my guests in Baghdad an assistant to the minister of antiquities. He saw the brick on my hearth.

"What are you doing with this brick? It is a brick from the first diggings, and I remember well when we uncovered it. It belongs to the state."

"You may have it," I said. "It was given me by Professor Mallowan's houseboy. Do you wish to take it with you?"

"Not now," he returned. "Bring it to the Museum one day."

He was a guest in my house and, like all Arabs, very sensitive to what politeness demanded. When I left Baghdad to return home, I wrapped it in a blanket and placed it in my trunk to be shipped home. Later I gave it to the Library at Sewanee. I don't believe the librarians really appreciate what a significant antique they have. It is interesting that the minister could not only read the inscription but write out for us with his pen the inscription and his translation.

The Museum of Antiquities in Baghdad is small. The collection there, however, is one of the finest. I saw there represented on a clay tablet the famous theorem dealing with the square of the hypotenuse. The solution was written neatly in cuneiform and dated more than a thousand years before Euclid passed it on the the West. In many ways archaeological discoveries are changing our views of Greek originality. Much they inherited and passed on.

We took many trips into the country around Baghdad. Once when we were inspecting the two great burial towns of Kerbela and Najaf we passed by a migration of a tribe to the winter pasture lands near the confluence of the Tigris and Euphrates. What a sight! More than a thousand camels were strung out across the desert. The old women and the babies rode the camels. The strong walked. They were followed by flocks of sheep and goats. Some of the baby camels were tied to their mothers' backs. Old men carried cocks and hens. All of the belongings of a people were being transported across this dry land. I took the picture of an old man on a fine grey Arabian horse. The picture is now in my study. These same people will make the trip back to southern Iran when the season for travel comes.

I was paid for my work in dinars, each dinar worth $2.80 in American money. Each time I received my check I took it to a bank in Baghdad to be cashed. The bank was something out of Dickens. There were no adding machines, you can bet. A Turk with long mustaches and heavy jowls was the cashier. All of the ledgers were kept by young men perched on stools before their high tables. I always took my money into the suq to the money changers. Here I would get a portion changed into dollars for my trip home.

The speed with which they make the calculations mentally is unbelievable. I always got out my pen to figure whether or not I was short changed. This always amused the money changer. "Can't you Americans count?" he would say with a superior air. Each part of the suq is devoted to a different business. All of the money changers were together. It is a highly specialized operation and one with its own life. A rumor can pass in a moment from one end to the other.

We were desirous of visiting Istanbul while we were so near. I was able to buy Turkish lira on the black market in the suq for eight times less than the official rate. When we did go on a visit to this city, I put my lira in my shoes and about my body. Since it is unlawful to import lira into Turkey, I took a chance. I was, however, never searched. Thus we were able to stay at the Istanbul Hilton in a sixty-dollar room for an eighth of the cost. For one on a Fulbright allowance, it was a great advantage to have broken the Turkish law.

In June we left Baghdad. We had determined to buy a car in Rome and return home by way of Europe. We left the airport after a long delay and headed for Jerusalem. For some reason our plane landed in Amman, Jordan. At the time the political situation there was very tense. We were quickly and quietly brought by the airline personnel to a hotel. The next morning we were sent by a special car to Jerusalem. We welcomed the opportunity to travel in this fashion. We were able to see first-hand the jaunty men of the Arab Legion at the check point on the Jordan River and to observe the ruined city of Jericho whose walls came tumbling down. The road was winding and narrow. From time to time we stopped to permit herds of sheep to pass us. We stopped briefly at the Dead Sea. Rachel and Tine waded into the dead and salty water and found that the water is indeed buoyant beyond expectation.

We ended the journey at a monastery situated in the Old City that offered economical board and room. We spent the next few days exploring this city that carries so many memories and is such hallowed ground for Arab and Christian alike. Since we came from Baghdad, we entered the Arab section of the city and were consequently unable to visit the New City then in the hands of the Jews. It is the Old City, though, that embraces the historic places. Somehow we found Jerusalem disappointing. Competition among the many sects of Christians and rank commercialism have destroyed for many its religious appeal. Our admiration was excited by the Dome of the Rock and the site of the Temple of David, by the beauty of the structure, by the great extent of the courtyard, by the aged olive trees. We visited the manger at Bethlehem, Golgotha, the Stations of the Cross, saw the brook Kedron, saw where the angels rolled away the stone that sealed the tomb of the crucified Christ. All about lay the gaunt, emaciated land. No wonder that all great religions of the West have emerged from the desert or from stony, infertile earth where men suffer and die and wear themselves out in a fruitless struggle against a grim land. In such conditions men become introverted, fanatic, and look to a source of power outside themselves.

At this point perhaps it is the time to inject my own assessment of the politics and culture of the Arabs. My experience was limited but rich, and I think I have some understanding of the problems of the area, though my travels did not take me to the Nejd, or Arabia proper. For many hundreds of years the Arabs have slept, worn out from the expenditure of energy that sent them from Arabia to Spain in the west and India in the east as a conquering people who brought with them their faith and their language. They are now rubbing their eyes from that long sleep. Nowhere in the world can be found a more independent-minded, deeply individualistic people. All attempts at Arab unity are bound to fail on this historic rock of individualism. The Arab League is a failure. At this moment Syrian troops fight on the side of Christians in Lebanon against Palestinian Muslims. The only unity that exists has at its root an enduring hatred of Zionism. The Arab does not hate the Jew as such. He holds grudges, he is incensed that Arabs were so taken in by the West after World War II, when a national home for Jews was carved out of land the Arab had held since the seventh century and even before. Even this hatred is not enough to fuse into a united people the various Arab states.

A common language and a common faith are not yet enough to insure the triumph of any Pan-Arabian movement. The rank and file of Arab people are more deeply committed to their faith than are the rank and file of their Christian brethren. Their faith is simpler, less priest-ridden, far less hierarchical than Christianity. All one has to do to become a Muslim is to testify by saying, "I believe there is no God but Allah and that Mohammed is the messenger of Allah." This is the first of the five pillars of Islam. The others are simple as well: Pray to Allah five times a day; observe faithfully Ramadan, that is, abstain from food, drink and sexual intercourse from dawn to sunset during this sacred month; travel to Mecca once during one's lifetime if this is financially possible; give alms to the poor. These are purely religious duties and they are observed. I have watched poor workmen in the street at the stated time bow in prayer. This religious loyalty and an observance of Islamic law that itself emerges out of the teachings of Mohammed have bound the Muslim for these many years, and these bonds are still strong.

In the West Christianity is languishing under the kiss of death from Science. That Christ is the risen Son of God is no longer believed except by the fundamentalists. A faith that no longer sustains cannot through good works or an altruistic, humanitarian philosophy maintain the strength and vigor of the Christian religion. Religion defines man's relation to God. It does not merely assuage the wounds of society. The Arabs may be the last great religious people, for their millions still believe there is no God but Allah and Mohammed is his prophet. In the modern world this is both a strength and a weakness. Strong in that it gives peace and satisfaction to the believer. Weak in that it inhibits the advance of the secular state founded on science and technology.

Not only are the Arabs deeply individualistic, they are also at times violent and cruel. They are especially heavy-handed with animals. They have lived in Baghdad for so long accustomed to the sights and sounds of suffering that they have grown callous. They are an emotional people easily given to excesses. During a revolt a few years ago, Nuri Pasha, probably the greatest of the modern Arab leaders, was cornered in a telephone booth by a mob that tore him limb from limb.

I am told that pieces of flesh and bone were strewn for more than a mile from Acadamain to Raschid Street. The mob literally ate him up. Had he been able to escape to the tribes he would have been safe, for he was universally admired by the nomads.

The Arabs have always tolerated in their midst people who do not share their religious heritage. They are second-class citizens, but they are permitted a life of their own. The small Christian section of Baghdad is still inhabited by descendants of first-century Christians. Here the streets are so narrow as to be easily defended by a few men. They even tolerate the Yezidi sect, sometimes known as devil worshippers.

On one of our trips we visited these people at the time they were celebrating their new year. The Yezidis are a sect founded by Sheik Adi. They are a strange people, many of them blonde and blue eyed. Their religion is a combination of many beliefs and practices. They practice baptism in running water, believe like many Persians in the eternal struggle between good and evil, revere the color blue and the peacock. They seek to appease the devil in various ways. Christ is a God of love, say they. No need to worship him. The devil, though, is powerful and strong. He is evil and treacherous. Better appease him with song and dance and worship.

We were there at a special occasion, the annual cleansing time. The tribesmen had gathered to go through the annual ceremony of cleansing and to feast together and exchange goods. The day was perfectly clear and fortunately rather cool. Little blonde girls with silver bells tied to their hair went tinkling about. On carpets grain and food of every sort were exposed for sale. Early in the morning the tribesmen had formed a ring and danced in the circle. Many of them had bottles of araq tied to their belts, from which they fortified themselves from time to time. A drummer stood within the circle and beat time on a highly ornamented drum. They danced all day until exhausted. Some became rigid and fell in hypnotic trance. At eventide the women shyly formed their own ring and danced the same shuffling dance. The purpose of this dance was to cleanse every individual from the sins of the past year. All was forgiven. If men had quarreled, the quarrel was wiped out. If a woman had strayed from the way, her husband forgave and presumably forgot. The slate was wiped quite clean. On the morrow every person came to the new year with a clean record. It appeared to me then and still does that we need something of this kind in our own society. Imagine being able to start a new year with a clean mind and a pure heart. The devil whom they seek to appease must have been highly incensed.

Chapter Eleven

Lectureship in Korea

In 1964 I applied for and was granted another Fulbright lectureship, this time to the College of Arts and Sciences and the College of Law in Seoul University in Korea. We had never been to the Far East, and we looked forward eagerly to the experience. It had been exactly ten years since our excursion to Iraq. We knew what to expect in the matter of adjustment and conditioning that accompanies an involvement with a new people and a new culture. This time Rachel, who was in college, and Ulysse, who was by now married, did not accompany us. We flew first to Hawaii for a few days of sight-seeing and enjoyment of the island. We had reservations at the old and lovely Hotel Halekalani on the beach. We arrived late in the evening. Lei laden, we found we were expected at our hotel. We went immediately to bed.

I awakened early in the morning to the sound of the surf and went immediately for a plunge into the rolling waves of the Pacific. I got the shock of my life. The water was cold. Within a moment or two the body becomes accustomed to the temperature, and there is an exhilaration both mental and physical from an early morning dip. The surf on this beach was strong. Great white-tipped waves beckoned to hardy trials. Soon Tine joined me. Nothing excited her more than the sea. Within a short time she had engaged a surf boy to take her for a trial on the board. She did well. I was more timid about such an attempt, doubting my ability to hold the balance necessary for such a ride.

We explored the city and ate for the first time with chopsticks. The fruit was marvelous, especially the fresh pineapple. The people were on the whole a motley crew, especially on the street. The great informality of dress does nothing for the American tourist, of whom there were many. The native boys and girls, though hard to find on the streets, were magnificent.

How glorious they must have seemed to the early explorers! The girls with their supple, youthful bodies and their long hair were especially charming. In age they tend to grossness. A fat woman was highly prized, I believe. At any rate, the older they grow the fatter they become.

I was anxious to see Pearl Harbor. We took a tour of the area. Even now to see the rusting hulks of great ships sunk by the Japanese is to regain that rage and frustration that came to many Americans when they learned that our navy had been decimated on the fateful day, December 7. These hulks stand as a reminder that we must ever guard against the stratagems of our enemies.

The islands we saw were green, mountainous, and lovely. At almost any moment of the day a misty rain may gently water the earth, capriciously, silently, wantonly. My impression gained from so brief a visit was of lovely islands, magnificent seas, beautiful sunsets, motley tourists ill-clothed, and native peoples perverted beyond redemption by the white man's greed and cunning and the missionaries' puritanism gone to seed. They say that when we first came to the islands the white man had the Bible and the natives the land. Within a generation the natives had the Bible and the sons of the missionaries the land. I am opposed to missionary zeal. Too often the old religion and culture that integrated the lives of natives crumbles and a kind of ersatz religion and culture takes its place. Nothing is gained but the destruction of the old and a perversion of the new, which is neither uplifting nor ennobling.

One day we left Hawaii for Japan and Seoul. It has always been an exciting moment for me when the sight of a new and unvisited land slants into view. So it was with Asia. We stopped briefly in Tokyo and within a short time landed in Seoul. We were met by representatives of the Fulbright Mission to be steered through customs. One newsman, having read my name, Lancaster, thought I must be a brother or at least a kinsman of Burt Lancaster, the actor. I told him that Cousin Burt was not with me this time. He insisted in being helpful. This did not prevent, however, customs from holding up my trunk. They found and confiscated the shotgun that I had disassembled and hidden among my garments. He was of no help with this.

There were several Fulbright grantees arriving at the same time. We were introduced to each other and taken away to our separate homes. Since Tine and I had no children with us, or for some reason I know not of, we were assigned the upper apartment of a vertical duplex at the top of a steep climb to Itewan, a kind of American compound near the Han River. There we were welcomed by our maid, Mrs. Cho. The furniture was adequate but spartan. One entered the door at the top of a flight of stairs. On the right was the bathroom. Through another door one entered a room separated into dining room, and living room with a kitchen annexed. Off this room was a bedroom. The beds were low and hard; the furniture consisted of a wardrobe for suits and dresses and a small dresser. It was enough and Mrs. Cho made up for whatever was lacking in comfortable equipment, though we thought those who had drawn more comfortable houses to have been more fortunate. All Fulbright grantees are paid in native currency. Here the won reigned, and it proved to be a stable currency. We paid fewer won for our apartment than our colleagues. This proved to be an advantage.

Our first few days were taken up with orientation sessions designed to introduce us to Korea and prepare us for whatever difficulties lay ahead. All of this was expertly done. I discovered that I was to teach two classes in American government at the College of Arts and Sciences and give two lectures a week on American jurisprudence at the College of Law. We were introduced to the respective deans. I liked immediately Paul Ryu, dean of the Law School. We became in time good friends.

Korea, as so many American soldiers can testify, is mountainous land. My first impressions were of a down-at-the-heels city, old crumbling monuments of the past, and shifty, bad-breathed people. Like many first impressions mine were faulty. I soon learned to respect the gentle manners and the hard work of the typical Korean student. Most of my students spoke passable English. Many of them had learned German and French as well.

Since we were not affiliated with the armed forces or aid, we were unable to buy at the post exchange. In a way, this was a great deprivation. We were allowed to buy at the commissary run by the American embassy. Here one could buy almost any American canned or processed goods. The prices were not high since no taxes had to be paid. Whiskey and almost any wine sold at an unbelievably low price. I could buy a bottle of Johnny Walker Red for $1.60. At my first visit I ran into Mr. Waldemar Gallman, who had been ambassador to Iraq when I was there ten years before. From time to time we saw the Gallmans. He was there as an adviser, paid by the Korean government for his counsel about their foreign affairs and personnel.

Since we had no car all of our travel was by bus or in the automobile of a friend or by taxi. We often walked down the steep hill to the bus line. Small buses always attended by little girls ran all over the city. Since we knew no Korean we sometimes took the wrong bus and with many a gesture and impossible Korean had to work our way to a section of the city we knew.

I very early made friends with a certain Captain Kim, who was the librarian at Korea Military Academy, the West Point of Korea. Kim loved to hunt pheasants. A month or two after my arrival he invited me to go hunting with him and a friend who had a jeep. My shotgun had been confiscated at customs and was at the time in the custody of the superintendent of police of our district. One day Kim and I went to the headquarters of this area to try our luck at obtaining my gun. We sat waiting for some time. A police headquarters is an interesting place. While waiting I listened to, or rather watched, the attempt of a prostitute to regain her picture or rather to remove it from the police book. She was to be married, Kim said. All of her cajoleries were getting her nowhere. The officer had the book open. Suddenly with a quick movement she snatched it from the book. The officer made a halfhearted effort to regain it but in the end let her depart with her picture. Both Kim and I were much relieved that she succeeded. The girl was young and pretty. Her record as a prostitute might have stood in the way of a happy marriage.

After a time we were admitted to the superintendent's office. He was very gracious in his welcome to us both. Kim explained the situation. I was a professor, a Fulbright grantee in his country under the auspices of the Department of State. He simply could not understand why a professor should have brought a gun with him to his country. He even mentioned to Kim the assassination of President Kennedy. Eventually he agreed that I might borrow the gun for two days if we promised to bring it back. He feared lest he get into difficulty if the gun were not returned.

We went into the country near Seoul. It was my first journey into the rice fields and the cultivated country. The rice had scarcely begun to turn its golden color. I learned that wherever there was a trickle of water, it was contained for a paddy. At the top of a steep hill a small trickle from a spring emerged. From its rise to its confluence with the Han River it was partially dammed, time and time again, for the raising of rice. At the top the paddies were small, some scarcely larger than a small garden plot. Below the paddies were increasingly larger, some covering as much as five acres. The hills were steep, but the people, old and young, were active and vigorous, small and wiry.

We got up a few pheasants. They were principally too young to be killed. This meant little to Kim, for they were food. I killed three small birds about two-thirds grown and one fine adult cock. Later I had many hunting trips, but this first one was memorable for the paddies, the fine views from the mountain tops, the warm companionship with new friends.

Upon my return I took the gun to the superintendent. From time to time thereafter I visited him. He usually called in an interpreter so that we could talk. He asked many questions about my life in the United States. Finally one visit I asked for the gun to see its condition. It was getting rusty. I pointed this out to him and decided to keep the gun. I told him I must clean it up and left the office with the gun. He insisted that I return it. I was noncommittal. I never returned it and he never sent for it. I think he was convinced that I was a strange scholar who liked guns.

Before going to Korea I talked with a colleague on the faculty, Don Webber, a retired lieutenant colonel of the army. He had been an instructor at Fort Leavenworth to a contingent of young Korean officers who were being trained in the United States. From this contingent of officers came many of the powerful people in Korea. He suggested that he write me letters of introduction to Korean generals whom he knew. I agreed. Knowing that letters sealed with wax and adorned with ribbon carry great weight in some foreign places, I sealed the letters with the seal of the university. Upon reaching Korea, I found that one of the generals whom he had taught as a young officer in our country was now the prime minister. I mentioned to a certain Captain Yi or Lee that I had such a letter. From time to time thereafter Korean agents would call at our apartment, ostensibly to ask about our quarters or to inquire into the state of our happiness in Korea. This was not without significance, I later learned. From the superintendent of police or from some source there arose the speculation that I was an agent of the CIA. One day I had a telephone call from the Blue House from the PM's office. A secretary suggested that I call at a fixed time and the prime minister would be available to talk with me for a few minutes. If I had a letter of introduction, it should be brought along.

I went at the appointed hour and was at length ushered in to the outer office of the minister. After a time, a secretary came for the letter of introduction. Shortly afterwards I was invited into the PM's office. As the door opened there was a great splash of intense light that blinded me momentarily. I recovered to see the prime minister smiling and affable at his desk. He arose, greeted me warmly in English, and bade me be seated. He explained that every stranger who entered his office was photographed for security purposes. He reminisced about his life in the United States. Webber had been gracious enough to get him out of some small scrape. He was grateful. He had been Ambassador to Turkey, the United States, and Germany, I believe. He was as well a fervid supporter of President Park with whom he had served in the officer corps. Later he was gracious enough to invite Tine and me to lunch in his home. He sent for us in an official car and returned us to our spartan apartment. Such is the efficacy of a letter of introduction if it is done up right.

The same Captain Lee took me later to interview General Tiger Sung, who was at this time out of prison but under house arrest for opposing the program of President Park, his enemy. Sung had commanded the Korean armies that under the support of our naval guns had bulled their way up the east coast of Korea during that war. He was an immense man, standing over six feet two, which is tall for a Korean. Once upon a time he had been a corporal in the Japanese army. Now he was out of favor, ill, and suspect.

I arrived at his compound in a jeep driven by Lee. Sung was suffering from swollen legs caused by the irons of the prison in which he had been confined, but he hobbled into the courtyard. Before greeting me, he shouted to the darkness, "Don't shoot me in the back. I am greeting an American visitor." Whether he was actually liable to be shot I don't know. Life is tough for an enemy of the regime who has been powerful in Korea.

General Sung was gracious and an attractive man filled with suppressed ambition and much talk of Korean history. He had suppressed the communist guerillas in Chegedo, an island offshore in which they were intrenched. He showed me his letter to General Taylor of our army, asking that he intervene to have Sung sent to Viet Nam to fight with the Americans. "I know how to treat guerillas," he told me. "Pin a few skulls to the ground with stakes and they will get the word."

General Taylor had replied, pointing out the political difficulty involved in acceding to such a request, praising the Tiger for his services during the Korean war, and expressing his admiration for the fighting qualities of the general. He showed me his swollen and still infected wounds on his ankles from the leg irons. He then recounted the history of a fourteenth-century Japanese invasion that was repulsed by the famous turtle boats of an ingenious Korean leader. Sung was an impressive man, once prime minister and now virtually an outcast in the land he loved.

The attitude of the typical Korean toward the Japanese interested me. They seemed to enjoy a kind of love-hate attitude. As their former overlords and conquerors the Japanese had respect, but it was a respect colored by pride and aversion and secret admiration for an Asian people who had modernized their state in the shortest time. The Koreans thought of themselves, however, as the cultural children of their Chinese mentors; they believed that Japanese art and culture had passed from China to Japan through the Korean bridge. Historically speaking, they may be right. Their real hate they reserved for their communist brethren of North Korea who had wrought such frightful and cruel havoc in the early days of the invasion from the north. They especially remembered the many children and intellectuals captured and taken north.

I lectured on jurisprudence in the College of Law. This was a difficult assignment. The Korean has never experienced law or the rule of law in the Western sense. The law has always been handed down from above. It has always been positive law. Total submission they understand, but they have no concept of the right-duty relationship based on law. Indeed, law is something to be avoided and feared; resort to the law always causes a kind of Oriental loss of face. The importation of codes and written law from the West has never been suited to the people who do not understand it. It is alien to the culture of the people, evokes no inherited response, does not reflect their traditions or customs. A living law must reflect the customs, the emotions, the community spirit of a people. The Western importation does not do this. Consequently lawyers and Western legalism represent a kind of social and political veneer at odds with their spirit and even hostile to their deeper aspirations that have emerged from their Confucian inheritance.

The Korean people have lived since the beginning of the twentieth century in a kind of trance. With the breakup of the Yi dynasty which ruled from 1392 until the Japanese became their lords and masters in 1910, and with the partition of Korea after World War II, the Korean has lived an unsettled and even desperate life. There has been no real stability, no real security. This fact is reflected in their attitudes and political postures. When one adds to this the great migration from the villages to the cities, especially Seoul, the capital, the vast and successful attempt to make literate the entire population and the swift advance of industrialization, with its impact upon village life and village economy, one can understand to better advantage the trauma of this hardy and cheerful people.

I found that most of my students were intrigued by and drawn to Marxism. It seemed to offer simple solutions to ingrained economic and political problems. Further, the Korean intellectual has gone to school in the West at the wrong time. No self-respecting student would dare expound capitalist doctrine. He has been taught its evils. As a Korean scholar explained to me, it would have been better had the Korean experienced capitalistic theory in the days of Adam Smith. What he advocated was the movement of Korea through the various phases of the Western experience but in shorter time periods. I could never understand the appeal of Marxism with its repression of freedom and its heavy-handed planning that has never produced prosperity and happiness for any people who have tried it. I insisted in my classes that they examine the doctrine not in the books but in practice. Measure it by its actual achievements.This they were loath to do because many of them thought learning reposed in books, in theories. During the short time that I taught, I sensed a great dissatisfaction and much tension in the student population. This tension was to break out in student riots in February and result in the temporary closing of many universities.

I was in Korea during the 1964 election that pitted Goldwater against Johnson. On the whole the Koreans supported Goldwater. They saw him as a prospective president who would take a more militant stance against the Communists and they expected greater support and more aid from such a man. In 1964 I voted Republican for the first time in my life. Indeed I was the only American professor who could be found to take up and argue the Goldwater cause. The American embassy supported the idea of a debate after the American example. It was held at the headquarters of the U.S. Information Service, and a large number of Korean editors were invited to the confrontation, which was carried by radio and spotted on television to the Korean people. We had a lively debate. Johnson was supported by the head of the Fulbright mission in Korea. I made a vigorous and typically political campaign speech that drew vigorous applause.

Later it stood me in good stead, for in a way it introduced me to the Korean people who would otherwise never have heard of me. It paid dividends in villages and in the city. I received invitations to hunt pheasants at places that would not have been open to me otherwise. The Johnson landslide, which even I had predicted, did little to still the admiration of the Koreans for a man whom they thought better suited to their own needs. When Johnson adopted much of the stance advocated by Goldwater, they were a little confused but very appreciative. Shortly after his election, it may be remembered that a Korean contingent went to Viet Nam to fight with the Americans. This was politically confusing to the students, who had not learned that campaign rhetoric and promises have little bearing on the making of policy after the event.

The customs and manners of the Korean people were of never-ceasing interest to me. Although Western dress is almost invariably worn by the city dweller, in the village the older and more typically Korean dress is often encountered. In the city it is not uncommon to see the older style, especially among the women. The traditional women's costume includes the trousers over which is worn the skirt. The upper body is covered by the *chogori*, or blouse-like coat fastened by two long strips of cloth rather than buttons. The color green is often preferred. The costume is colorful and quite becoming to women.

The men of the *yangban* class in the villages were continuing to wear the traditional white costume when I was there. It consisted of balloon-like trousers tied at the ankle, a kind of inner jacket and a coat-like garment tied at the neck. Yangbans are descendants of the former civil servants of the upper class who had passed the examination. Very strict rules of class inheritance and aristocratic lineage without stain limited this class to the few who could qualify. They wear horsehair hats with an exceedingly wide brim. I have seen them walking through the village streets clasping a long-stemmed pipe with their hands behind their backs, the very image of the old and honored. Everywhere in the village they are treated with deference. Children bow to them; ordinary folk pay them homage. They are the vestigial remains of a former day, replete with power and authority. Close conversation between two yangbans is difficult. The hat insures a proper distance; impaired hearing does the rest.

Traditional housing interested me. The old houses have a top-heavy appearance. The roof is too large for the under-structure. The elaborate roof style is a Chinese touch. The houses of the rich are invariably tiled with heavy black tile. The houses of the poor are small, thatched with ten inches or so of grass or rice straw. Seldom does a village house have more than four rooms. Usually one finds only two. The houses have small windows and doors, sometimes with glass panes but more often of oiled paper. The floors of the poorer houses are of clay, on which has been glued many sheets of paper finally covered by a hard varnish. Of course one removes his shoes before entering such a house.

Centuries ago the Korean learned the efficiency of radiant heat. The winters are severe. To keep warm they learned to build a flue at the end of the house where cooking might be done and to extend the chimney through a clay pipe in the floor. When I was in Korea they were using small cylinders of coal dust held together by oil and pierced by holes for draft. A small cylinder of the fuel would provide sufficient heat for the night. The Korean house uses or rather needs little furniture. They sleep on pallets on the floor, often using a wooden block for a pillow. They dine on a small table twelve inches or so high. Clothes, bedding, and such are stored by day in those lovely Korean chests that serve so many purposes. Naturally in the houses of the rich there may be found Western furniture commingled with the old.

Korean food is palatable but to a westerner strange and sometimes even unappetizing. The staple is rice, rice, rice. Along with this may go a soup of bean curds, and the omnipresent *kimchee*. If there is a national dish it is surely kimchee. It is nutritious and redolent. Kimchee is made by placing in a large jar in the ground Chinese cabbage, large radishes, bits of fish or even shellfish, along with salt water. It ferments slowly, develops a distinct odor and provides the vitamins and roughage necessary to sustain a Korean. In early autumn the streets of Seoul devoted to such trade were filled with tons of cabbage and radishes and peppers for the making of kimchee. I have spent delightful hours watching the housewives buy their kimchee ingredients. It is a colorful and human scene.

In all of Korea there are only about 250 surnames. Of these Kim, Yi, and Park are the most numerous. There are other common surnames like Cho, Song, Sin, U, Pang and Sung. My two closest friends were Major Kim and Captain Park.

In the city weddings are usually held at marriage parlors. They follow traditional Western patterns and are quite often love matches. The old rule, a Confucian rule, that boys and girls must not sit together after the age of seven is passing. In the villages weddings are still arranged by parents, or were when I was there. The groom rode on a litter or palanquin to the house of the bride, accompanied by kinsmen. Here wine was sipped and the vows said. After the wedding the groom remained three days at the bride's house. Here he put up with much spying and good-natured raillery. At the end of this time he returned to the house of his parents or, if he were lucky, the couple set up housekeeping in their own house. Sometimes mass weddings were held. While I was in Seoul the government sponsored the mass marriage of nearly five hundred former prostitutes to the same number of "quickie boys." The latter were skilled at pilfering, the former at lovemaking.

There were thousands of prostitutes in Seoul when I was there. The street just below the hill where we lived at Itewan was practically given over to their calling. The economy of the villages, disrupted by invasion and war, simply would not support the big families that were produced. Many girls were forced to the city by the hope of a living and found a precarious one in the oldest of professions. Then too, the presence of many American soldiers made the occupation both more stable and more profitable. I have known American GIs upon the eve of returning home to sell apartment, furniture, and girlfriend to an incoming soldier. Some GIs fell in love and made enduring matches. The oriental girls, especially the Koreans, are lovely, with the classic features and beautiful hair, and they are milder and more tractable than American women, more given by inheritance and training to spending their time making a man happy. If I were young and unattached I would be drawn to the Orient as a place in which to marry and live.

Once in the early autumn I went to the nearby officers' club to shoot skeet. In so doing I passed through the street of the prostitutes and by the army paymaster's office. The soldiers were being paid. I had to make my way through a throng of available girls drawn to the honey of money on GI payday. Several girls approached me for help and support. I passed them off rather easily because I was then fifty-six years old. One tall good-looking girl was persistent. She took me by the arm and said, "I like. I be your girl."

I replied that I was too old and too tired. "Not old. Just right. I make you little tired then rest." I must say the opportunity was tempting.

I believe the most beautiful girl I ever saw was on the street near the Fulbright headquarters in Seoul. I was sitting at a window watching the street. There came up that street a young woman of such graceful beauty that I went below to observe at closer quarters. Her hair was long and glossy, shining in the sun. Her features were regular and delicate. She walked like a young filly on parade. She was dressed in a beautiful Korean dress. Seldom have I seen so attractive a sight.

The Korean children are about the sprightliest children I have ever known. Hard living has weeded out, I believe, the weak and afflicted. At least they are not seen in public. In the winter, which is cold and often windy, they are all over the ponds and rivers and streets. They are usually clothed in a woolen suit knitted of yarn by their mothers or sisters. The conventional colors are red and green. They are lively and lovely and seem not to have the impudence of the usual street gamin. They fasten pieces of tin or other metal to their shoes and skate. They make ingenious sleds out of scraps or the lids of buckets.

The Korean child until about seven years of age is never disciplined except by habit. Older sisters carry them on their backs; mothers carry them slung on boards. They are for a time Lords of Creation. Unlike American children, they seem perfectly secure and unabashed in the presence of strangers. They know what is expected of them and do it. They are taught in the best homes what is proper and proportional to their place. Many know the different bows: for the strange guest, for the grandfather, for the yangban. My heart went out to the children of mixed unions with soldiers. Their lot was hard and their expectancies fragile. The government and various religious and charitable organizations did something to make their lot easier. But life was hard for these children with rickety bodies and pinched faces.

Before the weather became too cold for outings, the whole

Fulbright aggregation was taken on a trip to Cheju Island, which lies off the coast of Korea. The island is an extinct volcano that even in the fall wears a hat of hoarfrost. It is one of the most spectacular places I have seen. Water rushes from the mountain top in many directions and falls over precipitous cliffs into the sea. The terrain is extremely rugged in the upper reaches, but near the sea there are small plains suitable for the planting of almost any fruit or vegetables. Sweet potatoes are grown for their starch. When we were there the potatoes had been cut and lay sliced in the sun to dry. There is a starch factory on the island. Starch is about the only exportable commodity aside from fruit. A passable road traverses the circumference of the island near the sea. There are many colorful villages here. The women of the villages dive for shellfish and occasionally come up with pearls. They dive without oxygen to remarkable depths. The men work around the vineyards and gardens and help look after the small children.

Cheju Island affords wonderful pheasant hunting. Here the American Air Force had put up a radar tower as a sort of cover for a hunting camp and a refrigeration facility for processing the birds shot by the visiting officers of high rank. I noticed jeeps and other vehicles for hunting purposes. Some vans had pheasants painted on their sides. It was a little irritating to me, and more so to the inhabitants of the island, to see the destruction of so many birds. I had carried my shotgun. With help I found a native guide in the village. We went into the upper stretches of the mountain for birds. I killed four cock pheasants. I could have killed many more. One could hear the crowing of the cocks in the thick cover. Any imitation of the sound, however imperfect, would bring an answering challenge. Often in the higher elevations of the mountain one encounters wide fissures made by the volcano when active. Sometimes the ground is split open for a quarter of a mile or more. Often one must walk several miles to detour around such gaps in the earth. Without a guide a stranger would be in trouble.

With its spectacular falls of water tumbling into the sea, with its sturdy women divers, its lovely scenery, its mild climate, Chejudo is a kind of tropical retreat in this cold and mountainous land.

In December Tine went with other members of the Fulbright mission and the American colony on a trip through Southeast Asia. This journey was sponsored by the Royal Asiatic Society. Because of the intense cold of the winters she decided to spend a few months in travel. Among the places she visited were India, Nepal, Cambodia,

Malaysia and Penang. I decided to remain in Korea for the Christmas vacation. In any event my vacation was for only a three-weeks period.

Major Kim had planned for us a hunting trip into the mountains of the eastern coast to pursue the elusive red deer with the great antlers. There are many marsh deer in Korea, a small species without antlers, especially in the demilitarized zone, which has become almost an animal sanctuary. There are few of the great red deer yet remaining in the country. They are mostly found in the high mountains. These were the deer we sought.

At a nightclub with Major Kim and his wife. Mrs. Kim had never before been to such a place.

Since I had no jeep we determined to go by train to Pusan and there rent a jeep or other sturdy vehicle for travel up to the high villages. I had never taken a trip by train in Korea. I spoke the language scarcely at all. I made arrangements with Mrs. Cho, our maid of all work, to escort me to the station early and help me buy the ticket and carry the luggage. I awoke early on the morning of our departure to await Mrs. Cho. Time passed and no Mrs. Cho. I was greatly chagrined that she who was usually so faithful did not show up. At length I was forced to carry my luggage down the hill to the main street and hail a conveniently passing taxi.

My driver spoke no English. I managed to convey to him where I wished to go. When I arrived at the station I found myself in a great press of Koreans intent on boarding the train. With much difficulty I found a Korean who spoke passable English. I gave him a handsome bit of money to buy my ticket and see me launched on my journey. Major Kim, his wife, his brother, and a family friend had agreed to meet me on the train, which they had to board at a station further up the river in Seoul. I found them finally several cars from the one I had entered. My tension vanished. I was in the midst of my new family.

We spent a pleasant day on the train to Pusan, eating apples and pears which they had thoughtfully provided. I had made sandwiches of ham and cheese which they preferred to their own rations. I had also brought a bushel of rice which, as events had it, turned out to have been a most fortunate purchase. The train was crowded with Koreans going to Pusan and elsewhere. It ran through remarkable scenery at times and stopped now and then at dingy towns, for the Pusan express then made many stops. I noticed with distaste how littered were the aisles with the refuse and the baggage of the travelers. They lived in so much litter that they never thought to use the receptacles provided on the train.

We arrived at Pusan in the late afternoon. No jeep could be found nor any vehicle to be rented for love nor money. The buses that came by headed north were packed with people like cans with sardines. There was simply no way up the coast. Night was coming. We were far from hotel accommodations and I grew a little desperate. I noticed a weapons carrier standing at the curb with a Korean army driver. Kim, who was a major, approached the vehicle and inquired of the driver the name and rank of the user. He turned out to be a captain with a vehicle to be used for providing venison to the officers' mess in Seoul. He had been away from his unit for two months engaged in this enterprise. Kim, who outranked him, practically commandeered the vehicle. Captain Sung agreed to take us north to a village where he had friends and where he thought we could find both accommodations and good hunting. So we set out, the driver, the captain, and I in the cab, the others, including Mrs. Kim, perched in the back in the open. The weather had turned cold. The sky was pale mackerel. The sun shone feebly through a frigid cover. For a few miles the road was fairly good but soon it turned into a rutted pathway. We jerked and bounced our way through the coming darkness. Captain Sung knew of a village where he had found a friend who he said would provide us with supper. About dark we arrived at a compound near a clear mountain stream. The master of the house was away but his wife agreed to provide us with supper. The Korean is seldom in a hurry. Our hostess possessed this frustrating quality. She went leisurely about her tasks, boiling rice, dipping out the kimchee, all the while engaged in a running conversation with Mrs. Kim. We cleaned our guns, oiled them thoroughly, warmed by the heated floor on which we sat. I went with Kim to look at the stream. We took our guns. Two ducks sprang from the water. In the gathering darkness we missed.

At length dinner was served. We ate our rice and the kimchee. For dessert we were provided with the largest and juiciest pears I have ever eaten. Unlike American pears, they were large and round. This hospitality was provided gratis, nor would our hostess accept money when I tried to pay. I did manage to slip a won note to her young son.

We left the compound about nine in the evening. The cold had become more intense. I feared for Mrs. Kim who, though tough, was thin. I suggested to the captain that he drive and that Mrs. Kim join us in the warmer cab. He agreed and we all cuddled up for warmth. Occasionally the private in the back would attempt to spot deer with his light. When he did, the captain would stop and take a shot. Several times feeding deer were spotted by the light but only once did he manage to kill one, a small marsh doe that perhaps weighed forty pounds. We continued north, climbing ever higher over a road that only a vehicle such as we had could have traveled. Now and then we passed through forested areas. Most of Korea has been denuded of trees, but in the area where we were going there are large trees and some forested areas, about the only ones in South Korea.

About two in the morning, cold, weary from long travel, bruised by heavy jolting over make-believe roads, we arrived at a village, quiet except for the barking of dogs who smelled strangers. The captain took us to a small house of two rooms by a frozen brook. He hailed the owner, disappeared inside to at length emerge to inform us that the woman who lived there with her daughter and two young children had agreed to move out of one of the two rooms and leave the other room for all seven of us. They moved their gear and we moved in. Fortunately I had brought a sleeping bag. The others had only blankets, but the ondol-heated floor was warm, and wearily we all lay down like puppies in a basket for a few hours of sleep.

Morning came. I lay among my companions taking stock of my

situation. I was in a room about ten by fourteen feet. The floor was warm and covered with many a layer of paper varnished together to make a very smooth surface.

The walls were papered with nondescript pieces of paper, obviously gathered here and there. There were two receptacles in the walls containing the tiny oil lamps used in the Korean village houses to provide just enough light to see to eat and to undress. On the wall was a faded photograph of *Halmoni* (grandmother) in her wedding dress. There was a single chest by the tiny door leading to the other room. The entrance door was about three feet wide and four feet high made of thin strips of wood. Outside a cock crowed and the *kae* (dog) whined to enter. This was the establishment of the grandmother who owned the small house and a plot of earth about forty feet square through which ran a now icy brook.

With the coming of day the spirits rose with the body. We had not undressed except to remove our shoes. We went to the brook and broke the ice to wash our faces while Mrs. Kim helped Halmoni prepare the breakfast. My rice was a godsend, for it was hard to come by in the village.

Halmoni was a poor woman with little to sustain her except her tough spirit and her determination to survive. She owned this small plot of ground that produced a few vegetables in the summer, a pink little sow who had three pink piglets, a dog that slept in a basket of rice straw beside the house, and a cock with only three lazy hens. The cock was forever asserting his marital rights to such an extent as to impede all development except his crow and his masculinity. I offered to go to the village to buy a few more hens. "Kim," said I, "tell Halmoni that her cock needs more hens, and I will buy her some."

He told her. She replied, "Tell that redheaded ugly American that my cock is a weak bird already. I'd rather have the money."

We remained with the family for seven days. Each morning we would rise, have breakfast, and climb the hundreds of stone steps to the top of the mountain to hunt the deer and the wild boar. By the time I had climbed the steps I was almost done in, but to my companions that was like going up the steps to an upstairs room. Kim's wife was assigned to me as gun bearer, and though I carried my own gun, she was a delight to be with, even though she spoke no English and I spoke no Korean.

Once we flushed a great buck. The other hunters were below me.

We were standing on the top of a knoll that provided a grand view of the valley. A village boy had joined us and in spite of all my gestures he would not be still. Suddenly I saw the great antlered buck running toward us. I motioned to Kand, the child, to be quiet, but he was so excited by the spectacle that he could not be contained. When about fifty yards away the buck sighted us and turned. My gun was loaded with buckshot. It was a long shot but I fired. The buck staggered and fell. I fired again but somehow he managed to get up and go. We tracked him by his blood for a mile or two and lost the trail in a creek. The next day we heard that a village boy had found him dying. The whole village came out to rejoice. The blood was drunk by the old men and the meat provided a feast. The antlers, we were told, would be ground up to provide sexual stimulation to the old men and even the young, for the Koreans consider the horns of the deer to be very potent.

At the end of a week of hard hunting I badly needed a bath. Halmoni heated water and poured it into a pot near the little stream by the house. Several villagers showed up to see what I looked like under my shirt. It was with some embarrassment that I shed down to my drawers. The Koreans are never embarrassed at the naked human body and could scarcely understand my modesty. They laughed at my pink skin and ugly white body. Nevertheless they were kind and considerate of my foreign customs.

Only once did I become ill. Unfortunately I developed a bad case of diarrhea from perhaps the rice beer. Since we all slept together on the floor like so many sardines, it was extremely inconvenient to get out of a sleeping bag or from under a blanket and visit the john. Incidentally, the john was a hole in the ground with two planks arranged for the business. On one of my excursions into the cold, I dropped my glasses into the excrement. There was nothing to do but return to bed and wait for the coming of day. When first light appeared I got up to retrieve my glasses from the dismal hole. Kim assisted me. Finally with two sticks we managed to retrieve them and place them in the running current of cold water, where they remained for several hours. My disability grieved Kim even more than me, for he was by nature more squeamish than I.

At the end of the week the captain, whose vehicle we had almost appropriated, had to return to Pusan. When we left the morning was extremely cold. Halmoni openly wept. Villagers gathered to tell us farewell. The trip back to Pusan was cold and wearying. Once we stopped to pick up an old woman who was going afoot to a village twenty miles distant. The road was so rough that she became violently ill from the continuous up and down motion of the vehicle and elected to get out and go afoot rather than suffer from the motion sickness. We deplored leaving her on a lonely road in zero weather, but there was nothing else to do as she positively refused to ride further.

We made it to Pusan barely in time to take the train to Seoul. I had desired to have one of the small lamps, such as was used in the villages to provide a dim light for the houses, as a souvenir of my adventure. Mrs. Kim set off to find one for me in the market and by her desire to please me almost caused us to miss our train. Captain Kim dressed her down for the delay but I was pleased by her solicitude for my every want.

We arrived in Seoul about midnight of the last day of December after a long journey. I was dirty, tired, and half sick from exposure and the rigors of the trip. There was no taxi available at the crowded station. There was no way home but by foot from the station all the way to Itaewon. I looked forward to the comfort of my own bed and abode. I had told Mrs. Cho to leave me a key at a certain place in the bathroom, which was at the top of a flight of stairs and apart from the living room. When I made it loaded with gear to the top of the steps, I was distressed to find that the key was not available, and I could not get into my house. I spread my sleeping bag in the warm bathroom, took a sleeping pill available in the medicine cabinet, and slept until Mrs. Cho came about ten o'clock the next day to go back to work. I scolded her severely for her negligence in forgetting to take me to the train upon my departure and her untimely negligence in failing to leave a key. She moped around for a day or two, but within a short time recovered her spirits. I have never understood what actually happened to her, for she was a reliable and likable woman. She attempted to appease me with much attention and favorite dishes.

After Christmas vacation school opened for a day or two and then, because of student unrest and the threat of violence, all the schools and colleges in Seoul were closed by government order. There had been unrest among students for some time. Much of it was caused by the failure of the government of Park Chung Hee to move toward a more democratic regime. Some of it was attributable to the general student unrest of the sixties. Perhaps much of it was occasioned by crowded classrooms and the general frustration over the lack of proper jobs after graduation. Some of the unrest was the result of communist agitation. In any event great masses of students congregated in the downtown area of the city. Perhaps as many as twenty thousand students gathered in the streets. Mob violence was in the air. I watched from a safe perch in a window the government police break up the mob. They did it effectively and with a minimum of violence. Teams of police in wedge-like formations broke up the crowd into manageable pieces, then with truncheons and strong arms loaded the most unruly into police vans for prison. Some heads were broken and students made much of the strong-arm tactics of the police, but it worked. After a short time all but the most truculent of the students were released, but colleges were not reopened.

Since there was no teaching to be done, the Fulbright Commission looked for tasks to which the grantees might be assigned. I had gained some fame from the election-time debate at the American embassy. It will be remembered that I supported Goldwater, whom the knowing Koreans preferred to Johnson. Perhaps as a result of this I was assigned to go out into the villages of Korea and lecture to meetings called to hear me tell about American life and democratic processes. I enjoyed this work very much. I was provided with a jeep, a driver, and an interpreter. The gathering places were cold, the roads bad, the difficulty of speaking through an interpreter almost unsurmountable. Yet I was always cheered by the size of the turnout and the great warmth, unfailing hospitality, and curiosity of the people. The difficulty with an interpreter is that one loses spontaneity and one never knows just how what is being said is being rendered. Then too, because of the slowness of the process, I found it difficult to speak with coherence and authority. Yet when it was all over and we were seated in the warmth of the headman's home enjoying the comforts of a kaesang party, it was worth it.

The kaesang party is a Korean version of the Japanese counterpart. I was first invited to such a party by Paul Ryu, the dean of the Law School at Seoul University. When we entered we were greeted by our hostess, a mature and pleasant Korean woman. She introduced us to her girls, of whom there was one for each guest. They were both waitresses and entertainers. The party started without any awkwardness. Each girl attached herself to a guest and with some little joke or playful prank made him immediately at home. Always at such a party one sits on the carpet and dines from tiny tables only a few inches high. The meal is preceded by ceremonial wine-drinking in the lovely little cups—hot sake. Games are played and the loser penalized by having to drink a larger cup. Slowly and inevitably the heated wine does its work on hostess and guest alike, although hostess is more noticeably restrained in her imbibing.

The meal proceeds by courses, all deliciously prepared. A girl may offer you a tidbit held in her teeth. Each guest is encouraged to sing a song, do a dance, or do anything to free him from inhibitions. Before the end of the party a warm glow permeates the establishment. The girls are never wanton, merely exciting. They have learned in a long apprenticeship how to maintain the delicate balance between decorum and indecorous conduct. Before you know it a bell rings. The party is over. If your hostess has been pleased with you, a telephone number may be discreetly slipped into your hand or pocket. The kaesang party offers a well-earned end to a hard day.

From Christmas time until I had to return home Tine was travelling in Southeast Asia. I seldom heard from her and I seldom wrote, for I never knew where she would be. In late February I had a cable from Bishop Juhan asking me to return home if possible to help in Sewanee's campaign to raise money to match the Ford Foundation offer. Obviously things were not going well and I was needed. Since schools were closed anyhow, I felt no obligation to remain in Korea. I asked for and received a release from the Fulbright Commission. I sent Tine a cable in Hong Kong to return to Seoul. I knew not whether she would receive it, but I had determined to return to Sewanee in any event, as she could very well handle her own traveling affairs. Fortunately she received the cable and soon joined me in Seoul for the packing up and the trip home. I had originally intended to return home by Hong Kong, Bangkok, India, and the Philippines. The necessities of my early return denied me much in the way of touring the Orient, and I have always regretted it. We headed for home one cold day in early March by way of Tokyo. We did spend a week in Japan before the long flight to Chicago.

We were welcomed home by a number of friends who had opened our house, prepared a party, and were making merry before a great fire in the living room. We returned to the warmth of our own house and friends and to the uncertain prospects of a campaign for funds, my role in which was as yet undetermined.

Chapter Twelve

Milestones

The year 1979 brought great changes in my life. I retired as professor of political science, after forty-six years at Sewanee, and that summer my wife, Ernestine Desporte Lancaster, died of ovarian cancer. She had a short year and a half after its discovery, and in her last days she endured great pain. For the last two months of her life I slept on a cot by her hospital bed. We had lived together nearly fifty years.

Tine was talented and courageous. She was direct and plain spoken. She was a woman of many enthusiasms. Sometimes she was collecting sea shells. Another year it might be mushrooms. She loved to travel, and she visited many exotic places. I have rubbings she made at the temple of Angkor Wat in Cambodia at a time when few Americans knew of its existence. We had difficulty living together, but we made it for nearly half a century.

When Tine died, we scattered her ashes on the waters of the gulf in front of her mother's house at Biloxi, Mississippi.

In this same year the university conferred on me the honorary degree of Doctor of Civil Law. In many ways I considered it an earned degree. Wholly unexpected, however, was the degree of Doctor of Letters conferred on me by Hampden-Sydney, my alma mater. The citation is especially lovely—written by my friend Josiah Bunting, a most articulate man. Whether or not I deserved his praise, I liked it.

Here is the citation:

The brilliant but disarmingly modest Louis Pasteur often insisted that his achievements were the product of chance; but, being not naive, he qualified that disclaimer with an aphorism: "Chance favors the prepared mind." As it is true with men, so it is true with men's institutions. Thanks to a discerning headmaster, the Sewanee Military Academy, the preparatory school operated by the University of the South, in 1932 engaged a twenty-three-year-old Hampden-Sydney alumnus, who had in 1929 graduated magna cum laude after only three years, to organize and preside over a lower school: and so almost a half-century of service to the the Sewanee family began and yet continues from a chance encounter of a teacher and a headmaster.

Vital in him are the qualities that have made him an institution within an institution—dignity, good humor, prodigious intellectual powers, sympathy, and the supreme, informing quality he himself has so often used to capture the essence of his adopted university: the elusive grace we call civility. He and Sewanee are traditionalists in the most positive, authentic sense; and he said in paying tribute to his own Sewanee mentor, Bishop Juhan, "Like Burke, he realizes well that 'in what we improve, we are never wholly new; in what we retain we are never wholly obsolete,'" and, "Like Chesterton, 'one should refuse to surrender institutional values to the arrogant oligarchy of those who merely happen to be walking around.'"

In college he had intended upon a career in law, and during his days of preparatory school teaching he studied law and was admitted to the Virginia Bar; not content with this diversion, he acquired a master's degree in English literature, and then, having in 1948 joined the political science department of the University of the South, in 1952 he earned a Ph.D. from the University of Michigan. But then came full and taxing recognition of his generous but quietly exercised gifts: he became successively dean of men, dean of the College of Arts and Sciences, and director of development; in each office his contribution was not only competent for the operation but seminal for the future of Sewanee: academic departments strengthened, scholarships multiplied, buildings erected and restored, a Ford Foundation matching grant more than matched, extraordinary problems and challenges accepted and more than successfully addressed.

And so we salute a paradigm of our own vision of producing men fit for the world's fight, and the pride we take in sharing this illustrious son with the University of the South we seal today as I, under the authority vested in me by the laws of the Commonwealth of Virginia and by the trustees of Hampden-Sydney College, admit Robert Samuel Lancaster to the degree of Doctor of Letters: in token of which I present him with his diploma and he will be hooded.

Soon after Tine's death I married her friend and traveling companion Elizabeth Gewin Craig. Some say Tine passed me along for my own good to her friend. They are wrong. I passed myself along to a woman of beauty and wit, of splendid character and never-failing compassion. We were married on January 4, 1980, by Bishop Girault Jones. Our lives have been happy and serene.

Elizabeth Lancaster settles affairs of church and state (speaking to Presiding Bishop Jack Allin and Vice President George Bush).

Chapter Thirteen

Whimsical Thoughts about Dogs

The first dog that I could call my own was a black and tan hound whom I named Lead. My Uncle Albert had rescued him as a pup from the wet basement of a vacant house being demolished in Martinsville, Virginia. He brought him to me on a hunting visit to Floyd. The pup was about four months old and small and wiggly with a loud mouth. I was about fourteen, callow and wiggly with a mouth too that sometimes said too much. We got along famously.

Lead grew to be a fine hunting dog with a long mournful mouth that ranged into a chop mouth when he was not on a fox trail. At this time in my county in Virginia, foxes, after a long absence, were returning along with raccoons. Our neighbor, Murphy Thompson, raised turkeys. Fox began to raid his turkey pens. He borrowed my father's Ithaca shotgun and killed a fox on a raid. He gave me the fox tail. I dragged it all over the hills; then I put Lead on the trail. He opened up his mouth, gave one of those mournful horn-like cries, and traced the course I had taken with the fox tail. I knew I had a fox hound, but there were still too few foxes to run.

About this time I learned of a man in the county who had dug two kits out of a den. I bought them and built a house for them in the old yard and put them on chains attached to a wire. One of them had an injured leg. I called him Crip. The other was Renard. Lead got used to them and they to him. They were young and playful and foxy.

Sometimes they would lie in wait and pounce on one of my mother's Rhode Island red hens. Mama didn't like that. I kept these foxes until 1926 when I went away to college. I left Lead at home. His prowess as a hunter was well know by then, and one day he disappeared, stolen, we thought. I was not home to search for him, and he disappeared into history and memory.

In the early fall of 1932 my cousin Dr. Bob Phlegar gave me a setter pup we were to call Rodney. This first Rod was a great dog. He looked the part of a black and white Llewellyn setter, but was actually a dropper, the offspring of a setter father and a pointer mother. He was trained by Webster Price of Iuka, Mississippi. Mr. Price had a son in the academy who needed tutoring in mathematics; so he and I traded off. He taught my dog; I tutored his son. I got the better part of the deal, for Mr. Price trained Rod to perfection. Often Rodney brought me birds that had been crippled that he alone knew about. He would go into a stream to get a floating bird. Once I killed a quail across a wire fence in a posted field. The warden was standing by the woods watching. I did not dare cross the fence to get the bird, but I sent Rodney across. He leaped the fence, got the bird, and sailed back over the fence. I have kept this picture in my mind for fifty years.

In addition to being the best field dog I ever had, Rodney made a perfect pet. I could read the newspaper in my office, give it to Rod, and he would take it to our apartment, scratch on the door, and deliver it to Tine. He went to class with me, lay in the corner, and absorbed much classical learning. He spoke many languages. He understood moods, gestures, glances, and orders. All dogs do. I am told it comes from their long experience in the pack when a lifted ear, a sudden turn, or a quick glance had meaning. Anyhow, Rod was a dear dog, better at finding the covey than the singles and the best retriever I have ever seen.

We always went to Sophie's in Biloxi for Christmas. Even after Ulysse came we took both dog and baby. She admitted him to the house like the understanding mother of Tine that she was. She arose early each morning to do the shopping for the day. Rod sometimes accompanied her. Rodney did not like the beach, but he did like the piney-wood hunts with my friend Champlin Gay. In these days there were many coveys of birds in the woods back of Biloxi. Champ Gay's father had a crew of blacks working a turpentine still in the woods. They always knew where the coveys were. Many a bird we killed, with

Rodney the finder. He stayed under our bed in an upstairs room at night, but when I let him out early in the morning he would go find bottles of milk in the neighborhood and bring them to Sophie's front porch. These were the old glass milk bottles; so he must have had a time lugging them. At the complaint of neighbors I made him sleep late.

Rodney, 1932-1940

I still had Rodney, as well as another setter named Rip, when I went to Virginia to practice law. Both dogs rode from Sewanee to Virginia on a trailer behind the car. When I got a house in Floyd they lived there or at Mama's on the farm. I had few clients my first year of practice, but I had many hunts with my friend Chris Harmon. Once while in Floyd Rodney appeared one day with a country ham. I was certain it came from the smokehouse of my neighbor, who hated my dogs. We ate the ham. I think it was not stealing but a subtle way of preserving neighborly friendship. Nevertheless we felt a little guilty when the neighbor accused his yard man of the theft.

When I went to practice in Pulaski, Virginia, I left the dogs with Mama on the farm. Here Rod came to his end. An irate neighbor shot him with a .22 rifle for getting into his chicken mash. I was never told of his end until long afterwards, lest there be trouble. Rip returned to Sewanee with me, lived with Everette Myers during my war years, and was still a good hunter and recognized his master when I returned to Sewanee after the war.

The very first Rodney in the family was my Uncle Albert's dog. He was named Rodney because the famous Prince Rodney was his progenitor. He was white with black spots and a patch of liver over each eye and around the ears. He became a famous working bird dog around Fayerdale, Virginia. Then just before World War I Rodney was stolen. Three years later my Uncle Albert moved his medical practice to Martinsville, and one day when he went to his car he found Rodney lying on the seat. Evidently he came upon the scent of his master and returned home. Where he had been we never knew. He was still a great bird dog. It was over this dog that I shot my first bird, and it was this dog that provided the name for so many Rodneys I have owned.

Once in the sixties I gave up bird dogs for beagles. Beagles are even tempered like all hounds, fine companions and great hunters. I got a pair of beagles from my cousin Bob Phlegar when they were pups. I named them Bugle and Trumpet. They became great rabbit dogs. Felix Long, my hunting friend, had three or four beagles. Together they made a fine pack. Some had chop mouths, some long bugling high notes. Some were jump dogs, some slow trailers. We had many a fine race and killed many rabbits over this and succeeding packs. Thinking of beagles reminds me of a story.

Once we had to dinner Steve and Upshur Puckette and Henry and Harriet Hutson. Harriet was a Charlestonian and a splendid lady. Harriet was seated by me. Tine had prepared rabbit in some elegant way for the entree. Harriet confided to me that she liked all game except rabbit. When she was served she ate rabbit with gusto.

"Oh, this is so good!" she said. "What is it?"

"This is wild goose," I replied.

"I do like goose," she said.

Steve Puckette observed, "This is the strangest shaped goose leg I have ever had."

"Geese sometimes have strange shaped legs," I replied. We let the conversation about roast goose lapse.

On the way home Steve told Harriet she had eaten rabbit. She called me, furious. "Red Lancaster," she said, "I am going to invite you to my house for chicken sometime and serve you snake."

After Bugle and Trumpet I had a succession of beagles. Once I had two litters of pups at the same time. At my lunch hour I would eat a hasty lunch and go to see the puppies nursing, pushing with their fat paws against their mothers' breasts. Then filled to overflowing, growling their small growls, and gamboling and playing—they were a delight to behold.

I once had to take a business trip to New York and left a litter of half grown beagle pups. While I was gone they followed their mother through the woods and fell over the cliff by our house into the Alto Road. Joe Long, Sr., ran over them with his truck. He killed two and carried off two others. Upon my return I learned of the loss. I went to see Mr. Long. He was apologetic, but I gave him a piece of my mind. I did not know then that he had carried off two pups. I learned from Felix Long the true story. One of the pups he had given to the man who ran the Alto Store and gas station. Felix urged me not to try to recover the dog. The proprietor of the store, he said, was a violent man and easy to anger. I thought the matter over at length. I realized that I must do something about it if I was to live with myself. Having made the decision, I felt better. I left immediately for the store.

I entered. The man asked me what he could do for me. I looked him in the eye and said, "You have my beagle puppy, and I have come for him."

He looked at me squarely and silently for a long moment.

I said, "Where is the dog?"

"He's over in the yard." he said shortly. "A chicken hen pecked out one of his eyes."

"Let's go get him," I said. We went to his yard, and there was the one-eyed pup. I picked him up and said, "I know your son likes him. I would have given him to you if you had called to tell me you had him. You know he was mine."

"Yes," he said, "I knew it and I ought to have called you."

Some years later I was in Mobile for a Carnival Ball of which Bowden Mitchner, Elizabeth's niece, was queen. At supper in the hotel I related this story. Sitting near us were a table of four. I paid little attention to them. Later that night I was introduced to a gentleman. He said, "Yes, I know about you. You are the man who once had a puppy that had an eye out from an angry mother hen." I was mystified. It turned out he was one of the men who were sitting at a nearby table at supper and had overheard the story.

Eventually I gave up beagles and returned to English setters. I believe it was principally on account of Shirley Majors coming to Sewanee to be coach of our football team. Shirley Majors was an avid

Two war chiefs of the Sewanee tribe, Shirley Majors and myself

bird hunter and a setter dog enthusiast. With him I began to hunt quail again and once more to have English setters. Shirley had the best strain of registered setters I have ever seen. They were docile, easily trained, spirited long-range hunters. They all went back to a female white setter called Old Dutch. She was a streak of white in the field, but she had bird sense. She knew where to hunt. When she disappeared you might as well look until you found her for she had birds. I think she was the best bird finder I ever saw.

All of the dogs descended from her were high-spirited long-range hunters. When first in the field, Shirley hunted some of his dogs with trace chains attached to slow the dogs down. I have seen him thrust the front leg of a dog through the collar and seen the dog hunt too fast even on three legs. This was an extreme resort only and used sparingly.

I had many happy hunts with my friend Shirley and a great hole was left in my life when he died. He was a loyal friend, a good coach, and a man who knew his mind and spoke it. His boys learned more than football from him, and he had the knack of getting more from boys than they knew they had.

His son John, coach of Tennessee, and one of his four all-American football player sons likes to tell the story of a hunt Shirley and I had one snowy day. The day was cold, the roads were icy, the sun shone bleakly. We were on a country road somewhere out of Manchester. Shirley drove with too much abandon anyhow. He came around a bend where the sun had not melted the snow. The car went off the bank and landed on all four wheels in a stubble field. The impact had caused the trunk lid to pop up. Out came the dogs ready to hunt. I leaped out of my side and called out, "Hunt, dogs, hunt!" Shirley got out slowly. He was much impressed with the way I took the mishap.

We hunted until nearly dark. When we returned the ground had frozen sufficiently for us to drive the car to a point where a road led from the field to the highway. We killed some birds, but it was not one of our better hunts. On our way home we gave out of gas on Monteagle Mountain. I remained with the car, and Shirley got a ride with a man in a Cadillac who took him to the gas station at the top of the mountain and brought him back with a can of gas. We got home late that night. Now most of my hunts and most of my friends are memories. They have gone on the last long hunt.

In 1965 or thereabouts I met O. D. Carlton, called Peck by his friends. He owned a fine quail-hunting and working plantation in Albany, Georgia. He invited Bishop Juhan and me to hunt quail with him. He had and still has one of the finest quail plantations anywhere, with many dogs, fine walking horses, and a dog wagon pulled by two matched mules driven by a black retainer. He carried four dogs, hunting two at a time. The dog handlers and a couple of outriders looked after the hunters and hunted pointing dogs. Sometimes a day's hunt would bring in nearly a hundred quail.

For twenty years or more Peck invited me to hunt. A couple of times I hunted with Shirley Majors, a couple of times with Heck Clark. Once he invited David and Rachel Tyrrell along with Elizabeth and me. His wife, Kathleen, was a splendid hostess. The hunt was medieval. There were the hunters on their horses, the wagon for dogs and elder shooters, the outriders, the racing dogs, and the sound of rising birds, the gun fire. Any hunter and his lady lucky enough to be invited to Oakland Plantation in Albany is fortunate.

In 1977 Shirley Majors gave me a setter pup, all white and black ticked, who became Rodney V. He almost didn't make it. He disappeared with the older dog, King. For three days he did not appear. I hunted for him high and low and finally gave him up as gone. On the evening of the third day he appeared barely crawling. He had a great hole in his side as though he had fallen on a sharp spike. I hurried him to the vet who gave him antibiotics and told me to take him home and look after him. We took him home and placed him on a small bed in the garage room. He lay there mortally ill for a day of two and then he began to heal. Within a fortnight he was almost his old self. I sent him to a trainer in North Georgia to be schooled, but I was disappointed in the results. When Tine died I needed companionship, and Rodney V gave it to me. He followed me, obeyed me, and chewed up every thing in sight.

That fall Peck Carlton invited me to hunt, and I took Rodney with me. He was out of his element with all the dogs and horses. In the field he sometimes took a flying leap to sit by me on the wagon. I gave him

Pearl, first Rachel's dog and then Charles Harrison's

to Peck when I left, knowing he would often be in quail. On my seventy-fifth birthday, Peck flew up in his plane, bringing Rodney as a surprise to me. He was newly washed and had a big red ribbon tied around his neck.

I kept him. He was the most intelligent dog I ever had. He knew his rug, he anticipated my commands, he knew my moods. He talked with me, the only talking dog I ever had. He smoked my pipe when I was not looking—a very remarkable dog.

Dogs love Sewanee when school is in session. Many students adopt stray dogs left on the mountain by miscreant dog droppers. Those dogs still wander freely over the campus, interrupt chapel, beg at Gailor dining hall and are generally quite friendly and gregarious. Football games have been interrupted by dogs excited by the play. Several professors have been dog lovers, and dogs have often attended classes.

When I first came to Sewanee, the most famous dog was Fitz, an off-color collie owned by Dean Baker. The dog was as grave and dignified as his master. He wandered about the campus with a slow gait and an upright tail. He is the only dog I ever knew with a charge account at the Supply Store. At precisely 10 a.m. he would make his way to the Supply Store and ask for his daily ice cream cone, which was invariably delivered to him. He would take it tenderly in his mouth, seek some shady spot and spend a quarter of an hour enjoying it lick by lick.

What happened to Fitz I don't know. He just faded away. Since we seldom attended dog funerals, our memories of their passing are nebulous.

Pearl, a collie of questionable ancestry, became Charles Harrison's dog and is ever immortalized in a cartoon strip called "Sam's Brother," prepared for the Sewanee *Purple* by Leonard Trawick. First, though, Pearl was Rachel Lancaster's dog. She was given to Rachel as a young puppy by Andy Stevens, who worked at SMA and with whose children Rachel played. Rachel brought her home one Sunday morning very early and flung her on her father's bed, saying, "Daddy, Mr. Stevens gave me this puppy. Can I keep her? He says she can be fixed." I could not deny her. We had her spayed and she grew into a wise and noble animal. Twice she was hit by cars. In one of these accidents she was almost mortally wounded. She learned how to avoid cars and was as careful at a crossing as an old man. For a time the Sewanee children each Saturday morning had a circus at which they would make their dogs compete. Pearl's specialty was jumping rope.

She came to be Dean Harrison's when we left for a year in Iraq. We put her out in the country with a reliable farmer, but Pearl was a village girl. She came to the Harrison house in the company of two crude country dogs, leaped his fence, growled at the two companions not to follow, and announced to Charles that she had come to stay. She lived there the life of Riley, with her own sleeping bag and dog biscuits. She came to his classroom, knew her place in the corner, and absorbed more Shakespeare than some students. The "to be or not to be" question she had solved long since. Occasionally she stayed with Eugene Kayden and often visited her old home at the Lancaster house. She too, like Fitz, passed out of all except memory. Her grave is unmarked.

There have been so many splendid campus canine personalities. There was that jaunty terrier Johann Sebastian Bark, who belonged to Brinly Rhys. Bark knew he was special and played to the crowd. Then there was the famous Myers dog, Hrothgar the Dane, a bulldog of ferocious mein and mild disposition. Once I saved his life at the cost of a sprained back. He got into a fight with Dr. Henry Kirby-Smith's setter, Fighter. Fighter was all his name implied. He was choking poor Hrothgar to death when I pried his jaws apart. He snapped at me, and I leveled a kick that wrenched my back.

There are dogs now on the campus. Dog policy is ever debated in the community council. Leash laws are enacted and access to dormitories forbidden, but to little or no avail. Sewanee dogs march on. After all, in the old football yell "Sewanee was Sewanee when Vandy was a pup!"

Chapter Fourteen

Sewanee
Then and Now

M y life at Sewanee embraces two different eras: Old Sewanee and New Sewanee. The change came during the sixties with the great social revolution of that decade. The Old Sewanee was small, formal, provincial, distinctly southern, still aware of the suffering of Reconstruction, oriented to low church, honoring plantation life and the professions, and expecting all students to be gentlemen, not only by virtue of a code of conduct but by an aversion to giving pain. There was expectation of a certain dress code that indicated an outer awareness of an inner grace—all a mark of attachment to civility and its close relative gentility.

It was still the Sewanee that cherished memories of the founders and looked to the past rather than to the future for example and guidance. There were still the matrons who exercised great influence on the students, older ladies whose decorum and grace came from a family security or a sense of worth. Old ladies, like Miss Celeste Wicks and Miss Kathleen McCrady, demanded and received respect and attention. Mrs. Hale, a Kirby-Smith, still drove her buggy to pick up mail or visit the village. There still lingered at Sewanee the aroma of the early boarding houses as opposed to the later dormitory life. Hunters from the valley still sold rabbits and quail to Mrs. Hale and Miss Johnnie Tucker, and to Mrs. Eggleston, who ran the dining hall and prepared every salad with her own hands.

Discipline in the college was in the hands of the matrons, proctors, and gownsmen, and overall the dean. The college was small. The professors, few but demanding, often taught long hours on small salaries. The faculty thought they ran the place, and the administration was wise enough to leave them with this belief. The committees of the faculty did their work under the leadership of the dean, who, if he were wise, saw to it that the committees were made up of men who could be convinced of a proposition if they could be shown the rationality and the necessity of its adoption.

Since the college was small and since there were few who did not share an understanding of its mission, its necessities, and its options, there was very little major disagreement among those who lived and worked at Sewanee. Major disagreements usually broke out over minor matters. So steam was let off and the engine worked.

Sewanee in those days was a relaxed, rather laid-back college. We thought we were good. Our students thought we were good. This lent a kind of self-satisfied air to the place that curiously enough led some students to fulfillment. The college, the seminary, the military academy, and the community embodied a place that had little in common with the world around it. We had a few very superior students who were as good as the best anywhere and with perhaps a little more freedom. The rest earned a degree, and many of them went on to real achievement.

The graduates went to the professions, to the Church, to the banks, to the plantations. They carried with them an abiding love for the place and its people. They carried with them, too, a certain flavor of gentility that lasted them a lifetime. Sewanee did for them precisely what the liberal arts were supposed to do to people who would exercise authority and who had a stake in society—civilize them, make them aware of the responsibility of those who had a place to those who had none. Not that it always worked; it did not. But it worked often enough in some to lend approbation and distinction to the whole class.

The faculty, aside from Professor Eugene Kayden, was politically conservative and Democratic. If anyone was typical of the age it was the inimitable Major William H. MacKellar, orator, old-fashioned fire-eating southerner who once challenged Professor Kayden to a duel. Major MacKellar nearly always addressed the football team on the eve of the Thanksgiving Day game with Vanderbilt. Like an Indian chief he would recount the exploits of teams and heros of old and, remembering accrued wrongs, whip his hearers into passion for justice and revenge. The next day the whole of Sewanee, town and gown, would board the train to Nashville and Vanderbilt stadium where the cheerleaders, led on by Miss Johnnie Tucker and Miss Eva Colmore, pleaded for a touchdown and victory—which seldom came.

Some men, like Tudor Long in English, had no advanced degrees but were magnificent teachers at a time when teachers were expected to teach as much by example as by formal instruction. William Lewis is another example of an old-fashioned scholar without a Ph.D. who made a mark in his day, as a teacher of Spanish, and is remembered.

Gaston Bruton belonged to two eras, but he was beginning to make

Three Sewanee deans: John Webb, left, Gaston Bruton, and...

his way at Sewanee as a gifted mathematician and formidable debater, often engaging Kayden at E.Q.B. on such ideas as: There is nothing in poetry that cannot be better expressed and understood in plain prose. He delighted in pointing out inconsistencies and posing dilemmas. He had the lead part in many plays and, along with Esther his wife, led the Little Theater group in Sewanee.

George Alexander was dean of the School of Theology during my time as dean of the college. He was a good dean with a balanced mind and a fine speaking style. I remember yet a sermon he preached in All

Saints' Chapel on Marcus Aurelius. It is not often you hear a preacher base a sermon on a Greek or Roman philosopher. Marcus Aurelius was an emperor and a Stoic, and he believed all men were sparks from a divine fire.

George liked to dove hunt. Once with Gilbert Gilchrist and me he was hunting doves in a corn field. A bull and several cows were gleaning in the field. I am afraid of bulls, and I said to George, "Doves are flying in the corner of the field, but I am afraid to go there."

George said, "I'm not afraid of bulls; I will take that stand."

I thought to myself, "The Lord be with you." He was. The bull charged at the first shot, and George cleared the fence with a leap that was especially vigorous for a clergyman of his age. However the bull somehow got through the fence and presently headed in my direction. I was close to the car and escaped as he scattered corn stalks close by. In the meantime a young heifer was following the bull's every step—too young to breed but old enough to adore. I let them move along a hundred yards or so, and before long George appeared.

"The Lord saved you that time for better sermons," I said.

"I'll work on them," he replied.

George Alexander is gone, but Sewanee owes him remembrance.

There were many more at Sewanee then whom I have not characterized, men like General James Jervey and George Myers who brought to Sewanee an air, an élan, a touch of elegance and gracious living that rubbed off on students and made their lives richer, more responsible.

Vice-Chancellor Edward McCrady's tenure at Sewanee was for me the golden years. He was a man of so many talents, so many sides one could devote to him a chapter or many chapters. In the context of my story, I prefer to let his record speak for itself.

There were men in the village who contributed to the Sewanee scene. Among them was my special fishing friend Cotton Terrill. Cotton was a man of many parts, businessman, trader, politician, benefactor of students, teller of tales. In his later years, Cotton bought the old railway station. It became a hangout for the older men of the village. Some told stories; others dozed in their chairs. They interfered with business, but the real purpose of the place was not business but lounging, reminiscing, organizing hunts that never took place, catching fish without wetting a line.

Then there was Tom Hawkins. The Hawkins family lived in the

Sewanee area long before the university was founded. Tom sold dry goods in the Supply Store—everything from golf clubs to shoes. He knew the students by name, and they loved his banter. Once he promoted a chicken-plucking contest between a black chicken picker from the SMA kitchen and another who worked at the meat shop in the Supply Store. I witnessed the flying feathers and the laughter of the on-lookers. I believe the contest was a draw.

Tom too was a promoter of the Purple Tigers. Once or twice during the fall season a football team made up of blacks who worked on the campus as waiters or handymen put together a football team—convened on the spur of the moment. They would play a team from Winchester or some other neighboring area. What a contest. They were cheered on by wives, sweethearts, and village folks, as well as a few adventurous sorts from the "gentry." The name of the team came from their purple sweatshirts, castoffs supplied by the athletic department.

These were the days of the great orchestras. Many times Francis Craig and his orchestra played at Sewanee. His "Near You" became the number one hit in America for a while and still brings in royalties. I know, for I married his widow Elizabeth Craig, a woman of style and character. Of all the orchestras to play at Sewanee perhaps the favorite was Kay Kyser, with now and again a Jennie Simms or a Dorothy Lamour. The old gymnasium was the scene of these lovely parties, a gym all decorated and festive. Many a southern belle prized an invitation to the Sewanee dances above all others. There were three occasions during the year when the student mind was not on studies: openings, midwinters, and spring festival.

The songs and music of the era are now the golden oldies. Who of my vintage can resist the charm of "Night and Day," "Smoke Gets in Your Eyes," "Begin the Beguine." Of course then we had no Sewanee Summer Music Center to bring to Sewanee people the thrill of classical music. We made do with the radio and the phonograph and looked forward to the next touring band to come to town. Sewanee was quiet in the summer. There were no regular sessions of summer school.

In Old Sewanee we were playing big-time athletics without the means for sustaining our position. We remembered ancient days of glory, but each Saturday in football we were reminded by the score that we could not win. A succession of coaches and teams had their hearts broken on the cold rock of reality. Alabama, Tennessee,

Vanderbilt, LSU were headed for big-time football. They had the resources to sustain it. Sewanee had not.

When I came to Sewanee, Heck Clark was head football coach, and Gordon Clark was athletic director. The team was good, well-coached, valiant, but simply not able to compete in the Southeastern Conference. For half a game we could usually hold our own, but by the second half the lack of replacements spelled defeat. Eventually a wise Dr. Guerry took us out of that conference and insisted we play in our own league.

I have always supported athletics at Sewanee. Seldom have I missed a home football game. I like football because it is a contact sport that requires skill and finesse. It teaches lessons not found in the classroom: to take a blow, to learn the limits of courage and stamina, to subordinate self to the efforts of the team, to learn to win. There is little value in losing. Lose with truculence, but be graceful in victory. Life grants its favors to winners.

Looking back, it was a different world we lived in. There were relatively few automobiles owned by students. Travel was by train. Men like Cotton Terrill kept a fleet of taxis busy carrying students to and from Cowan and to here and there. Sewanee was no suitcase college; so fraternities flourished. The long winters, cold, wet, sometimes creating a November of the soul, were hard on faculty and student alike. Fortunately there were picture shows, and Tony Griswold somehow brought the latest hits straight from Atlanta. There were also many parties, especially bridge parties among the faculty and residents. Everybody had shifted from auction to contract and were busy with Culbertson and point counting.

An invisible barrier existed that separated the village from the hill, or university. The faculty member knew it, and the villager knew it. Few were the persons who could live on both sides of the barrier. However there were a few who enjoyed ease and prestige on both sides. The barrier was seldom talked about or even resented. It was like a fact of nature. It was there; it had been there. A Martin Johnson or a Doctor Lear might ignore it, but they knew it was there. Similarly a barrier lay between Winchester and Sewanee. They might poke fun at those silly impractical people who lived at Sewanee, but in Winchester they were most proud of the fact that the University of the South lay in Franklin County. Again there were a few who were able to ignore the difference, but again these were few. All of this had something to do with the Episcopal Church, with a ritual so unlike Presbyterianism and Methodism, so strange to the frontier community that took its religion like its whiskey, straight. It had something to do with an aristocracy of learning, with difference in speech and dress. It had something to do with human nature. I took pride in the belief that I could live on both sides of the street.

There was no word that could so arouse anger and cause trouble as *covite*. It carried with it on one side the image of rough, redneck, untutored ignorance and lack of grace. For the dweller in the cove, it violated his sense of worth, his dignity, his innate feeling of equality. It carried a connotation to him somehow different but worse than that fighting term *son of a bitch*. From the use of the word came violence.

Old Sewanee like New Sewanee centered on and reflected the values cherished by the Episcopal Church. Chapel attendance was required of all students. Both the number of Sunday attendances required and the number of daily attendances required were changed from time to time. As I remember, the requirement for daily attendance was three times each week and seven Sundays a semester. Proctors collected the attendance slips that were signed by the students, and records were kept in the office of the dean of men. For a long time there was no objection voiced by parents or students. Like mathematics and English, chapel attendance was simply a requirement. Perhaps the questioning of the chapel-attendance rule was a first mark of the difference between then and now. Students sometimes read newspapers, sometimes slept at the service, but the words of morning prayer and its ritual rolled on, leaving on nearly all a deposit of rich language and stately dignity—this even though they knew it not.

Then Sewanee was male. It exuded masculinity from its athletic fields to its fraternity houses and even to its sounds and smells. Its voice was a male voice, its dress was male trousers and coat, its classrooms provided rough benches and writing boards unsuited to the female form. Furthermore it rejoiced in its maleness. When women came at party time it went mad with drink, with display, with competition. Like the male grouse in drumming season, Sewanee drummed. There was a need for the admonition, "Gentlemen, gentlemen, you are gentlemen!"

It is astonishing to remember that Sewanee, in at least half of my lifetime at the academy and college, afforded a farm of about 800 acres, including a dairy that provided milk for the mountain and part of the county, a laundry employing a comparably large number of workers, and a supply store affording everything from men's shoes to golf clubs and groceries, the latter delivered to your door. It included a bookstore, which turned a handsome profit, and a pharmacy. In addition to all this there was a hospital, the only one between Nashville and Chattanooga; a sawmill that sold lumber commercially; a dining hall run by the university that served good food—albeit with some students grumbling; and a press that actually printed books. All of this has passed away as though it were a dream in the night. Quietly, slowly the old merged into the new. One knew not whether to attribute the passing of the old ways to lack of energy and will, to changing times and modes of thought, or to a developing technology that made the

Arthur Dugan and myself. In Dugan's class if you dropped your pen you lost the lecture.

old inefficient, unaffordable, even undesirable.

The experience of World War II brought a change. Students had lost time, and they were in a hurry. They had experienced war, and it had made them less civil, rougher of speech, cruder of manner, more competitive. The GI Bill opened opportunity to the sons of carpenters and plumbers. The professors recognized it immediately and made adjustments. New blood flowed in new ways through our minds and lecture notes were updated, new techniques of teaching were tried. There was more research. The library became more important.

The emergent New Sewanee became apparent in the sixties. Perhaps the first harbinger of a new way, a new style, could be detected in the music that students listened to and apparently enjoyed. It became louder, more raucous, wilder. Naturally, to dance to such music required hops, jumps, unpatterned movement. The old formality in dress and movement gave way to the informal, the spontaneous. Hair became longer and dresses shorter and shorter.

During the time of change the university generated great energy. Much money was raised and virtually a new plant was built. From 1950 to 1970 the campus took on today's appearance. The building process started in the early fifties with Gailor Hall, a dining hall and dormitory, and ended with the Bishop's Common just out of the twenty-year period. This building period coincided almost exactly with the administration of Edward McCrady as vice-chancellor. A combination of people and circumstances made it possible. Arthur Chitty, director of public relations and alumni affairs, with imagination and great energy, created an alumni affairs office with the records and the techniques necessary for fund raising. To this office as director of development came Bishop Frank Juhan, retired bishop of Florida, a man of controlled energy, wide vision, and many friends and acquaintances among a wide range of people, some of them like Mrs. Alfred duPont rich and powerful. He proved to be a dynamic fund raiser. I was joined with him in the Ford matching grant campaign. Then there was Bruton to administer and alumni like Cecil and Albert Woods and Kemper Williams to take the lead. Altogether it was a great team.

During this period, we built the Woods Science Laboratories, duPont Library, Guerry Hall and Auditorium, Juhan Gymnasium, and the new Sewanee Inn. We renovated St. Luke's Hall and Walsh Hall, completed All Saints' Chapel to its present splendor, and added dormitories such as Cleveland, Benedict, Hunter, Trezevant, and Courts. At Sewanee Military Academy were built Hamilton and Cravens Halls and a new football field. This was a remarkable achievement. Most of the buildings were paid for when built. A few awaited the great fund-raising performance of the Ayres administration to be fully funded.

Perhaps the greatest change in my Sewanee experience came with the admission of women students in 1969. Exactly how it came about is hard to explain. First and foremost it was a time of change, of radical ideas, of unparalleled social movement. The drive for change in the status of the blacks of America may have been at the roots of change. Flower children, student rebellion, violent protest, long marches for freedom were symptoms of a deep-seated revolution that was taking place in America.

It was in this context of change that Sewanee Military Academy was demilitarized and women hastily admitted to the college. No time for preparation of dormitories or for psychological adjustment was permitted. The trustees, one summer day, simply said, "Let it be done," and it was done. It was done over the objection of many in the administration, but it was done. I was against the admission of women, but no professor liked it more than I did after it became a reality. Girls quieted down our hectic weekends, brought academic achievement to a new eminence, filled the campus with new voices, new beauty, and fulfilled the mission of the owning dioceses to provide a Sewanee education for their young people, men and women alike.

When Sewanee was smaller and younger, Sunday night visiting was an established institution. The professor and his wife prepared some light refreshment for some of his expected students. They came sometimes few, sometimes a dozen, to visit, to talk, sometimes to listen to music, sometimes to join the family in games or singing. It was a humanizing experience. The professor took the measure of his students, and the student learned what his professor was like. A bond of more intimate understanding was formed, and an easy congeniality made the student's life easier and more productive. Like many other practices, it has passed on, and life has become more impersonal, teachers less involved with students. A part of the appeal of Sunday night visiting came from the fact that in the past there were fewer things for students to do. Now there are concerts, plays, lectures—more choices for the students. None of them contribute so much to character formation and easy relations between faculty and students as Sunday night visiting once did.

An example of the difference between the past and the present are the changed circumstances of the E.Q.B. (*Ecce Quam Bonum*) Club. Once it was a faculty social club, a literary club, and place for gathering and enjoying a communal life. I am told that W. P. Trent, the first editor of the *Sewanee Review* had listed among his attainments recorded in *Who's Who in America* his membership in the E.Q.B. Club. Admission was by vote of the club; an annual program was printed; and care was taken to see that refreshments were at least adequate. The club was well attended; some meetings were eagerly awaited. Every two weeks a member of the faculty, who had spent an enormous amount of time in preparation, gave a "lead," a paper dealing by custom with some subject outside his professional area of study. Once the lead had been given, the leader was immediately available for questions and discussions. There was no hesitancy to take issue. I have heard some heated, even angry exchanges. Once Kayden and Ware almost came to blows over the role of Bonaparte in the development of European politics and culture. For a time the club owned its own meeting house; later it met in faculty homes; finally the present clubhouse was built. I was chairman of the building committee. It was financially possible because Ben Cameron, who ran the College Board in the area, agreed to lease rooms for his operation to be built for that purpose.

Now professors seldom join the club. It has become a gathering place for residents, particularly new residents of Sewanee. It has lost its magic. Occasionally a professor, who would not deign to join, gives a paper, but on the whole the faculty have turned it down. Whether this is due to scholarly disdain of a more pedestrian club than once it was, or to the fact that the age provides many other diversions, or to the unwillingness of professors presently to bind themselves to prearranged time schedules, or to some other reason endemic to a restless and discordant age—I do not know. The E.Q.B. Club is not what it was. So it is with God's creation; only the bare outlines of nature seem to last, and they are not impervious to time.

The E.Q.B. Club for many years was a men's club. In recent times it has opened its membership to men and women alike, another nod toward the homogenizing process so typical of a society without distinctions. I voted against it. Later I said in jest that I would make application for membership in the ladies literary society, the Fortnightly Club. All in all I expect the most significant change of my lifetime is the changed status of women. Surprisingly, I am for it, though *chairperson* still seems to me awkward. I think both men and women may be subsumed under the general term *mankind.*

Once faculty members, both Democrats and Republicans, agreed on what then appeared to be fundamental propositions basic to our corporate life, that we were supported by and owed our existence to a form of capitalism in which gifts from accumulated wealth in the hands of individuals and corporations made our college possible. Consequently the world of business was respected and admired. Businessmen were, indeed, symbols of our national achievement. Today in our college and in the academic world generally, business has a bad name. Economic ideas which have become bankrupt in practice seem to have found a last comfortable resting place in the universities and colleges of America. Especially the great foundations funded by grants from the business world are often in the hands of directors and executives who scorn the system that enabled such wealth to be put together. The state has become the dispenser of charity on such a scale that private organizations are left behind in the competition. When Sewanee was as I once knew it, this could not be said. Conservatism has lost the day in academia, and so prejudiced are those who scorn it that they sometimes deny its spokesmen the basic rights of free speech and hoot them from the platform. It has not come to such a pass yet at Sewanee but the liberal voice has risen in intensity and volume. A Dean Baker or a Dean Lancaster would have all he could do to run a meeting with dispatch.

The college has risen in size to more than 1,000 students. There are more departments, many more course offerings, many more faculty members, many more academic options. Whether there is a better education for a life of choices, I do not know. Certainly there is a better understanding of the new tools for solving problems in the sense of getting quantitative answers. Whether there is sounder morality or a better understanding of the right-duty relationship or a more attractive sense of style and joy in living, I doubt. I think it possible that Sewanee could become just another liberal arts college, its peculiar and distinctive style gone, its memories of whence it came dim, its mission active but its mode of life undisciplined and ragged at the edges, its once secure inner life monotonous, vague, uncertain.

After waging successful campaigns for funds, it has been typical of Sewanee to go on spending binges. Three times I have seen it happen. Each time it ended in financial difficulties that plagued the administration. Our last campaign raised more than $50 million. This was an incredible amount of money to be raised from so small a constituency as Sewanee enjoys. Meanwhile the budget has skyrocketed. In a few years we have gone from a comparatively low standard of living to one that is very high. You have seen the same thing happen in families that have inherited wealth. In the feeling of happy satisfaction lie dangers. Already tuition charges are too high; scholarships are too few, the administration too fat, the faculty possibly too large. Sewanee must ever keep in mind the necessity of operating a lean and well conditioned enterprise. This need not affect the academic excellence we expect. Sometimes we have produced better when we have been poorer. We must continue to give students an education worth the cost lest we price ourselves out of the market. I fear this will be harder and harder to do.

It can be done, though, not by becoming big or more like other colleges but by maintaining the style and particularities that have marked Sewanee from the beginning. Sewanee's appeal lies in its respect for the past, as well as a concern for the future. The traditional organizations, the concern for civility and manner, and a sturdy moral code must continue to be cherished and encouraged. This also means that Sewanee must be very careful in its selection of faculty. We can tolerate a few burrs under the blanket, but the great majority of professors should have, in addition to splendid scholarly qualifications, an appreciation for Sewanee's cultural environment, her Anglican outlook, and her historic interests. In their lives and in their conduct, they should be worthy role models. This does not require that every professor be Protestant or even Christian; it does require that the greater number be men and women whose heritage is like our own. Sewanee must anchor herself firmly in the heritage that gave her birth and makes possible her existence.

A good example of the value of maintaining a college with a difference is Hampden-Sydney College. In addition to maintaining its other traditions, Hampden-Sydney decided to remain an all-male college. The results have been gratifying. It has grown, improved in nearly all respects, maintained a steady increase in applications for admission, expanded and rebuilt its plant, and balanced its budget. Its appeal lies in its difference. After all, there should be a place in our educational system for a few all-male and all-female colleges.

My message has been repeated often. It is that memory civilizes us, because attachment to place and people develops the moral sense, a feeling of obligation for the past and responsibility for the future.

One thing is not as good as another. There can be bad art and good art; there can be poetry that trivializes and poetry that lifts us beyond our moorings. Push pen is not as good as poetry.

People are never equal except as they enjoy a common humanity. By nature and by training, some are better than others.

The end of education is the production of excellence in mind and body. This necessitates the acquisition of skills as well as achievement of knowledge and wisdom.

Happiness results from freeing ourselves from the shell of our egos and pushing out into a greater freedom.

Good judgment is be cultivated by an awareness that all experience has meaning.

Men and women, knowing right from wrong, must be led by authority to pursue the right. People in authority have an obligation to speak out and, if necessary, act to preserve the true and the good.

Knowledge of the true and the good passes from generation to generation by an education that preserves the sound traditions and the worthy beliefs in the culture of a people.

Variety in ethnic origins enriches our national life, but care must be taken to see that immigrants meld into and accept the cultural heritage of the English language and literature, the social forms, and the ideals inherited from our Western past.

I am in my age impressed by a quotation from Marguerite Yourcenar, with whom we once journeyed in a small boat up the Nile before I had come to know of her power and grace. She quotes from the Latin of Pico della Mirandola's *Oratio de hominis dignitate:*

> I have given you, O Adam, no fixed abode, no visage of your own, nor any special gift in order that whatever aspect or place or talent you yourself will have desired, you may have them and possess them wholly in accord with your desire and your own decision. Other species are confined to a prescribed nature under laws of my making. No limits have been imposed on you, however; you determine your nature by your own free will, in the hands of which I have placed you. I have placed you at the world's very center that you may the better behold from that point whatever is in the world, and I have made you neither terrestrial or celestial, neither mortal nor immortal, so that like a free and able sculptor and painter of yourself, you may mold yourself wholly in the form of your choice.

While I subscribe generally to the doctrine of free will, that by our choices we make ourselves what we become—for any other doctrine would leave man without moral responsibility—nevertheless the quotation from Pico seems overstated in a world of gene-splitting and alteration of both plants and animals. I do believe we must take care what we want lest we get it. I started out in life loving books and desiring, above all, an education. For what it is worth, I ended up Robert Lancaster, B.A., M.A., Ph.D., D.C.L., D.Litt.

What have I learned in this long journey through schools, academies, and universities? Of it all I will tell you one thing. It is at once simple and profound. It is that the final purpose of education is to produce just men and women. Just persons create a just society. Justice is the highest virtue; it produces civility, without which men cannot live happily and productively. The concept of the just man is at the base of the best Eastern, as well as Western, thought. For Christians it is summed up in the teaching of Jesus in his second great commandment: Love thy neighbor.

All the Lancaster children: From left, standing, are Attaway, Grace, Albert, Maude, and Red, and seated, Mary, Annie, Virginia, Helen, and John.

Ten Little Indians

Floyd County lies atop the Blue Ridge in southwestern Virginia about thirty-five miles from Roanoke. In summer it reminds me of Switzerland. Its people are principally Anglo-Saxon yeoman farmers, though foreigners are coming to discover its charm.

In these green mountains I was reared with seven sisters and two brothers, one of whom, the eldest, Albert, died in 1985. All of my sisters are strong, intelligent women who made their own way in the world. At one time or another all of them, except Mary and Helen, were teachers. Years ago teaching was about the only way for women, especially women from rural areas, to make a living.

My sister Attaway is the eldest of ten. She started out a teacher. As a matter of fact, she got me started. Attaway is the genuine article. When she means to have a thing done don't bet against her. As a private nurse she has served the people of Knoxville, Tennessee, for half a century. She lives today in the affections of her friends. At ninety-one she has the energy and imagination of a much younger woman.

My sister Grace sought her fortune in New York City as a musician, met a Brazilian intellectual, married him, and still lives in Rio de Janeiro. She had two intelligent children, Luzia and Jose. Jose earned his Ph.D. in geology. His adventures and exploits would make exciting reading.

My sister Maude earned her degree at the University of Mexico. She of all my sisters is the most exotic and dramatic. Her son Louis McClung is one of the best sleight-of-hand magicians in the country. He can pull a duck out of your ear, or if you prefer a chicken. Give him a deck of cards and his magic is better than Aladdin with his lamp. I have never seen him bring a genie from a bottle; only I can do that. His sister Helen Harvey is the softest-spoken woman in Virginia.

233

My sister Mary is redheaded, shrewd, and puckish, with mercury in her blood. I once saw her change from laughter to tears on a trip down the stairs. She is said to be like me. Once when Presiding Bishop John Allin was visiting her church in Richmond she came up after the sermon to meet him. He saw her coming and said, "Don't tell me who you are. You are Red Lancaster's sister."

My sister Annie started out a teacher. She got tired of it and took secretarial training. She spent the greater part of her life working for the Red Cross here and there in the world. Annie is bighearted and sensitive, with a temper you had better watch. For undue provocation she might hit you with what comes to hand.

After my sister Virginia's children were well up she went back to college, got her degree Phi Beta Kappa from the University of Georgia, and that year was Woman of the Campus. She did graduate work and taught English at Georgia for many years.

My sister Helen became an army nurse in World War II. The stress of her work brought on a nervous breakdown, but out of chaos she has made a life. She is the most courageous of all my clan.

My brother Albert was a careful, conservative, and respected businessman in Roanoke, Virginia. He had to leave college after a single year to help my mother after Papa's death. He was the family head.

My brother John, the last of the ten, attended Sewanee before enlisting in the air force early in World War II. He flew several missions over Germany. On one mission he was briefed and ready to go when by chance he was ordered to fly a black B-24 by night on a highly classified mission to Sweden. He was lucky. His old crew was shot down on their mission over Germany. John survived the war, came home, and eventually was graduated in forestry at Georgia. He worked for Georgia Craft until he retired. A good man in a dove field or behind a quail dog and pure hell for a gobbler in turkey season.

Acknowledgments

I thank all those who have helped to make this memoir into a book. I especially thank my wife Elizabeth, who first urged me to publish it, George Core for his guidance, Elizabeth Chitty for checking my memory of Sewanee names and other references, Alex Standefer for his copy editing, and Latham Davis for his encouragement and direction through each phase of publication.

235